OCR
/EMENT

HODDER
EDUCATION

Official Publisher Partnership

OCR Media Studies

for AS

Third Edition

Julian McDougall

HODDER
EDUCATION
PART OF HACHETTE LIVRE UK

Orders: please contact Bookpoint Ltd, 130 Milton Park, Abingdon, Oxon OX14 4SB. Telephone: (44) 01235 827720. Fax: (44) 01235 400454. Lines are open from 9.00am–5.00pm, Monday to Saturday, with a 24-hour message answering service. You can also order through our website www.hoddereducation.co.uk.

If you have any comments to make about this, or any of our other titles, please send them to educationenquiries@hodder.co.uk.

British Library Cataloguing in Publication Data
A catalogue record for this title is available from the British Library.

ISBN: 978 0 340 95898 8

First Edition Published 2008
Impression number   10 9 8 7 6
Year   2012

Hachette UK's policy is to use papers that are natural, renewable and recyclable products and made from wood grain in sustainable forests. The logging and manufacturing processes are expected to conform to the environmental regulations of the country of origin.

Cover photo from Photolibrary.com/Stockbyte (Title: 'High-tech background.' Photographer: John Foxx)
Typeset by Servis Filmsetting Ltd, Stockport, Cheshire.
Printed in Dubai for Hodder Education, An Hachette UK Company
338 Euston Road, London NW1 3BH.

Contents

Acknowledgements

For Lyd, Ned and Alex.

Thanks to the grandparents—Jan, Val and Barrie—for time and space. I am also grateful to Alison Walters and Lavinia Porter at Hodder and Paul Dodd at OCR for help with the process.

The following have provided ongoing inspiration: Dave Trotman, Wayne O'Brien, Pete Fraser, Jenny Grahame, Roy Stafford, David Buckingham, David Gauntlett, Andrew Burn, Nick Peim, Mark Reid and Nicky North.

I am indebted to Ben Andrews, Doug at Finders Keepers, Jim at Ghost Box, Basil, Huw and Somak. And I wish to make special mention of the late Jacquie Bennett, a huge loss to media education, who provided invaluable guidance as always.

Thanks also to Bruce Johns, Rome consultant.

Photographic Credits

The author and publishers would like to thank the following:

Illustrations

Foreword

Media Studies occupies an unusual space within the education system, offering you as a student many opportunities to discuss the kinds of thing that you would choose to consume anyway: films, TV programmes, newspapers, magazines, radio, music, videogames and websites. The OCR specification offers you the chance to study examples from many of these media at AS level, with a concentration on radio or TV drama and at least one contemporary media industry.

On this course, you have the opportunity to analyse media texts in depth and to find out more about how they are produced. With production work, there is additional scope to develop a whole set of skills involving teamwork, research, planning and organisation as well as the particular techniques involved in using the equipment and computer programs.

The new A level for 2008, with 50 per cent devoted to coursework, is designed to build upon your existing knowledge and understanding of media from past experience and to raise questions that you might not previously have considered.

For example, you may be very familiar with broadcast drama, but have you thought about how editing contributes to storytelling in subtle, often 'invisible', ways? Similarly, have you ever considered how social groupings, such as age, gender and ethnicity are represented through these dramas? How are the media texts you consume, such as the videogames you play, the films you see at the cinema or the magazines you buy, produced, funded, marketed and distributed? These are the kinds of question that the course will encourage you to consider.

In the Foundation Production unit, you will have the opportunity to develop quite sophisticated skills. Whether you work in video, radio, web design or magazine production, you will have the chance to build up through a preliminary task into a main project, which should allow you to demonstrate a high level of understanding of conventions as well as make something of which you can feel proud. You can also build upon your existing knowledge of the internet by undertaking research and planning in electronic form via a blog, wiki or podcast, for example. Additionally, the practical work will enable you to reflect upon ideas encountered in the exam unit for you will need to analyse and evaluate your own production in similar ways to those used for the exam.

Media Studies is a 'living' and ever-changing subject and keeping up-to-date is crucial. Reflecting on your own media use, both as a consumer and as a producer of texts like YouTube videos and MySpace pages, is a key part of the course. This book and the resources provided in the Student Online website (see the inside front cover for details) will give you much of what you need to support your studies, starting from your own media experience. The book covers a wide range of up-to-date and accessible case studies and offers lots of useful tips for both coursework and exams, some of which are also designed to prepare you for the A2 course. Student Online shows you some model coursework assignments to which you can aspire and takes you through some of the key steps in how to make the kinds of product needed to do well on the course.

I wish you well in your studies and hope that you enjoy taking the course and that this book and disk will prove useful in structuring your progress.

Pete Fraser
Chief Examiner, OCR
Jan 2008

Introduction: Media Literacy for AS

In order to establish what makes *studying* the media distinct from *experiencing* the media, it is helpful to use the relatively new concept of 'media literacy'.

Literacy is a term that is used all the time in education these days—from the literacy hour in primary school to 'functional literacy' key skills in further education. Usually, we think of literacy in terms of reading and writing the written word in printed text. But in recent years, the world of education has started to accept that other forms of literacy play a very important role in people's lives. Young people in particular are spending less time reading novels and newspapers and more time watching films, reading magazines and accessing online media and videogames. Rather than disregarding these media experiences as being nothing to do with literacy, or even an obstacle to it, a subject like Media Studies sets out to engage with these more popular textual forms. And to do this, we need new ways of thinking about literacy, one of which is media literacy.

Burn and Durran (2007) offer a clear idea of what we might mean by 'media literacy':

> Media literacy allows us to engage in cultural practices through which we make sense of and take control of our

world and ourselves, in expressive practices in which we
represent ourselves, and in critical practices in which we
interpret what we read, view and play.

(Burn and Durran, 2007: 16–17)

Buckingham (2003) focuses on the inter-related nature of these
practices:

Literacy clearly involves both reading and writing; and so
media literacy must necessarily entail both the interpretation
and the production of media. This model of 'media learning'
attempts to provide a more dynamic, reflexive approach
which combines critical analysis and creative production.

(Buckingham, 2003: 49–50)

Advanced Media Literacy

According to OFCOM, the regulatory body for broadcasting and
communications, there is a distinction between simple and
advanced media literacy:

At its simplest level media literacy is the ability to use a
range of media and be able to understand the information
received. At a more advanced level it moves from
recognising and comprehending information to the higher
order critical thinking skills such as questioning, analysing
and evaluating that information. This aspect of media
literacy is sometimes referred to as 'critical viewing' or
'critical analysis'. © Ofcom 2007.

(*Source*: http://www.ofcom.org.uk/advice/media_literacy/of_med_lit/whatis/)
(Accessed 21 September 2007)

An AS Media student will of course be working at the advanced
level, so he or she will be developing a critical approach to media.
But this is not a purely theoretical, analytical pursuit. We should
think of advanced media literacy as being a combination of
'thinking' and 'making'; of responding to media and creating
media. You may well already be doing this—web 2.0 technologies
allow ordinary people to become media producers very easily, by
creating and sharing words, images, films and music on social
networking sites on the internet. As a result of this development,
many commentators and academics suggest that it no longer
makes sense to think of producers at one end of the media
process and audiences at the other. So we certainly need to think

of theory and production as mutually dependent and connected and *not* as separate from one another.

The OCR AS Media Course

The OCR AS Media course is arranged into two *units* that cover three *areas* of study, as reflected by the structure of this book. You are required to create two pieces of media and evaluate the process and the outcomes. You will study a range of media texts from either television or radio. In addition you will research an area of media in relation to institutions (the people, companies and organisations who make, distribute or regulate media) and audiences (people making use of media in various ways). Before embarking on these key areas of study, this first section of the book introduces you to the key concepts and ideas that you need to have at your disposal as a kind of 'toolkit' for developing your media literacy. It is important to start here, because the sections of the book that relate to specific OCR units of study will refer to a range of terms and concepts covered in this introduction. The OCR specification stipulates a range of 'performance descriptions' for AS students. These indicators establish how important it is for students to understand media forms, codes and conventions and a range of media concepts. The remainder of this introduction will get you started with these, so you can apply them more thoroughly in the sections that follow.

Media Language

When we usually think of language, we tend to think of spoken and written words. Media language refers to written, verbal, non-verbal, aural and aesthetic communication and usually a combination of these. For example, in television drama, a phone conversation between two characters in different locations can only be understood by the audience because of the relationship between the camera angles (close ups, head and shoulder shots or longer shots showing location context), non-verbal performance (facial expressions during the phone conversation), dialogue (what the two characters say), lighting (to provide a meaningful atmosphere), editing (so that we can follow the conversation and so that continuity is correct) and sound (atmospheric music or 'diegetic' sound such as a door opening or slamming shut). When we watch television, we don't need to think about these things, so they are unobtrusive. What we see appears to be straightforward and conventional. Over time, we come to expect certain styles of filming, acting, editing and sound for certain types of programme. So we can 'read' the media language as easily as we can understand our friends in conversations without having to recall the meaning of every word.

Form and Style

The form of a media text is its shape and structure and the combination of the 'micro' elements such as dialogue, sound effects, editing and ambience in the case of radio drama. The form of a text is instantly recognisable to the audience—for example, soap opera or historical drama. The style of a text is the way the text uses this form. For example, the Channel 4 television drama *Shameless* has a particular aesthetic that makes it unique within the genre—which writer Paul Abbot describes as 'Little House on the Prairie on Acid' (see Figure 1).

Figure 1 *Shameless* has a unique style within the broader form of TV drama.
(*Source*: John Wright/Channel 4)

Convention

Conventions are usually described as the 'ingredients' of a particular form or genre. For example, if you make a news bulletin for your production work, you will have to observe a range of 'rules of engagement' for news broadcasts, or, in your evaluation, justify breaking or challenging them. And if you study the videogame industry, you will see that the way games are marketed shares a range of conventions with Hollywood film franchises (see Figure 2). Another example is period drama, a sub-genre with a range of necessary ingredients which are expected by the audience, making conventions 'contractual' in nature.

Signification

Signification is often applied within a theory called semiotics, the study of signs. Everything we see is a sign and carries a meaning.

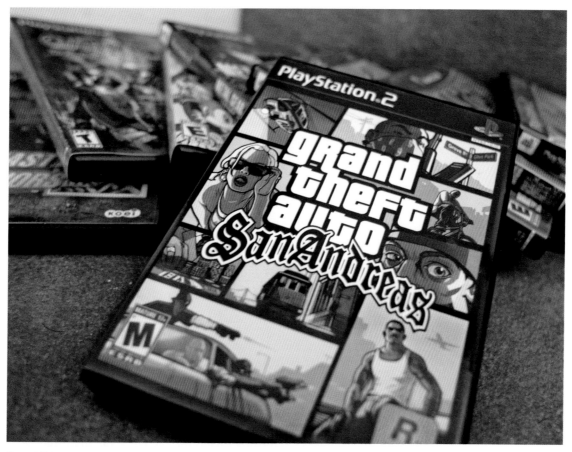

Figure 2 Videogame promotion shares conventions with Hollywood film campaigns.
(*Source*: AP/PA Photos)

The basic meaning of the sign that most people can recognise and agree on is known as the signifier. The more complex individual meanings that people give to signs are known as the signified. Look at your shoes. What image do they create of you? As a signifier, they are just a pair of shoes. As a signified, everyone who sees them will construct their own meaning; this is a matter of taste. When analysing media meaning, we deconstruct signs for what they might signify, but we must always remember that meaning is polysemic—every signifier has the potential to be given meaning differently by every person who sees or hears it.

Representation

The section on television and radio drama begins with a lengthy exploration of the concept of representation. Put simply, it is the 're' part of the word that is important. We no longer believe that media texts simply offer a transparent 'window on the world' or that audiences passively receive fixed messages which they accept and believe without question. Instead we see media texts as mediating between our sense of reality and the fictional or factual representation of reality—of people, places, ideas, themes, time periods and a range of social contexts. How the text presents 'reality' is always a 're' construction of a mediated version of the real world. The media student's job is to deconstruct representations at the 'macro' level of a text. For example, does the videogame *Def Jam Icon* represent black hip hop male artists in negative, stereotypical ways? Does it merely reproduce these representations already in place from the music or does it just represent 'reality' as it is? The subject is open to debate and is a very complicated issue.

Audiences

The section on institutions and audiences includes a detailed consideration of contemporary audience theories and approaches. The simplest way of analysing this concept is to look for a 'target audience' for a media text or product. But it is often more interesting than that—many texts appeal to a range of secondary audiences and the ways that different people respond to texts often challenges expectation.

So while on the one hand it is fairly easy to differentiate the audience for Radio 4 drama from pirate radio playing mostly reggae music, on the other hand the 'remixing' and uploading of *Lord of the Rings* scenes set to music on YouTube is unexpected

Production Tip

Whether or not you are going to work with film or video for your production work, uploading video to YouTube is something you should experience as it helps you to understand how the notion of media audiences has changed. You will also realise that there are different intentions behind the huge array of moving image material that appears on the website.

- Much is existing commercial material
- Some is existing material 'remixed' by a DIY enthusiast (like the *Lord of the Rings* example mentioned in this section)
- Some is amateur material posted only for family and friends to view
- Some is amateur material seeking a wider audience and 'playback' — see the Martinez research from Barcelona on pages 73–74.

Consider this description from Italian student Federico Leppene, who, at the start of an exchange visit to England, wanted to communicate with his friends back home in Bari, and used YouTube to do so.

'When I was in Roma Fiumicino Airport, I decided to make a movie to share on YouTube because, before I left my hometown, everybody told me they wanted to know about Birmingham, what the college looks like, what the English weather is like, etc. So I decided to include all the possible answers to my friends' questions in a video. The only problem was that I did not have a camera with me. So I decided to take a lot of photos and to make a video with them, and then to record an introduction using my webcam when I got to my room.

'For the editing I used Windows Movie Maker and then Nero Vision Express (just to add some extra effects). I chose some pics and I put them in chronological order. I chose background music, and I added some funny sentences and writing to make the video less boring.

'After that, I recorded the introduction using my webcam and a microphone, describing briefly those first days in Birmingham and sending greetings to "my audiences" back home.

'When my video was done, I uploaded it on YouTube and sent e-mails to all my friends I wanted to see it! I asked them to send me an email in return to comment on it (and everybody did!).

'I think to phone Italy is too expensive and to chat by MSN messenger (or similar) is almost cold. So I think a video is a great idea to get my Italian friends involved in my "new British life". And, of course, the images are powerful and easier to remember than simply spoken or written words (that's the power of the image).'

If you are a 'YouTube virgin', then you should experiment with the kind of social video networking undertaken by Frederico, and if you get playback or comments posted in response, this will give you an important insight into 'web 2.0'.

audience behaviour that is hard to analyse, as it doesn't have a tangible purpose either commercially or culturally beyond 'fun'.

Narrative and Genre

The news is packaged every day into the same amount of time or pages. This is not because the same amount of stuff happens every

Figure 3 *Lord of the Rings*: remixed 'just for fun' on YouTube.
(*Source*: New Line Cinema/Ronald Grant Archive)

day; it is because the news is presented through a particular narrative structure. Fictional TV and film tends to operate on a simple structure of balance, conflict and attempts at resolution. Narrative describes the process of balancing what we actually see or hear and what we assume in addition. It is fundamentally to do with order, usually linear, and the relationship between information and enigma.

When a range of media texts share form and conventions and the audience for this type of text develop certain expectations, this is referred to as genre. Whether genre exists more in the minds of producers or audiences is open to debate but the media is dominated by formats and when a format is seen to work (e.g. reality TV), then we are treated to a huge plethora of examples within a short space of time. But within a genre things tend to be more interesting—genres shift over time, producers and audiences subvert and parody the conventions and hybrid fusions of genres develop.

Creativity

Famously hard to define, creativity is a key 'performance descriptor' for the media student. Creative skills operate on two levels: first, the ability to use digital technologies to make meaning so that the audience can respond easily to the text and second, the ability to engage and interest the audience.

This doesn't necessarily mean originality—it is perfectly creative to imitate the conventions of a media form in a new configuration and this is a form of parody which is complex and fascinating. What it does mean is simple—for example, if you produce a website, the visitor needs to enjoy the experience of using it. This will only happen if the construction was creative. Media products emerge as a result of hundreds of creative decisions. When you analyse texts you will work out what these decisions were. When you make them, you will account for and evaluate these decisions from your own personal experience.

Connecting the Micro to the Macro

In this book the words micro and macro appear frequently in relation to textual analysis. The micro elements of a text are the technical and symbolic features which you will need to identify, recognise and describe the function of. These micro elements can be treated separately—for example, lighting has one range of meanings and editing has another, or speech in radio as separate to sound mixing. But when these elements combine they add up to an overall representational 'world' that makes sense and is believable. We call this plausible macro sum of the micro parts 'verisimilitude' and it will be your job to describe how this process works in specific cases.

Multimodal Literacy

Media literacy is changing in the context of web 2.0 technologies. As the technology allows us to read and write and create in new ways, so the theories we need to understand these communication processes also have to adapt. Critical multimodal literacy is about users making their own trajectory through hypermedia environments. What does this mean? Well, it means we have to be careful about theorising simple producer–audience relations and creator–consumer patterns of behaviour, because it is possible that HTML, web navigation, 'wikinomics' (Tapscott and Williams, 2007) and the general 'wall-less' nature of the internet are actually changing the way we 'read' texts altogether. It's worth bearing in mind!

Section 1
Foundation Portfolio

For most Media students, production work is what engages them the most. The opportunity to use new media technology to create media texts and gain feedback from an audience is rewarding, exciting and valuable as a way of acquiring transferable skills in creativity and communication.

Here, Steven Goodman (2003) describes the importance of practical media education by warning of the dangers of not including media production in the school/college curriculum:

> The failure of schools to address the media as the predominant language of youth today, or to recognize the social and cultural contexts in which students live, has resulted in a profound disconnect. It's a disconnect that occurs between the experiences that most students have during their time in school and those they have during their time outside of school. Until corrected this disconnect will lead to increased alienation.

(Goodman, 2003: 2)

Your media production work allows you to at least partly reduce this 'disconnect', the idea being that you can actively rework your existing media literacy (that you have developed through accessing various forms of media and by studying media theory) through practical implementation of creative ideas.

While digital technologies have undoubtedly made it easier for Media students and the wider general public to switch between media consumer and media producer—see YouTube (Figure 4) for evidence of this—it is really important to establish that AS Media Studies requires more than a hastily constructed amateur film, blog or music mix. To succeed in this part of your course, you need to combine practice with theory.

Media production and media literacy are connected. To become a more literate and critically engaged student

Figure 4 YouTube: web 2.0 applications allow media consumers to become producers.
Source: Courtesy of YouTube

of media it is essential to experience the creative process. Indeed, being creative with digital media—having initial ideas in response to a production brief, researching the subject matter, experimenting with form and style, considering audience responses, making changes to the initial design specification in response to unforeseen events or forks in the creative road or editing a text in post-production—is itself a theoretical series of activities. So it is best not to consider your AS studies as being a 'game of two halves'—theory on one side (analysis and knowledge) and production on the other (making a media text)—but to always see them as interrelated.

Burn and Durran (2007) summarise the mutual dependence of theory and practice by saying that:

> . . . the development of a critical grasp of the systems of meaning-making which operate in media texts is best achieved by making them.

(Burn and Durran, 2007: 169)

Process and Outcome

For the Foundation Portfolio, you need to think about process and outcome. *Process* is about engaging with the preliminary exercise as a place for trial and error, experimentation and learning the craft of the medium you are working in. This is where you get a sense of how many creative, technical and symbolic decisions are made by media professionals during their working practices.

Outcome is more important for the main task. This is where you 'deliver' the skills acquired in the preliminary activity. And along the way you will need to maintain a portfolio of production research and evaluative reflections on the work in progress—asking yourself questions about media conventions, representation, audience and your technological skills development from the preliminary task to the final product.

Disciplined Creativity

Writing in *Media Magazine* (the English and Media Centre's publication for media students), Pete Fraser, Chief Examiner for OCR Media, elaborates on the idea of disciplined creativity. He establishes a set of fundamental principles for media production work. These state that students should start with research into real media texts, consideration of audience awareness and careful planning of interim stages and deadlines (see Figure 5). These things have to happen (and be conducted methodically) before you get your hands on a camera, microphone or mouse. Following this pre-production research and planning, the

Figure 5 Media students planning for production: disciplined creativity in action.
Source: © Ian Shaw/Alamy

generation of simple ideas is more sensible than great ambition (however much you might want to film and edit a car chase!).

The effective combination of simplicity and originality is thus the key to a creative project, alongside rigorous attention to detail. For example, in the case of video, Fraser points to planning the minute details of each shoot meticulously to avoid wasting time on location, testing batteries, lighting and microphones before setting off and planning to improvise when group members are absent. Equally, time is needed for post-production—the final editing, laying out or uploading as well as testing the material with the audience and in many cases making last minute changes in response to their feedback. This can only happen if you have left sufficient time. These less 'sexy' aspects of media production, then, are actually the crucial building blocks for your creative genius.

So, if we take on board Fraser's advice we can say that a really important aspect of practical media work is the combination of motivation and organisation—aspects of discipline—and you can't achieve creative material without both of these. Media professionals (whose approaches to their work you need to imitate as far as possible) need rigorous attention to detail, planning, health and safety and time management, and from these elements creativity may flourish, but it won't the other way around. As Fraser says:

> Treat your project with professionalism and organisation and you will not go far wrong! Enjoy your work. Being creative is brilliant—but you can't beat being organised.

(Fraser, 2002: 42)

This section of the book provides a framework for approaching the three elements (preliminary task, main task and research/evaluation) for each of the set briefs. As textbooks are of limited use when tasking new media production in technical terms (most software is fairly easy to learn through play and experimentation), the emphasis here is on *disciplined creativity* in each medium, arranged around five key themes:

Activity 1.1

This activity links with your Television or Radio Drama work.

Select one of the drama sequences you are analysing for Key Media Concepts (see Section 2 for a range of examples). In a group, imagine you are at the first planning meeting for this drama—either the episode in question or the whole series, depending on what suits the activity more.

List ten key decisions you think must have been made at that meeting that are concerned more with planning and research than the creative process.

For each of the ten decisions you come up with, discuss what would have been the implications of that decision not being made—what might have gone wrong, what wouldn't have worked so well, how would the final outcome have been different?

1 Working with existing forms and conventions— *reworking the familiar*
2 Working in media production contexts— *professional practice*
3 Using technology—*creative tools*
4 Thinking about audience—*making meaning*
5 Representing—*constructing 'the real'*.

You are required to maintain an ongoing record of these evaluative reflections for assessment. This can be electronic or via a scrapbook or portfolio. In this section you are provided with a generic framework for this process for each brief, with the emphasis on the critical questioning and theoretical analysis of your own work, rather than the technical or formal aspects of how it is presented.

Chapter 1.1
Print Production

Preliminary exercise: front page of a school/college magazine.

Main task: front page, contents and double page spread of a new music magazine.

Technology: digital photography, desktop publishing.

Theoretical understanding: print conventions, audience and mode of address, making meaning through still image media language, semiotics, layers of interpretation, media and identity, the music industry and the music press, popular culture and youth representations.

Links with other units: Key Media Concepts: representation, music industry and audiences.

Composing Digital Images

As all of the images that will appear on your print products for both the preliminary and main tasks must be original, photography is a critical part of print production for AS. You will need to use a digital camera so you can easily download your images in order to work with desktop publishing software. There is a long-running debate amongst the photography fraternity as to the relative merits of traditional film and darkroom work versus digital manipulation. Digital photography does of course open doors to cheap and instant creative activity, as described here in some valuable advice from Huw Meredith, professional photographer:

> Any camera (film or digital) is just a capturing device, but saying that, the technology in a modern digital camera is just fantastic. The ability to see what you have just taken is a really useful tool, but don't let it make you a lazy photographer! You still have to use your eyes and your brain, there are great photographs waiting to be taken all around you. But get your photographs printed! Too many digital images just remain on a disc somewhere or are only ever seen on a screen. It is so easy to plug your camera into a portable printer, or take the memory card to a shop. Get out and use that camera, but use the prints as well!

The technical skills that you need to develop in the preliminary activity and improve upon when you step up to the main task are linked to the four production tips below.

Generating a Front Page

A quick glance at the magazines on display in a newsagent or supermarket reveals instantly the importance of the front cover design in either introducing or welcoming back the existing or potential reader to the world of the magazine. This is a world where identity is clearly constructed to make the reader feel a

Production Tip

Conception

You need to ensure that the images you develop are appropriate for the product being constructed, so how you conceive of the intended images is paramount. Spend adequate time planning your images and don't start taking photographs until you have produced a basic 'mock-up' design for the front cover and other pages you will create. Knowing roughly where the image is going helps a photographer with the 'instinct' for the right shot.

Framing and composition

This takes practice and you should expect to take far more images than you need. Framing can be adjusted through cropping at the design/editing stage, but good framing in the lens leads to a better quality image. The photographer is in ultimate control of what the viewer sees: by choosing the angle (framing and composition are to do with arranging the subject of the image); by deciding whether the subject in the photograph will be close to us or further away; looking up at us, down at us or away from us. What do you want to be the focus? Place this in the centre of the viewing lens. Compose your shot as an artist would a painting—it might sound slightly pretentious but some famous photographers talk of a photo being like a canvas, so imagine your images this way.

Shot distance

There is little you can do to alter this in editing, so this needs to be 'spot on'. Depending on the effect you want, using the zoom function will allow you a variety of possible distances from your subject. For this unit it is highly likely that you will be working mostly in medium close-up—this is required for the preliminary task. For the main task, many shots of bands or artists also use medium close-up, so it is a good idea to follow this convention.

Mise en scène

This is a term you will be familiar with when you get stuck into your TV/radio drama work. Meaning 'putting into the scene', it describes all the creative choices made by photographers, designers, and directors when creating an authentic atmosphere. For still images, this is partly constructed at the photography stage and partly through editing. You need to make clear creative decisions about lighting (trial and error is the best way of getting this absolutely right), costume, appearance, props for the shot, background imagery and colour.

Production Tip

Colour and resolution

Remember that how an image looks through a digital camera will not be the same as how it appears in print. The computer you use for downloading and editing and the printer you use will both influence the final quality of resolution and colour. It is sensible, therefore, to trial the process first so you get a sense of how the 'reality' of what you photograph will translate into a printed outcome.

sense of belonging, or a desire to belong to the community of readers that is established. Magazines adopt a template approach in the main, meaning that the cover model or image and text linking to content will change but the essential design is reinforced for each issue to secure familiarity and brand recognition. Your school/college magazine is, of course, slightly different in that this product will not be commercially available, but in order to use this developmental task as a productive stepping stone to the main print project, you should adopt this approach.

Semiotics

A basic familiarity with semiotics is useful for this task. Semiotics is the study of signs and meaning and can help us to analyse seemingly obvious meanings and interpretations that circulate everyday in the visual world. Rather than learning the theory of semiotics first and then trying to apply it to your own work, it is easier to learn semiotics through basic digital image manipulation, which the preliminary task is all about. If you place yourself on the cover of your school/college magazine you will immediately situate yourself in terms of choices you make about clothing, facial expression, posture and location (i.e. 'studio' or external background). After selecting a still image for editing, it is a good idea to use an interactive whiteboard for some peer feedback.

Having carried out this image manipulation and peer review work, you are now ready to use semiotic terms. Semiotics arises from structuralist theory and the key players in this kind of theory are Saussure (1954) and Barthes (1972). It is best to use semiotics as a way of developing your own thinking about 'polysemic' meaning (the way that the same sign can mean lots of different things to different people) rather than assuming that signs mean

Activity 1.2

When you have taken digital images which you intend to manipulate with software and use on a magazine cover, it is useful to stop at this early stage and focus on the importance of the image. The danger otherwise is that you get to the end of a larger project and much of the hard work is undone by the poor quality of the primary images.

However user-friendly technology becomes, image creation and manipulation require cultural knowledge (knowing what range of things your images might 'mean' to people), intertextual understanding (knowing how existing magazines work) and aesthetic competence (being able to construct images which are appealing, well composed and are clear and fit for purpose).

Download your images and present them on an interactive whiteboard, using the notebook tools to present the image and a colour pen to annotate the image to show intended cropping, enlargement, further manipulation and text.

Next, ask your fellow students to offer some critique and further suggestions, and use another colour pen to further annotate the work on screen. These ideas are visual representations of feedback and can be saved and printed out for evidence of the creative and evaluative process. To take this further, pair up with another student and follow this two stage process:

First, present a descriptive account of your own work—what do you think your image is going to represent/mean to the reader?

Second, respond to your partner's image from your own personal, subjective interpretation—a summary of what you think of when you look at this magazine cover.

Activity 1.3

Categorise these signs into iconic, symbolic/arbitrary and indexical:

A man's tie
A Manchester United football shirt
The Nike logo
A photograph of you
Your name, spoken or written
The words zoo and chair
A no smoking sign
A no entry sign
A crucifix
A picture of Harry Potter.

single things to everyone. There are three kinds of signs in semiotic theory:

1 **Iconic signs** which actually look like what they represent.

2 **Symbolic/arbitrary signs** which have a meaning that must be culturally learned because they don't actually look like what they represent.

3 **Indexical signs** which have a connection to what they represent and are suggestive rather than directly resembling what they represent.

Taking the example of a man's tie, the right answer is that this piece of material, worn around the neck for certain occasions (a meeting or interview, a wedding, but not watching TV at home) is symbolic/arbitrary. If you study in a school or college where the male teachers all wear a tie, this is likely to be a dress requirement. Would it make any difference to the teachers' skills if they removed their tie? Probably not, but it might make a difference to your perception of them, as the way they are dressed represents/symbolises a set of cultural ideas about formality, professional conduct, respect and care.

Motivated signs

When signs are in circulation they can be more or less *motivated*. More motivated signs are images which have more of a fixed meaning (but we must remember that no meaning is ever totally fixed as each human being will have a slightly different take on what they see as a result of their cultural experience). A photograph of David Beckham is much more motivated than a piece of Tracy Emin artwork (see Figure 6). The latter takes a lot of individual interpretation—it doesn't mean any one stable thing. A picture of Beckham is iconical and to most people on the planet, instantly recognisable. So the Beckham picture is much more motivated than the Emin artwork.

However, at the level of connotation (the individual meanings that people draw from images), how you feel about David Beckham (which might range from feelings of desire to intellectual superiority or distaste at the excesses of his lifestyle) will 'kick in' and influence your response. A more motivated sign just has a more limited range of possible interpretations.

Figure 6 Tracey Emin's infamous piece of art (her own bed)—a loosely motivated sign. (*Source*: Photo by NILS JORGENSEN/Rex Features)

Activity 1.4

Having completed Activity 1.3, you are now more familiar with semiotic terms. Display a range of images you have taken in your class around a room and spend a lesson moving around collecting examples of each type of sign from your fellow students' digital production work.

Using captions

For magazine production, the most common way of 'holding down' the meaning of an image to make it more motivated is to use text alongside an image or as a caption. This has the obvious effect of making the meaning less abstract and in semiotic terms this is known as 'anchorage'. So a picture of a two-year-old boy with long hair will, on its own, be fairly motivated. We will recognise the image as a two-year-old boy with long hair and maybe make a judgement about what he is wearing and how interesting/amusing he looks. If we add a caption—Ned Kendall, aged 2—the sign becomes more motivated, anchored by this new information, but still only loosely motivated to everyone who doesn't know the child. Change the caption to 'Ned Kendall, aged 2, son of the author of this book', and you are now thinking very differently about the image (see Figure 7). The sign is anchored by the caption, the meaning is pinned down.

Figure 7 Ned Kendall, aged 2, son of the author—a highly motivated, 'anchored' sign. (*Source*: J McDougall)

Designing the front page

With all this in mind, you need to decide on a name for your magazine that will work symbolically, perhaps as a metaphor. Here is an example—Newman College has a magazine named *Newsman* (see Figure 8).

You might decide on a less obvious, more abstract title—this will be a sign which will signal and connote various ideas in the mind of the potential reader. As the reader for the preliminary task will be a student, this range of meanings does not need to be obvious to the 'outside world'. The decisions you make about font size and colour will also be symbolic. Once you have decided on these, you need to create the text that will appear on the cover,

Figure 8 *Newsman*—the magazine of Newman College.
(*Source*: Newman College)

which needs to have a narrative form, drawing in the reader to the contents with the most attractive material being signposted first. This can be achieved either at the top of a list or in a larger font or in a different colour—study the way that existing magazines do this.

Developing a Music Magazine

It is sensible to study the ways that the music industry use music magazines as a form of promotion before starting work on your own product. Section 3, Chapter 2 of this book will help you with this. Each music magazine will have a clear definition of its reader and how they fit into the global music industry market. As the activity below suggests, it is sensible to begin by accessing information for advertisers as this will present an idea of the reader which is reflected in editorial decisions (what to include), design principles (how things should look), mode of address (the tone and style of language—how the reader is 'spoken to') and crucially, the balance of promotion and critique (most features and interviews are really a form of advertising for the musicians, but elsewhere in the publication reviews can be very negative).

Activity 1.5

In your production group, provide between you a range of popular magazines and after studying the cover, contents page and one feature, answer these questions about the reader of each magazine:

What breakfast cereal do they eat?
What car/mode of transport do they use?
What accommodation do they live in?
What do they drink?
What TV shows do they watch?
What music do they like?
What is their favourite meal?
What sport do they watch and what sport do they play (if any)?
Who is their partner, or are they single?
Where do they go on holiday?
Do they vote, and if so who for?
What type of bar/pub/club do they go to (if any)?

You can add four or five more categories to this list. You should find it fairly easy to answer these questions and the reason for this is straightforward. Magazine publishers work hard to create a notion of their 'ideal reader' and, in order to sell this readership to advertisers (from whom publishers generate far more income than they do from sales) they go as far as to develop short narratives about their typical reader. If you visit the website of a popular magazine and search for the material for advertisers, you should be able to download this information.

The front cover of a music magazine is distinguished from other magazines as the specific artist or band featured may attract particular readers and turn off others (this is not an issue for magazines like *Men's Health*, *Nuts* or *Cosmopolitan* where a generic approach to cover models is taken). Increasingly, a CD is offered with music magazines which is another example of the mutually beneficial relationship between industry and media (see Figure 9).

You are required to use original images, so, for the cover, you may use images of a real band or artist or images of you and your friends posing as musicians in a band, and then make decisions about what kind of magazine would feature this kind of music. Remember that your decisions about the double-page

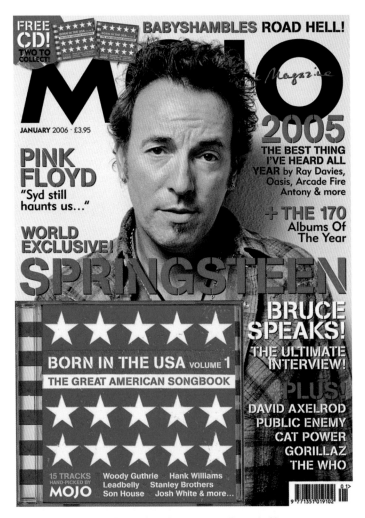

Figure 9 Music magazines strike a balance between promotion and critique. (*Source*: © EMAP Metro)

Writing skills

For the double-page feature, some journalistic skill is required. You should study music journalism and look at the blend in features on bands/artists of quotation, paraphrase and journalistic prose. You must ensure that spelling, grammar and punctuation are perfect, and while this is likely to be a group task, it is useful to identify the student with the most accomplished writing style for this kind of material (perhaps a student of English), so that you can all generate the ideas for the feature but she or he can put them into words. Media students sometimes neglect this area of their work, getting carried away with the technical side and forgetting that a crucial element of a magazine is the words on the page.

spread (which will be for the same band or artist, as this is the established convention) and contents page will need to be in keeping with this approach.

You need to ensure that the language used, mode of address, layout, font and colour range are right for the audience you have identified. One aspect of mode of address is the style of language you choose, or 'register', and this will either secure or alienate your readership. The register of *Word* magazine is very different to the *NME*. It would be productive to prepare some information for advertisers for this magazine, as is the industry convention. Use peer review throughout the project to test out these approaches, and with this in mind it might be more fruitful to identify an audience group which you have access to. If you are based at a school or college and surrounded by people in their late teens, this won't be difficult.

Desktop publishing and design principles

You will need to become competent with some desktop publishing software for this task. Much-used applications for print production are Adobe Photoshop and Quark Express, but your school/college may use another application. This book cannot teach you how to use these applications, so we will focus here more on the decisions you will make.

You will have the option to frame text in boxes, use layering to work on multiple elements of a page, insert backgrounds and make changes to colour, lighting, contrast and tone. You will work in grids and templates for each section of your print product. The crucial thing to remember is that the

Design principles

The key principles to apply are:

- Separate the most important aspect on a page from the rest.
- Spend time on tightly cropping and resizing images and use clipping paths so you can work on an image but not the background.
- Experiment with filtering and other effects to create impressions of motion or to soften focus but never use these for the sake of it—only when the effect is essential for the meaning you wish to suggest.
- Use a range of fonts and sizes but remember most magazines use two or three fonts in total, with distinct contrast between each font and its purpose, for example, one font for headings and titles.
- Use a pyramid approach for margins—the margins at the bottom of a page should be broader than those higher up.
- Use the DTP software's guidelines facility to keep text and images neatly arranged.
- Experiment with colour, black on white and white on black for contrast.

technical stuff is a means to a creative end, so refer back to the information on semiotics throughout and don't let the technical learning override the decisions you are making about signs, symbolic meaning, anchorage and mode of address. There are a number of design principles which you must apply.

Coursework Practice: Critically evaluating print production

Here are some key questions to ask about your print work as you progress with both tasks:

Working with existing forms and conventions— *reworking the familiar*

1 How do your school/college magazine and music magazine relate to existing examples of these media forms?
2 What conventions have you observed in terms of design, mode of address and use of imagery?

Working in media production contexts—*professional practice*

1 How have you approached the two tasks individually and in groups, and how have you managed time, each other, equipment and other resources?
2 Can you provide examples of creative problem-solving decisions you have had to make in relation to the development of ideas, still photography, image editing, desktop publishing, printing and trialling your work?
3 How did you organise your human resources, i.e. the people involved in the production?
4 How did you manage locations for photographs and any costumes and props? Remember that deciding not to use a particular strategy (not to use any props in photos, for example) is also a creative decision.
5 You should also reflect on the importance of design drafting and how the final outcome related to the draft layout in each case.
6 Finally, while not the 'sexiest' element of creative media practice, time management is possibly the most important—how did you manage your time, and with what success?

Using technology—*creative tools*

This is not about technical elements in isolation from the creative process. Instead, you need to be asking questions about how enabling the technology was in relation to your creative ideas.

1 Can you provide examples of the desktop publishing technology allowing you to do things that extended your creative control?
2 Are there examples of the technology obstructing or limiting the creative process?

Thinking about audience—*making meaning*

1 Throughout the two activities you will have been making creative decisions based on ideas you were developing about your readers. Where did these ideas come from and how did they influence the 'micro' detail of shot composition and framing, anchorage, layout, mode of address and register?
2 Did audience feedback confirm expectations or generate surprise?

Representing—*constructing 'the real'*

1 How did your ideas and their execution amount to specific representations of school/college life, music and the readers of music magazines?
2 What sense of reality have you constructed in each case and who is included and excluded as a result?

Chapter 1.2
Video Production

Preliminary exercise: continuity exercise.

Main task: titles and opening sequence of new fiction film.

Technology: digital video, non-linear editing.

Theoretical understanding: the language of film and grammar of the edit, making meaning through moving images, narrative and representation, action and enigma, plot and story, establishing realism and verisimilitude, mise en scène, genre, layers of interpretation.

Links with other units: Key Media Concepts: representation, the film industry and audiences.

Continuity

The preliminary task for this brief requires an understanding of continuity, which is a fundamental principle of moving image production. Watching a film or TV programme tends to be a fairly effortless pleasure because continuity is normally secured by producers following the conventions of the 'classical realist text'. As long as continuity rules are followed, plot and story can unfold in such a way that the audience can assume what happens in between each shot or sequence. For example, if a character boards a train in shot 1, is seen sitting reading a paper in shot 2, asleep in the same seat with the paper folded up in shot 3 and getting off the train in shot 4, the audience will not think the train journey was extraordinarily short. They will assume that in between shots 2, 3 and 4 the journey continued but nothing of significance to the plot occurred. However, if a continuity rule was broken so that the character appeared to move seats, this would disrupt the flow of the sequence.

Storyboarding

Whatever the nature of moving image production, storyboarding is vital. Artistic talent is not required and it is likely that your teacher will have a template for you to use for storyboarding. If not, five minutes with a search engine will lead you to a range of downloadable templates you can use.

Essentially, storyboards are more or less basic cartoon versions of what each shot will look like when filmed and edited (see Figure 10). In a box for each shot you draw the action, trying to make it as clear as possible for the crew where each character will be in relation to one another, the background and props. Most importantly, the shot type (close up, extreme close up, long shot, mid shot) and any movement (pan, zoom, tilt, track) must be clear to the camera operator.

Storyboarding allows you to visually conceptualise the flow of the action and to work through the important practical details. While you will almost certainly depart from the storyboard at some point, constructing one is an essential aspect of the disciplined creativity of moving image production.

The shooting script

The shooting script accompanies the storyboard and provides more of a schedule for the filming, usually listed in order of filming—for example a studio session followed by location work. The storyboard will be chronological in relation to how the narrative will unfold for the viewer, but the shooting script is arranged in order of filming, which is rarely chronological. It is usually more sensible logistically and financially to film all the sequences in one location at a time. The shooting script also lists equipment and people needed for each shot.

Figure 10 An example of a storyboard frame
from Film Education.
(© 2000 Film Education)

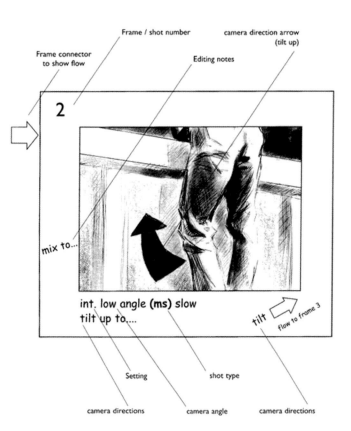

Every cell should contain certain elements...

Frame / shot number

camera direction arrow
(tilt up)

Frame connector
to show flow

Editing notes

2

mix to...

int. low angle (ms) slow
tilt up to....

tilt

Flow to frame 3

Setting

shot type

camera directions

camera angle

camera directions

Match on action

To use this technique, cut from one shot to another view that matches the action and pace of the first shot. This creates an impression of continuity although you may have filmed the shots weeks apart. If a character begins an action in the first shot and completes it in the next, a visual 'bridge' is created which acts to disguise the cut from one to the other.

Principles of continuity

The preliminary task requires you to produce a piece of film in which a character opens a door, walks across a room and sits down in a chair opposite another character and exchanges two sentences of conversation. There are three continuity principles to observe in this exercise:

- Match on action
- Shot reverse shot
- 180° rule (see Figure 11 on page 35)

Developing an Opening Sequence

Although there are some notable exceptions, in the majority of fiction films, not much happens in dramatic terms in the first couple of minutes. So your job here is to *establish* character and narrative context for the audience and to set up some degree of enigma (a question that the narrative will answer in time).

Rather than show the titles first and then some action, it is preferable to observe the convention of cutting between title/action, title/action. This can either be done by selecting the 'over black' option on the editing software you are using in the titles menu, or by positioning the titles over the action, which is usually preferred if actors' names are to appear alongside their characters.

Some of the most memorable film scenes are opening/title sequences. Some famous examples from different genres are: **Once Upon a Time in the West** (in which diegetic sound is amplified with a total lack of dialogue to create audience anticipation); **a Bond film (**the Bond opening sequence has become a recurring motif; an established convention expected by the audience); **Goodfellas** (in which we hear the lead character narrate 'ever since I can remember, I always wanted to be a gangster', thus situating us firmly in the mind of the anti-hero for the duration of the film); **City of God** (in which music, fast edits and clever narrative techniques introduce two inter-connected storylines and take the audience back twenty years in the process a strategy shared with *Goodfellas*); **Four Weddings and a Funeral** (in which the main character, Charles (played by Hugh Grant), and a friend swear a lot while rushing around getting dressed, thus establishing Charles as a likeable, though chaotic figure).

This list could go on for at least the rest of this book and all the examples would contrast with one another as there is no fixed approach to an opening sequence. Your sequence does, however, need to observe the one rule that every example follows: your job is to establish character and/or setting and to create enigma – to help the audience understand easily where we are, who is involved but, fundamentally, *why* we should be interested. It is likely that the time and resources available to you will determine a fairly economical approach to this. Bond-style stunts and explosions are unlikely. But if you watch a range of openings, you will realise that most of the time conversations dominate, along with continuity and cross-cutting. See *Grapevine*, an example by the Halesowen College Media staff, who made their own opening sequence in one day to show students how much better they could do with more time.

You will need to develop the idea for the film in broader terms before you can construct a plausible opening sequence (you need to have worked out what would happen later if you were going to produce the whole film). Your brief here is to show the audience a

Grapevine

We see through a range of different shot types a character preparing for a journey: making tea, picking up a wallet, a map and car keys. The destination is thus defined as Halesowen College. We never see the character's face, but we do see him using an asthma inhaler — an intertextual reference to the Harry Palmer character in *The Ipcress File* who makes coffee and cannot do so without his glasses (the students had studied this film). These shots are cut alongside shots of the rest of the staff team each in turn saying to an unknown phone caller 'I don't know who told me, I just know he is coming today.' Music by Cinerama plays in the background – a song with a 1960s spy film ambience, to aid the mise en scène. These shots and sounds add up to establish enigma. Who *is* the character who is coming? Why does nobody know *how* they know he is coming? And, of course, they anchor the title — *Grapevine* — that appears at the end of the opening sequence.

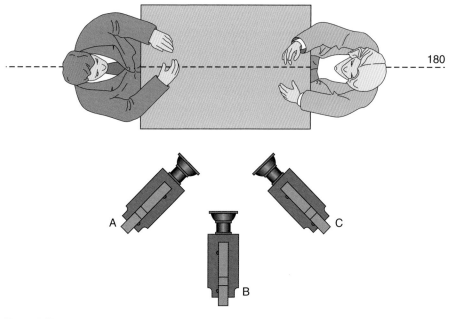

Figure 11 'The 180° rule'.
(*Source*: Barking Dog Art)

main character in a changing situation which will become dramatic. You must show her/him in their everyday situation and the representation must be achieved by a range of elements— appearance, costume, performance, location, dialogue, lighting, props, music and possibly voice-over. Here you will be constructing the 'micro' elements that you will be analysing for your Key Concepts exam, so you should refer to Section 2 of this book in detail. You will be combining diegetic and non-diegetic elements.

You will need to demonstrate both creativity (originating and executing the fictional narrative) and technical competence to be successful with this brief. The production tips provided relate to elements of video work that you will be assessed on.

Coursework Practice: Critically evaluating video production

Here are some key questions to ask about your video work as you progress with both tasks:

Working with existing forms and conventions— *reworking the familiar*

1 At a micro, technical level, how well did you observe the conventions of continuity, the language of film and the grammar of the edit?

Diegesis

A moving image media text creates meaning for the audience through the combination of diegetic and non-diegetic material, and particularly sound.

Diegetic material is that which exists in the world of the text itself, so that the characters are aware of it. Examples are dialogue, sound effects which are heard by characters (like thunder), background music which is heard by characters and dialogue between characters. Non-diegetic material is added purely for the audience, for example, atmospheric music, soundtrack music, voice-over or narration.

Some types of sound are both—for example, a character's thoughts in a voice-over are diegetic in that the character is aware of them, but non-diegetic in the sense that other characters are not. A good example of this is the film *Taxi Driver*, in which the non-diegetic music creates a haunting atmosphere while a voice-over of the main protagonist's thoughts situates us in the mind of a character losing his sanity (see Figure 12). This technique (by the director Martin Scorsese) makes highly effective use of diegetic and non-diegetic elements placed deliberately in a state of confusion to defamiliarise the audience.

Another interesting example of the difference diegesis can make is the film *Blade Runner*. The studio inserted a film-noir style voiceover narration from Harrison Ford against the wishes of the director Ridley Scott, and it was only years later when the 'Director's Cut' was released without the voice-over that the audience realised the original has a less anchored, more ambiguous narrative. In the meantime the film had become a cult classic with the voice-over, featuring lines like 'I didn't know how long we would have together, but then again, who does?', a major aspect of the film's popular appeal.

Micro and macro origination

In order to shoot material that is appropriate, you need to adopt the micro-macro strategy that is covered in Section 2. You may decide your fiction film will follow the conventions of a particular genre or style of film, in which case the micro elements—types of camera work, music, style of titles, dialogue, setting and pace—will add up to a macro theme and set of representations. For this reason it is important not to dive straight into filming the main task. Make sure you spend time with storyboarding and ideas development first, so you can ensure that your approach to filming is not out of step with the conventions of the type of film you are making. Put simply, if you are making a romantic comedy you need to follow a three-stage process. First, study romantic comedy conventions using the micro-macro strategy. Second, spend time developing a romantic comedy narrative that will be instantly recognisable to the audience for that type of film. Third, spend time planning to shoot and edit material which looks right for the genre, not only in terms of what is on the screen but also how it is filmed, edited and put together with sound and titles.

Figure 12 *Taxi Driver*: diegetic and non-diegetic elements situate us in the mind of a character en route to destruction.
(*Source*: Photo by Everett Collection/Rex Features)

2 How many mistakes did you make, and did you improve in the main task having made errors in the preliminary exercise?

3 At a more symbolic, macro level, how does your fiction film reflect or challenge the conventions of the genre or type you are working in? Will it fulfil the 'contractual' nature of film genre or will it subvert expectations deliberately?

4 Are there any elements of deliberate pastiche or parody, where you 'play' with the genre's codes and history? Are there any intertextual moments where you hint at a reference to another film?

5 What kinds of audience pleasure are you trying to provide, and how confident are you that you have delivered on this promise?

Camera work and framing

Holding a shot steady is not as simple as you might think and mostly you should be using a tripod unless a hand-held realist/documentary effect is required. Most of your shots should be filmed with a camera that is not moving, so movement becomes an effective exception to the norm. Zooming is rarely used in film so it is best to avoid it unless you want the appearance of amateur footage.

As you are working in the medium of film, select a widescreen framing if you can, and remember that film uses fewer close-ups than TV (simply because the viewing screen is much bigger). You can select long shots, extreme long shots, mid-shots, close-ups and extreme close-ups. For film, it is suggested that you mostly use mid-shots and long shots, with close-ups used sparingly.

The 'rule of thirds' principle is useful for framing your shots. Imagine the frame is made up of nine squares (three squares by three). The off-centre areas are where the eye is drawn to, so it is best to avoid the central square and position objects and people just off-centre as this aids concentration on the image.

Combining shot types and distances is essential to the 'language of film'. Effective combinations include going from long shots to mid-shots and then to close-ups. This enables you to establish action, emphasise location and then move to detail and cutting between two-shots, over-the-shoulder shots and point-of-view shots to situate the audience during a conversation.

As far as camera angle is concerned, you need to consider power and neutrality. High-angle shots reduce the power of a character and low-angle shots increase it. A simple principle of framing is to ensure that characters have room above their heads and are not made to look strange by objects behind them and have space around them to show direction if they are moving.

Here are some simple tips that will help you avoid 'unforced errors': practise moving shots several times before recording, shoot far more footage than you need to make editing easier, test microphones are working before filming so you don't end up with a silent movie by mistake, ensure you have switched off the date and time on the camera, be prepared to film several takes of each shot, be a perfectionist and re-film a shot if the camera shakes or someone walks through the frame in error and make sure your batteries are charged!

Working in media production contexts—*professional practice*

1 How did you manage the group dynamics, equipment and resources, interim deadlines and the necessarily collaborative nature of film-making?
2 What health and safety and logistical problems did you solve?
3 How did you organise your human resources—the people involved in the production?
4 How did you manage actors, locations, costumes and props? Remember that deciding not to use a particular strategy (e.g. not to use any props) is also a creative decision.

Mise en scène

Section 2 of this book contains guidance for analysing *mise en scène* in television. Here we deal with constructing it. *Mise en scène* is all about atmosphere and continuity. Working as a student without access to the expensive resources and amounts of time that the film industry enjoy, *mise en scène* is the most difficult element of production to get right, but probably the one that reaps the greatest rewards for those that do. Essentially it is about detail. Carefully choose costume, lighting (see the production tip below), locations and props to create the kind of 'feel' and verisimilitude (believable world of the text) that is required. Then ensure that this is maintained shot by shot. Simple mistakes that lots of students make are costume changes or haircuts mid-sequence, poor lighting or drastic contrasts in lighting mid-sequence, poorly chosen and unconvincing props and—as performance is another element of *mise en scène*—bad acting. Although not part of the assessment, poor acting skills will undermine the overall flow of the narrative and the realism of the *mise en scène*, so try to use students who are more comfortable with performance (preferably those who are taking Drama as well as Media) for the leading roles.

Lighting

Most Media students do not have access to industry standard professional lighting equipment and this can undermine their creative intentions. However, there are a number of ways that careful attention to detail can overcome this problem. Here are five tips, which are informed by an article by Michael Massey (2004) for *Media Magazine*. The fuller article is highly recommended. (See the Further Study Resources section for details.)

1 Use natural light—sunlight, in shadow, in mist, through rain—depending on the effect you need, and bearing in mind that you will have to be flexible about time if you need to wait for the right conditions.
2 Use cheap and cheerful artificial light—as long as you have carried out risk assessments, you can make use of candles, firelight, torches, car headlights, security lights, neon signs and street lighting.
3 Create colour filters—you can easily shine light through coloured liquids, vases, ornaments.
4 Position the light source for effect—lighting a scene from above, below or in an obscured way will create different kinds of atmosphere (*mise en scène*), so experiment with this using the kinds of light source listed above.
5 Ultimately, lighting a scene is a scientific process. Massey describes the equation in helpful, clear terms:

> **Once you have explored what your light sources can provide, experiment with the interaction of light with the objects in your frame.**

(Massey, 2004: 8)

Combining sound, image and titles

It is harder than it might seem to put footage together with appropriate sound and titles. You need to make very careful decisions about titles, choosing the most appropriate font, colour and size from the vast array that your software will present. In addition you must, though trial and error, end up with the most pleasing timing of titles for the audience. You will need to make creative decisions about where to place each title, whether to place it over black between shots or over the action and how long each title stays on screen. You also need to understand what contribution each title is making to the audience's understanding of the narrative, the genre and the representational aspects that you need them to grasp quickly since this is an opening sequence.

In addition, you will be using music to add ambience to the start of your film. Here you must think very carefully about the semiotic function of music and ensure that what the music suggests to the audience is in keeping with the tone and pace of the drama you are unfolding. It is a good idea to test this out with audience members at an early stage of post-production so you can make changes if they do not respond as you expect.

The grammar of non-linear editing

You will be using a non-linear video editing software package for your post-production work and you will be assessed on how well you can edit the material so that meaning is apparent to the viewer. To achieve this you need to observe the rules of grammar that apply to editing, creating continuity and the right rhythm and pace. Choosing the right kinds of transition is essential and the software you use is likely to offer an enormous range of effects. Avoid choosing transitions that are exciting to use but do not reflect the conventions of the type of film you are constructing. Most editing is simple—hard cuts. You should be using hard cuts for at least 90 per cent of your sequence. The exception is where you place a transition between a title and images, but you should still be consistent—do not use a different type of transition for each title.

Your job is to make the editing invisible, so that the viewer believes in the reality of the fiction that is unfolding. A fade might be used to portray the passing of time, and if you are establishing tension or action early on in the sequence, you may choose to use a greater number of edits. Editing is all about the manipulation of time and space. You will manipulate space by editing between two simultaneous pieces of action, and manipulate time by editing between two shots to move the narrative forward and bypass unnecessary time that is not interesting to the story. A standard industry technique is to cut from one shot of a subject to a different subject and then back again, rather than moving immediately to the same image.

Editing allows you to do things that you can't in real life. The careful execution of these forms of manipulation without distracting or confusing the viewer is what we call the 'grammar of the edit'.

5 How did storyboarding and creating a shooting script work in practice? Did you make creative decisions to depart from the original plan? For what reasons and with what outcomes?

6 Although time management may seem a less exciting aspect of creative media practice, it is possibly the most important—how did you manage your time, and with what success?

Using technology—*creative tools*

You will have used digital cameras, microphones, lighting and editing resources. Some of these will have been closer to industry standard (for example, Final Cut Pro) than others (for example, using a torch to light a scene).

1 How did digital technology enable you to develop creatively and are there examples of the technology obstructing or preventing your creative flow?

Thinking about audience—*making meaning*

1 How did you respond to the initial brief with the audience in mind?

2 How did your analysis and research into the type of film you selected impact on the creative process in pre-production?

3 In filming and editing, how did you ensure that the meaning would be apparent to the audience? What creative decisions did you make in planning, rehearsing, filming and editing that were influenced by your sense of the audience and possible layers of interpretation?

4 How did the audience respond when you trialled aspects of your film? Are there a variety of different possible interpretations of your opening sequence that will depend on the cultural situation of the viewer?

Representing—*constructing 'the real'*

1 Who and what (people, places, themes, ideas, time periods) have you represented and how in your film?

2 Who is included and excluded by the text you have created?

3 What form of 'realism' have you constructed, and why?

4 What role do the *mise en scène*, acting, dialogue, music and style of camera work (micro elements) play in the construction of verisimilitude (the macro level of the textual world)?

Chapter 1.3
Audio Production

Preliminary exercise: intro music/jingle, presenter/guest interaction and related sound archive for radio show.

Main task: 5-minute local radio news bulletin.

Technology: digital audio recording, non-linear editing software, music editing software.

Theoretical understanding: news values, local media and community/identity, radio news conventions, representation of region, audience and issues, narrative, making meaning with sound, auditory semiotics.

Links with other units: Key Media concepts: representation, the radio industry and audiences.

The software you use for audio editing will depend upon your institution and the resources it is able to provide, so the technical aspects of your audio production work will be treated generically here.

You may have access to a multi-track recording facility, or you may rely on sound recording software with which you are able to record separate tracks to edit from. Most audio editing software

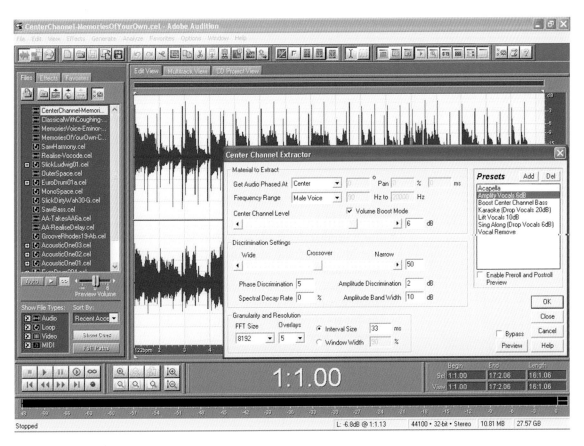

Figure 13 Adobe Audition® is used by the BBC. It shares features with many non-linear audio editing software solutions. (*Source*: Adobe)

shares some common features, with sound being represented on screen by sound waves which you can make bigger or smaller depending on the detail you need, and then edit by cutting, moving, pasting, stretching and manipulating in a range of ways (see Figure 13). You will be downloading and then mixing sounds and making an array of informed creative decisions about sound levels, effects, tone and pitch.

The main task is a news bulletin, so the most important skill is adherence to a range of local broadcast news conventions, always with the audience in mind. However, this bulletin will feature some aspects that are developed in the preliminary exercise, for example, opening music, an interview and sound archive are all possible features and, depending on the audience for the bulletin, you may also include musical motifs and sound effects.

Music Copyright and Radio

The MCPS-PRS alliance looks after the interests of musicians by protecting their copyright. A radio station needs to apply

Table 1 Commercial radio copyright rates from the MCPS-PRS.

'Net Broadcasting Revenue' (NBR)	Rate Of Royalty
Below £530,749	3%
£530,750–£1,061,497	4%
£1,061,498 and over	5.25%
Where the total music use is less than 15% of the broadcast then regardless of the level of the NBR the percentage rate to be applied will be	1%

Source: MCPS-PRS

for a licence to broadcast music. Table 1 shows an extract from the MCPS website indicating the payments made by broadcasters.

The MCPS-PRS Alliance was formed in 1997 between the two royalty collection societies and it collects and pays royalties to its members (musicians who have joined the Alliance) when their music is recorded and made available to the public or performed, broadcast or otherwise made publicly available. Money is generated through licences that are obtained by people wishing to engage in the public performance of music, whether live or recorded (outside the home) and from radio and television broadcasts and online.

Production Tip

Music, motifs and jingles

Jingles have one function: to be catchy. They must be so memorable that they instantly remind the listener of the station and/or programme they are tuned into. They do not have to be liked to be remembered, of course. Using a software package like Garageband, it is very easy to mix your own original jingle. Motifs are short pieces of music or sound that occur during a programme or news bulletin to signal the transition from one section of the recording to another—Radio 1's Newsbeat makes effective use of these.

Existing music must be selected very carefully—this production unit is not an opportunity for you to simply put together a collection of your favourite tunes. Crucially, the jingle you create must match the kinds of music the station is broadcasting.

Production Tip

Recording sound

There is, of course, a big difference between recording live sound and pre-recorded sound. The key with spoken voice radio is to avoid silence. Although pre-recorded material can be the outcome of several 'takes', this luxury is not available for live studio or location recording, for which rehearsal, a script and confidence on the part of the speaker or presenter are essential. With video, poor acting can occasionally be compensated for by visual elements and editing. Clearly this is not the case for radio!

You should wear headphones at all times when recording so you hear what the audience will hear, which is determined by sound levels, interference or background noise and ambience on location or in the studio. This is not easy to identify from the ear alone in the context of the event rather than through the technology. You should be using reasonable quality microphones—no longer prohibitively expensive for Media departments in education. Uni-directional microphones are better as they do not pick up background noise, but if this is the desired effect then go for bi-directional microphones. Make sure your microphone is about 12 centimetres away from the mouth of the speaker and it is best practice to position the microphone to the side of the mouth rather than directly below or in front.

An industry convention is to record a short amount of ambience from a location recording—the sound of the room or place you are in without anyone speaking, so this can be used in the edit to cover any gaps seamlessly. When recording interviews, use somewhere quiet, but for a vox-pop (where you ask several members of the public the same question about a current affairs issue), you need some location noise to emphasise the distinction between this section of a bulletin and the studio sections (but not so much that you can't clearly hear the answers.

Local News Values

Galtung and Ruge (1965) described the practices of journalists and editors as the use of 'news values'. These values help us understand why some kinds of stories appear more prominently in the news than others, and how the narrative of news, as a result, tends to have a familiar, shared structure. The news values shown below have been adapted to relate to local news in particular.

Frequency: news events that fit the schedule of the local news broadcaster are more likely to be given attention; events that have either several short bursts of activity or those that happen quickly are favoured.

Threshold: for local news, this describes the importance of an event to the local community rather than to the nation.

Simplicity: stories that are easier for the whole of the local community to understand are preferred, especially those with clear heroes and villains, winners and losers, culprits and victims, as opposed to more complex stories which may be given less prominence. This describes a rather patronising 'deficit model' of the audience.

Continuity: 'stories with legs'—those that will be on-going and will maintain their level of interest for the local audience over time, are favoured.

Elitism/celebrity: we are as a society, for whatever reason, drawn to famous people, those with power and those with celebrity status or infamy. News events concerning such people will always be given attention, especially when powerful people or celebrities visit a local community or when famous local people are in the news.

Human interest: this is the 'bread and butter' of local news, stories that create empathy or vicarious responses in relation to ordinary local people in a range of circumstances.

Negativity: it is a sad fact that things going wrong are the substance of most local news, and how the local community will be affected in negative ways by such events. Success stories are actually more common in local news than in national or global news, but they still play second fiddle to bad news on most days.

Local interest: many national news stories will be adapted to a local angle. An example of this, which also demonstrates a high level of negativity, would be the reporting of a local soldier killed in action in Iraq.

Activity 1.6

Listen to five local radio news bulletins from a range of commercial and public service broadcasters (those with advertising and BBC stations). Categorise each story according to the list of news values above. How well does Galtung and Ruge's theory seem to work for your local news?

Local News and Community

When the internet and rolling 24-hour TV news were introduced many media commentators assumed that local news in both broadcast and newspaper form would have a limited shelf-life. So far, however, this has not proved to be the case. In actual fact, the decline of newsagent delivery of newspapers (because people increasingly buy from their local Tesco Express) and free papers distributed on public transport seem to have posed more of a threat. So how has local news resisted decline in the online age? Activity 1.7 on page 49 may help you shed some light on this question.

Sound archives

Sound archives are holdings of recorded sound that a broadcaster will ordinarily pay to use. The largest is the British Library Sound Archive. The material held in archives ranges from all kinds of music to spoken dialogue, recordings of nature and sports commentaries—anything you can imagine that has been recorded in audio format.

For your preliminary task you need to create an archive sound clip that relates to your studio guest. This means a piece of sound recorded in the past that will remind the audience of the status of the guest. If this were a footballer this might be a piece of commentary on them scoring a goal; for a politician an extract from a speech they have made; and for a musician a piece of their music. A common technique employed in broadcasting is to play the archive sound clip before introducing the guest as this serves to engage and intrigue the listener and to establish a context for what follows. Here is an example from local radio. When Richard March, bass player with Pop Will Eat Itself, famous DJ and member of Bentley Rhythm Ace became a lecturer at Halesowen College in the West Midlands, a Birmingham radio station interviewed him about his new job for a midweek music programme. When the interview was broadcast, one of Richard's most successful recordings, 'Bentley's Gonna Get You', was played as an archive piece before the interview was introduced.

Interviews and vox-pops

Visit the BBC training online site (see Figure 14) and listen to the interviewing techniques and vox-pop guides, which are very useful. When interviewing, avoid closed questions which the interviewee can answer with one or two words, maintain eye contact and use non-verbal cues such as smiling, nodding and looking quizzical to encourage a fuller response. Try to elicit a descriptive response to create a verbal 'picture' of events or feelings.

Vox-pops ('voice of the people') are used to represent public opinion. So if your bulletin features an interview with a local head teacher about discipline in the classroom, you might ask twenty people on the street (in the centre of town usually) whether they think teachers have enough control over pupils and what should be changed. The crucial thing here is the cross section of the community. From the twenty recorded responses, you would select five or six and these should cover male, female, young, old, an ethnic mix and a variety of opinions in the responses.

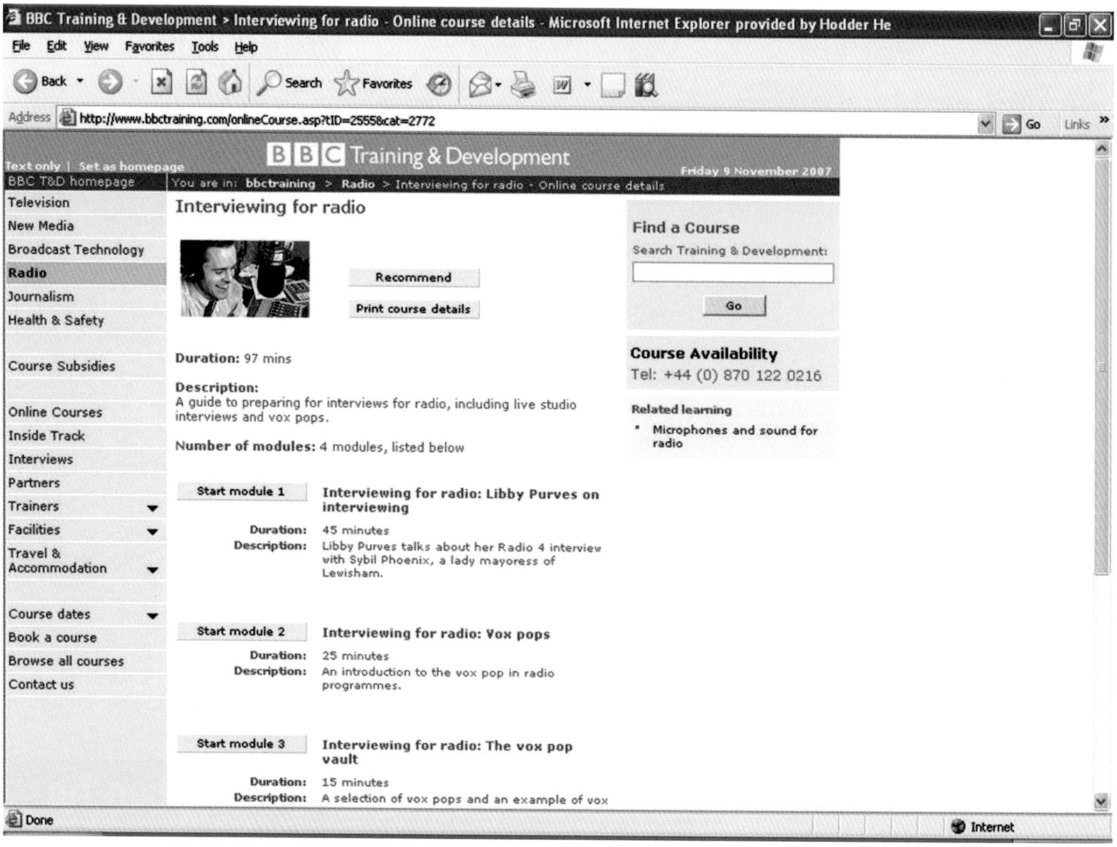

Figure 14 The BBC training online website is
essential for media students working on
radio broadcasts.
(*Source*: BBC www.bbctraining.com)

Production Tip

Specialist reporters

Spend a while listening to news bulletins on the radio and you will hear short contributions (sometimes pre-recorded and sometimes presented through a live link with the studio) from a variety of correspondents. There is a reporter for every area of public life—education, sports, music and entertainment, political, environmental, economic, celebrity, fashion, transport—that the station is likely to be reporting on. Depending on what stories you are going to carry in your bulletin, you will need to script, record and integrate contributions from two or three of these correspondents. It may be sensible for a specialist reporter to carry out the vox-pop and summarise its outcomes for the audience after it has been broadcast, so you can cover more than one of the requirements of the brief and also more accurately reflect industry practice.

Activity 1.7

Conduct a small-scale audience research exercise with local radio listeners— you will probably be able to select the sample from family and friends. Either through questionnaires or interviews, or both, ask a sample of listeners questions about what local news they listen to, how they access it, where they are when they listen to it (remember that, for now at least, radio still has the edge on TV for portability and you can't watch TV while driving) and what they get out of it.

When you have gathered your data, compare it to other students' findings and analyse it in the context of the local community: Did you find that a sense of community was important to the listeners, were there particular aspects of what they listen for that would not be shared by national news radio and what conclusions can you draw about the resilience of local news from this research?

Legal and Ethical Contexts of Local Radio Journalism

There are a number of laws that regulate journalistic practice. A useful overview of expectations is provided by the National Union of Journalists' Code of Conduct, updated in 2007. A journalist is expected to:

1 At all times uphold and defend the principle of media freedom, the right of freedom of expression and the right of the public to be informed
2 Strive to ensure that information disseminated is honestly conveyed, accurate and fair
3 Do her/his utmost to correct harmful inaccuracies
4 Differentiate between fact and opinion
5 Obtain material by honest, straightforward and open means, with the exception of investigations that are both overwhelmingly in the public interest and which involve evidence that cannot be obtained by straightforward means
6 Do nothing to intrude into anybody's private life, grief or distress unless justified by overriding consideration of the public interest
7 Protect the identity of sources who supply information in confidence and material gathered in the course of her/his work
8 Resist threats or any other inducements to influence, distort or suppress information
9 Take no unfair personal advantage of information gained in the course of her/his duties before the information is public knowledge
10 Produce no material likely to lead to hatred or discrimination on the grounds of a person's age, gender, race, colour, creed, legal status, disability, marital status or sexual orientation
11 Not by way of statement, voice or appearance endorse by advertisement any commercial product or service save for the promotion of her/his own work or of the medium by which she/he is employed
12 Avoid plagiarism.

Source: http://www.nuj.org.uk/innerPagenuj.html?docid=174

Key to this framework is the concept of the 'public interest' which often clashes with calls for a privacy law. One of the most contested elements of media practice in a democratic society is the relationship between the protection of privacy and the tolerance of intrusive journalism in the public interest.

Key Legislation

We must establish that the NUJ code of practice is a set of internal professional guidelines and is not in itself legal. Some key examples of laws that journalists must observe are:

The Official Secrets Act: This Act prevents people in the public sector from revealing information related to Government activity; in particular, matters of national security. Editors are sometimes served with 'D Notices' that prevent them from publishing stories which might breach the act.

Contempt of Court: This restricts any reporting that might impede the workings of the court in progress. For example, publishing a photograph of an accused person who has not yet been identified in court, or providing comment on factual information that is before the court, or criticising a judge while the case is being heard.

Libel and Defamation: Members of the public have the right to sue papers that print stories which damage their livelihood and/or character. While action is often threatened, newspapers know that most cases never get to court because of the expense involved. However, simply the threat of legal action does sometimes prevent a story from progressing further. In 2001 *The Sunday People* published a story about a footballer in a sex scandal without the names of the participants because the player had successfully applied for an injunction. This was the first case of this kind and concerns have been raised that, whilst this story might in itself seem a trivial, sensationalist example, a precedent has been created that may be a serious barrier to more serious investigative journalism.

Local Radio News Conventions

Local radio news tends to assume a cross-section of listeners and offers a more familiar mode of address than more formal national news broadcasts. The newsreader may speak with a 'soft' version of the local accent and local news bulletins are often shorter than national ones.

Within the broader category of local radio, however, your research into existing media will reveal specific contrasts in your local area between BBC news provision and that of its commercial counterparts, as well as between different news bulletins, on the same channel in some cases. There are some common conventions that are shared with national broadcasts though—the use of an emblematic theme tune, a degree of formality in comparison with other broadcasting, the hierarchical use of news values in the running order (see above), the use of specialist reporters, weather reports and travel news and the use of 'and finally' light-hearted concluding stories after the sport. It may be stating the obvious, but it is still worth reinforcing the fact that weather, travel and sport will always take a local angle, whereas other news events may be shared by national and local radio alike. In order to demonstrate this understanding of the interplay between local and national, it would be wise to include in your bulletin a local treatment of a national story.

Demographics, language and register

In any region, there is a range of FM, MW, LW and digital radio provision, as well as pirate stations. Some radio stations are 'badged' for a range of regions, which means they share a common style and format/structure but the generic programme is re-badged for each local audience.

Each station has a sense of its audience, but as radio is ongoing, it is crucial to consider who the audience is for your news bulletin in relation to the time of day you are producing it for. Rush hour news, mid-day and afternoon news, 'drivetime' news at the end of the day, evening news and late night news each have different conventions and the register and possibly the language may change for each of these. How (literally) the audience is spoken to is, naturally, crucial to radio as there is nothing there to compensate for this if it is misjudged. The register you choose will be more or less formal and the language style you adopt will cover a certain range of vocabulary. You will decide whether or not to translate some terms that are essential to each story and whether to explain some concepts. But this must not be guesswork. You must have a clear plan of who your audience is and base the register and the vocabulary you cover on research into existing radio provision for the same, or a similar, audience. You will alienate or patronise your audience, and thus lose listeners, if you get this wrong.

Coursework Practice: Critically evaluating radio production

Here are some key questions to ask about your radio production work as you progress with both tasks:

Working with existing forms and conventions— reworking the familiar

For both tasks, your research should have made you familiar with existing radio broadcasts that had the same intentions as your pieces.

1 What creative decisions did you make about content, structuring, links between sound sections, jingles and music and the integration of elements as a result of this research?

2 For the main task, it is important to clarify the exact intentions in terms of demographics and the intended broadcasting time as well as the station. It is probably less likely that you would aim to subvert or challenge radio news conventions than might be the case with a fiction film, but if you did, justify this in terms of informed creative intentions and the researched desires of the audience you were aiming to cater for.

Working in media production contexts—*professional practice*

To complete these tasks you should have followed industry practices in terms of selecting recording equipment, journalism, dealing with the public and interviewees, health and safety, sound recording and editing and studio management.

1 For the preliminary task, how did you go about selecting music and how did your understanding of copyright influence this?

2 In both individual and group terms, how did you work professionally in these various contexts and what challenges did you face?

3 What creative decisions did you have to make to solve problems and how did you depart from the original plan?

4 Which parts of the broadcast were scripted and which parts were developed as live? Remember that deciding not to use a particular strategy (not to use a bi-directional microphone, for example) is also a creative decision.

5 Within live elements, how much could be precisely planned?

6 The journalistic elements of the project should be evaluated in relation to legal, ethical and regulatory contexts. Radio journalists have to abide by a set of laws and codes of conduct that protect the public and people in the public eye from being misrepresented. How did you develop your stories with these in mind?

7 How did you organise your human resources—the people involved in the broadcast, from presenters to members of the public?

8 Time management is perhaps one of the most important aspects of creative media practice—how did you manage your time, and with what success?

Using technology – *creative tools*

1 Digital audio recording, music mixing and non-linear editing software, as well as hardware resources such as microphones, will have been very important to your work in this area. How did the technology enable the creative process—what could you achieve that would not have been possible without this digital technology?
2 Were there examples of the technology obstructing the creative process or forcing you into a particular approach which was not your original creative intention?

Thinking about audience—*making meaning*

Your jingle and selection of music in the preliminary task will have been in response to the desires and needs of a particular audience group. For a local news bulletin, a clear conception of audience—a demographic section of the local community—is everything. You need to reflect carefully and precisely on the decision-making process in relation to vocabulary, register and tone (the 'mode of address'—literally how your bulletin speaks to the listeners), news values, music and motifs and, story by story, the relationships created between events and local people.

1 Through the vox-pop you will have situated the audience in the text, by gauging the audience response to events or issues. How was this inclusive element constructed?

Representing—*constructing 'the real'*

In the main task, story by story, and overall in terms of the narrative structure of your bulletin, you will have represented a range of people, events, places and issues. You will also have represented the audience to themselves through the 'community ethos' of the local radio conventions you have observed.

1 In each case, what sense of reality have you constructed? How have news values been applied?

Remember that news is not just a transparent 'window on the world'. News is the outcome of journalistic, editorial and commercial/institutional mediation in response to events. News is selected (the stories chosen and those rejected) and then constructed (through convention—reporter, eye witness, expert, interview, vox-pop, studio presenter, sound archive) in such a way that the presentation of news becomes formulaic.

2 Through adopting these conventional approaches to news representation, who is included and excluded by your bulletin?

Chapter 1.4
Website Production

> **Preliminary exercise**: homepage for a school/college with hyperlink to Media department.
>
> **Main task**: campaign website.
>
> **Technology**: digital photography, web design software, digital video and audio editing software.
>
> **Theoretical understanding**: non-linear narrative, persuasive representation, navigation as narrative, layers of interpretation, semiotics, making meaning with still images and moving images, web2.0 and intermedial literacy.
>
> **Links to other units**: Key Media concept: representation.

Composing Digital Images

For the preliminary task, you will need to produce a range of digital still images from which to select the most appropriate to appear on your homepage and Media department page, alongside a range of other imagery which you will generate in other ways. For the main task, you will need a wider range of images related to your campaign. You will need to use a digital camera so you can easily download your images in order to work with web design software. The skills you will need in generating images for websites are linked to the four production tips that appear in Chapter 1 Print Production. Return to this chapter now and reread the production tips relating to:

- Conception
- Framing and composition
- Shot distance
- Colour and resolution.

For both of the tasks, the most important aspect of web design and one that takes a lot of careful planning is navigation. Navigation for websites is no different to navigation in everyday life; it involves finding your way around and locating things. The next activity asks you to think about how you navigate your own school or college and provides a helpful 'spatial analogy' for this.

Activity 1.8

Go to the visitor's car park at your school or college and find your way to reception. Ask the receptionist to select a random room and give you basic directions. Go to that room, making sure you take the route described at reception. Next find a toilet and the canteen/refectory, but you must do this by following signs only. Finally, make your way back to the car park, again only by following signs.

How easy was it to navigate, based on the instructions you were given and your institution's signage? If you found it easy to navigate your way around, then your school or college campus has been well designed.

The spatial analogy works like this: imagine the campus is a website. Each time you went back to a place for a second time without wanting to (and thus extended your journey time unnecessarily) can be compared to failing to reach the desired page on a website and instead going back to a previous page and taking more time. In real life if we have difficulty finding our way we cannot decide to instantly find a toilet somewhere else. However, when using the internet we can decide to leave a site immediately if we get frustrated with its site navigation.

Production Tip

Navigation

A user must be able to link to every important section of your site in two clicks. For the preliminary task it is a requirement that a user must be able to link in one click. Each section of your site must be distinctive and clear and follow existing website conventions. You must establish a uniform style that each page follows. Always consider how much control you are affording your visitor and think through the design of the site from the point of view of the user. The key questions a visitor will be asking during time spent at your site will be: Where am I? Where have I been? Where can I go next?

Production Tip

Design principles

Navigation cannot be thought about in isolation from design principles. To aid navigation, the design of your site should adhere to the conventions of websites favoured by the audience you wish to attract—you therefore need to research this first. The web is less straightforward than other more established media in terms of design conventions. The current debate over the merits of Facebook and Myspace indicate this, with some interesting demographic preferences being expressed in relation to two sites that at first glance appear to be offering the same things.

Font size and colour is crucial for attracting an audience, and it is also helpful to keep the size of files down to a minimum so you don't disadvantage users with an average connection speed or lower—remember the 'digital divide'! The design of your site must be constant and flow logically from page to page, so avoid changing font and colour. Keep the content and screen size inside the margins of the window so the navigation doesn't have to involve lots of time consuming scrolling. Think about the way you read—most people scan text and then go back and read it, so it is important to highlight key words, use lists of key terms and stick to one key theme in each section or paragraph of a page.

Web Design Theories

There are two kinds of design that you can choose from—structuralist design and presentationalist design, as Dixon (2007) explains here:

Structuralists are advocates of a conservative web, one based on the ultimate goal of simply driving information to the user, a tool void of artistic impositions that may inhibit the reception of pure information. They maintain that the web is intended as a universal platform for delivering standardised content, and that document presentation is better left up to the desires and preferences of the end user or the device on which it is being presented. Presentationalists see the web platform in a slightly different light. Advocates of this viewpoint maintain that the presentation of information is best delivered as an experience, rich with sensory feedback and interactive metaphors.

(Dixon, 2007: 3)

Screen layout

Dixon (2007) presents four commonly used designs for web pages (Figures 15(a)–(d)).

Each of these designs maintains symmetry to please the eye and aid reading, allows for logical grouping of information, leaves white space around the body of text to frame information, and avoids lumping together too much text or information. Significant content should, wherever possible, be organised at

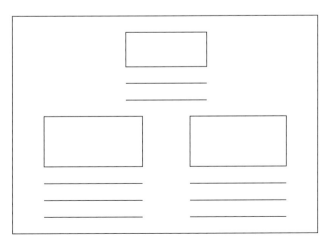

Figure 15(a) V layout pattern

Figure 15(b) A layout pattern

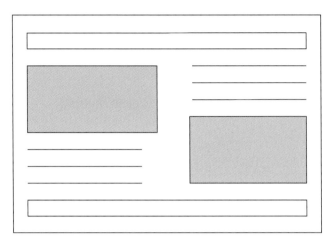

Figure 15(c) Z layout pattern

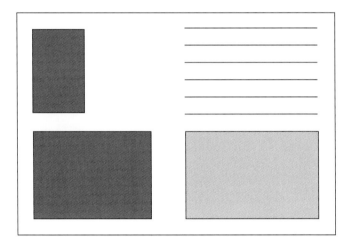

Figure 15(d) L layout pattern

the upper range of the screen, towards the left. As Horton suggests:

> **Design the display to direct the user's gaze to important information.**

(Horton, 1990: 109)

Developing a Campaign Site

The internet has provided a terrific 'shot in the arm' for people engaged in campaigning of all kinds. Here Gauntlett (2004) discusses the nature of political campaigning online:

> If we look carefully at the interactions between and around
> . . . the thousands of websites which can be called 'political'
> in the broadest of senses, we do find cultures of engagement
> and discussion. The fact that people who are concerned
> about an issue can create a website about it, and then find
> themselves in e-mail conversations (or in different forms of
> electronic conference) with people who are interested,
> curious or opposed to their views, or who run related sites,
> *does* create a climate of greater public discussion. Compare
> it to the days when all you could do was read about an issue
> in a mass-produced newspaper, and then discuss it with a
> handful of friends in a pub. We can hope that the greater
> engagement with political issues which the Web can bring
> will mean that more people become interested in politics
> generally; but this is far from guaranteed.
>
> (Gauntlett, 2004: 16)

All campaigning is political, but this doesn't mean that it relates to government or party politics. A campaign lobbying for a new music venue is political because it will be the local council that has to respond. A campaign to ban a violent video game is calling for legislation that only politicians can provide.

Once you have decided on your issue, the starting point for your campaign site must be research into successful existing sites that act as the 'hub' for a range of campaign activities. A campaign is not the same as a charity. A campaign is set up to try to create change, whereas a charity is usually a registered and established organisation that is supported by the establishment. An example of a campaign site is the website for Stonewall (see Figure 16).

Website pre-production work

Once you have decided on the details of your campaign (which can be an existing campaign or a completely new creation), your pre-production work will be concerned with audience and conventions. What balance of text and images will be needed? What similar campaign sites will be useful for context and conventions? And what is the ultimate goal of your site? For example, how will the visitor be 'helped' to join, lobby or donate (or, usually, all three)? To achieve this goal you will need to provide the right balance of pleasure and anxiety for the visitor—your site must be enjoyable to visit, but the outcome must be for the visitor to gain a sense of urgency to do something about a particular problem. The Stonewall site does this through balancing fun, vibrant imagery with more serious, informative text.

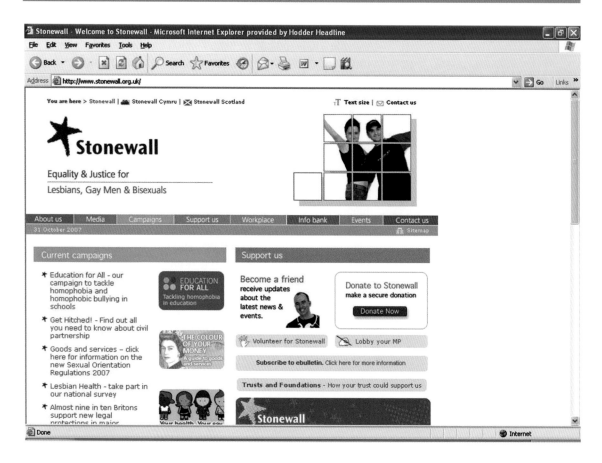

Figure 16 The Stonewall campaign website
(*Source*: Stonewall)

You will need to design a logo and a broad range of images that, in semiotic terms, signify the campaign. See the chapter on Print Production for a full introduction to semiotics and image construction.

As the campaign website requires sound and video as well as web design, you should refer to all of the chapters in this section of the book. These take you through the principles of video production, audio production and print production, all of which you need to observe. This chapter is concerned with navigation and page design and brings together these other elements, so the production tips on page 62 relate to the use of images, sound and video, once they have been constructed.

Coursework Practice: Critically evaluating web design

On page 63 are some key questions to ask about your websites as you progress with both tasks.

Stonewall

Stonewall is a lobbying group that campaigns for equal rights for lesbians, gay men and bisexuals. It was founded in response to a specific piece of Government legislation, Section 28 (which prohibited local authorities in England and Wales from 'promoting' homosexuality), and since its inception it has lobbied for equality on a range of specific issues. This campaign group is of interest to media students not only because it has a campaign website that offers a good example for production work at AS, but also because one of Stonewall's concerns is the representation of sexuality in the media. Here is how the organisation describes itself on its website:

> Stonewall is renowned for its campaigning and lobbying. Some major successes include helping achieve the equalisation of the age of consent, lifting the ban on lesbians and gay men serving in the military, securing legislation allowing same-sex couples to adopt and the repeal of Section 28. More recently Stonewall has helped secure civil partnerships and ensured the recent Equality Act protected lesbians and gay men in terms of goods and services.
>
> Stonewall also works with a whole range of agencies to address the needs of lesbians, gay men and bisexuals in the wider community. Our Diversity Champions programme offers advice and support to over 250 organisations including IBM, Barclays, Barnardos, DTI and the Royal Navy.
>
> Stonewall's Education for All campaign, launched in January 2005, helps tackle homophobia and homophobic bullying in schools and works with a wide coalition of groups.
>
> More recently Stonewall has formed partnerships with organisations outside Parliament to ensure the rights and needs of lesbians, gay men and bisexuals are addressed in the wider community.
>
> Stonewall has also raised public awareness in terms of civil partnership, through our Get Hitched guide, and on the changes to the employment regulations relating to sexual orientation through guides for both employers and employees.
>
> In addition Stonewall promotes new research, for example Tuned Out: the BBC's portrayal of lesbian and gay people and other research looking at homophobic bullying in schools, and has taken legal test cases that challenge inequality (e.g. on the age of consent and lesbians & gays in the armed forces).

Source: http://www.stonewall.org.uk/about_us/11.asp
(Accessed 18 August 2007)

Stonewall's homepage employs a colour coding design which arranges areas of content against a set of colours, and this coding is maintained throughout the site. Separate graphics for different campaigns and services are arranged in the middle of the homepage, and the visitor can navigate to these areas by clicking on these visuals. The organisation's logo and an accompanying semiotic image draw attention immediately on arrival at the site. This image changes when the user moves to each page, but the design (a set of boxes breaking up an image of a person or people) stays consistent in format and location. A list of current campaigns appears on the left side of the page (where the eye begins scanning); on the right is a further set of links to services and information and right of centre a 'Donate Now' button stands out.

This site is a very good example of the range and scope of a campaign site, and will give you a good idea of the techniques employed by campaign site designers to encourage the visitor to join the campaign and make a donation. However, the site does not always follow the design principles described earlier in this chapter, so you might want to be critical of some aspects of the site—for example, some pages are text-laden and others feature very little text. There are one or two places where it is easy to get lost—breaking the first rule of navigation.

Production Tip

'Bobby'

If you are using Windows, you can visit http://webxact.watchfire.com/ and then enter your web pages into a programme called 'Bobby' and have them scanned for accessibility. This will tell you how easily a person with a disability or reduced access to the internet can use your website. Making changes in order to be more inclusive is very good practice. Once your website is approved by 'Bobby' you can use the symbol as a 'badge' on your site.

Production Tip

Images, sound and video websites

When using images, it is easiest to save and upload them in the JPEG format. Diagrams, drawings or cartoon art are best saved as GIFs. For both, the most efficient resolution to use is 72 pixels per inch. You will need to experiment with levels of quality, colour settings, formal options and palette in relation to the software and hardware you are using and the needs of the user.

Although you are required to use sound and video, it is sensible not to include too much of either as the time it takes to download this material can be off putting for the user. For this AS task, one piece of video with sound or one of each is reasonable. Depending on your school/college's specific copyright and firewall policies, it may be possible to simply embed video from YouTube or via a moodle site. Otherwise you will be saving and inserting files using Quicktime or Media Player or Audacity, depending on what is available to you.

Crucially, you must return to the guidance in this broader Foundation Portfolio section of the book relating to semiotics, moving image narrative, combining sound with image and audio conventions, and ensure that you follow the same principles for the video and audio on your website as you would if you were producing a film or radio text. In other words, don't allow the technical detail of uploading to the web override the aesthetic, symbolic and creative integrity of your production work.

Working with existing forms and conventions—*reworking the familiar*

The web is clearly less familiar than other media because it has been around for less time. It is claimed that the conventions of a website are more fluid and dynamic than other media forms, that the user creates their own version of a site and moves between sites in such a way that they have far more control over the experience than, say, a radio listener.

1 How have you worked within this dynamic context?
2 How have you tried to 'control' the user experience?
3 How does your campaign site relate to the existing sites you encountered in your research? What features have you imitated in order to persuade the visitor to stay, to browse, to join, to lobby and to donate?
4 Which of the page designs did you opt for and why?
5 What creative decisions did you make in relation to the breadth and depth of your site, colours, text and image in combination, navigation and flow, and how do these decisions relate to the 'semiotics' of the web?

Working in media production contexts—*professional practice*

Arguably, it is harder to pin down professional practice in web design because, while there are professional web designers, there are countless thousands of amateur producers of websites. It is far easier to produce your own website and distribute it (as the internet is a distribution vehicle above all else) than for more traditional media forms.

1 How did research and planning, the generation of images, sound and video and the technical construction of the site itself fit together?
2 If working in a group, how were roles allocated and monitored?
3 How did you manage your human resources—the people involved in the production?

You should also reflect on the importance of drafting and layout design, and remember that deciding not to use a particular strategy (for example, not using extensive scrolling) is also a creative decision.

4 As stated in previous chapters, time management may not seem a very exciting aspect of creative media practice, but it is possibly the most important—how did you manage your time, and with what success?

Using technology – *creative tools*

1 You will have used different software for image editing, video editing, sound editing, graphics and animation, web design and uploading. In each case how was the creative process enabled by digital software and obstructed/limited in other ways?

2 Unlike other media production contexts, there is no 'before' digital technology with web design, so it is unlikely you would have found the technology limiting, but are there examples of the 'machine taking over' and leading you to particular decisions that went against your creative instincts?

Thinking about audience—*making meaning*

1 For a campaign site, the audience is everything. The sole intention and purpose of the site is to make that audience bigger, to raise awareness of the campaign and to raise money for it. How did you respond to this pressure?

Evaluate the success of the research, the initial testing of ideas, changes made to the creative plan with the audience in mind and the feedback from the target group. There will be three levels to this evaluative work: First, the design and navigation of the site. Second, the degree to which the content of the site was compelling and drew in the public sufficiently for the campaign to grow. Third, the extent to which the intermedial nature of the site—video, text, image, sound and graphics—in combination with the 'hyperlinked' fluid nature of the web, enables a meaningful experience for the site visitor.

Representing—*constructing 'the real'*

1 A campaign is all about representing a problem that needs solving. A campaign website will not aim for neutrality or impartiality, it will be emotive, arguing a case and demanding support. Who and what (people, places, ideas, themes, problems, victims) did you represent and how? Who is included and excluded from this?

2 Most importantly, how did you go about representing the site visitor, how did you locate/situate them in the problem and how did you attempt to convince them that donating/joining/lobbying will be part of the solution?

3 How did you represent a version of the 'reality' of both the problem and the solution?

A note about A2: Critical Perspectives

If you intend to continue Media Studies through to A2 with OCR, you will take a unit called Critical Perspectives. The first part of the exam for this unit requires you to write reflectively and theoretically about your production work at AS and A2. One element asks you to write about all of your production work (both Foundation Portfolio and Advanced Portfolio) in relation to how particular creative skills have developed. The other element is concerned with theoretical analysis of your own work, and you are required to choose one of your production pieces and to write about it in relation to one of the key media concepts—genre, narrative, representation, audience or media language.

With this in mind, your critical evaluation work at AS needs to focus on two areas: skills development (how have you developed your creative skills through the progression from preliminary to main task; what specific skills can you identity as the most developed?) and key concepts (how do the texts you have produced relate to key media theories, or in other words, how would a media student 'deconstruct' your production work?).

Section 2
Textual Analysis and Representation

Key Concepts: The *Representing* Text

Sohn-Rethel (2003) describes four forces at work in media production which we can use as a framework for analysis. These forces are:

1 Technological
2 Economic
3 Cultural
4 Regulatory.

In this section we will consider the key concept of representation and start to apply it to television drama. Representation is a cultural force as it relates to tastes, identity and interests that are shaped by the culture we inhabit. But representation is also related to regulation. People have legal means to respond to representations that they consider inaccurate or harmful and OFCOM, the regulatory body overseeing broadcasting, can intervene when programme makers represent issues in a controversial way. Representation is also linked to economic forces. When the BBC commissioned *Rome*, a very expensive drama to make, decisions will have been made in relation to the likely audience and future DVD sales. Representation is increasingly shaped by technology, as the audience is able to watch a series in a staggered fashion or all at once or with a range of interactive features that may not appeal to all viewers—this is described as a fragmented audience.

Textual analysis is an advanced form of media literacy. A basic level of media literacy allows a person to understand the narrative of a television drama and to make a critical response in relation to other programmes and to the ideas, themes and people represented. For example, is it realistic? Advanced media literacy enables us to 'deconstruct' a television drama—to understand how it has been put together. To do this well, we need to work at both micro and macro levels of the text.

Working at a micro level involves pulling apart the detailed aspects of the text's frame by frame construction—camera angles and movement, shot composition, use of point of view, specific edits and transitions, cutaways and visual effects, pieces of dialogue, music and sound effects, lighting choices, props and costumes. Doing this kind of work, you will need to play, pause and rewind a short second sequence several times just to observe the creative and technical decisions made in the production process. This builds up to work at a macro level. This is all about drawing conclusions from the micro work about how the sequence overall represents people, events, places and themes—how it portrays a sense of the 'reality' being dramatised. But of course, we must always bear witness to the complex range of interpretations that different viewers will create, as we know that watching a television programme is an active process and that it is the audience that ultimately makes the meaning. So we have a three-stage process here:

1 Analyse the micro elements of the text
2 Conclude from the micro elements a range of macro representations
3 Consider how different people might respond differently to these representations.

First we need to spend some time thinking about media *representation* as this is a key analytical concept that you need to be comfortable with.

Representation

The media do not just offer us a transparent 'window on the world' but a mediated *version* of the world. They don't just present reality, they *re*-present it.

(Buckingham, 2003: 58)

Even when you watch live sport, England playing football in the World Cup, for example (and losing on penalties, probably), you aren't really watching the match. If you are asked—'did you see the game last night?'—of course you will say 'yes'. But strictly speaking you should say—'no, I watched a mediated, constructed re-presentation of the match through the medium of live television.'

Take an example from everyday life—why do men wear ties on some occasions but not on others? At first the answer seems obvious—they do so to look formal, businesslike and professional; as though they have made an effort to look smart. But this isn't obvious at all if we take a step back from what seems natural. Why should a piece of material worn around the neck make a man more able to do his job or attend an event or function? Well, in our society a tie has come to represent formality. The tie is a sign or a symbol. In itself it makes no difference but it carries cultural meaning—we might call these cultural meanings *connotations*. Now let's extend this—your name is a symbol, it stands in for you; when people who know you read or hear your name, they think of you. And the clothes you wear don't just keep you warm and dry— they present an image of you as you like to be seen by others. The way your bedroom is decorated and laid out has been considered carefully—not just so you are comfortable in your space but so that a range of signs and symbols reinforce your identity to yourself (and to anyone else who enters).

Metaphor

Gauntlett (2007) has developed a research method using Lego. He asks people to make metaphorical models with Lego to represent their identity. The key thing here is the metaphor bit. He doesn't expect them to make models that actually resemble what they are representing. He says that this way, when he asks people to reflect on the models they have made, he gets a better sense of how people see themselves than if he asks them to just use language (to talk or write about their sense of identity). You may be thinking—what has Lego and identity got to do with media? Well, if you think about it, a lot of the time we are looking at things that represent something without actually resembling it—like the tie, for example. So maybe metaphor is actually something we use all the time without realising it.

Verisimilitude

Now let's think about TV programmes—a form of media text—in the context of representation. For example, in order for a character to be believable, she or he must wear clothes that you would expect that type of person to wear. When we look at how a media text represents the world, we are usually concerned with the representation of gender, age and ethnicity, social groups (or types of people), places, time periods and themes. This all adds up to verisimilitude—the construction, in a text, of a plausible, believable world. Such a world may have its own internal logic and therefore little similarity to our world (*Doctor Who* for example, where we come to see time travel as possible). Or it may share its logic with our world and attempt to represent our reality (like *Coronation Street*, which relies on a weighty sense of realism).

To explore representation in TV/radio drama, we'll be asking:

- What kind of realism is being attempted by the programme?
- Who is being represented in the drama (who is present), and how?
- Who is not being represented in the drama (who is absent), and why?
- Can we identify any characters that are stereotypical representations?
- Is there a dominant view of the world represented in the drama, or are there several different views to choose from?
- What different responses might audience members make to these representations?

The following example may help to explain the point about absence more clearly. Imagine watching a TV police drama with a detective as a central character. At the end of a busy working day he goes home for his evening meal and instead of a long-suffering wife taking his dinner out of the oven he is met by his gay partner. This situation is treated as incidental though, because the drama is not about 'gay issues'.

Does this happen very often? We can say that there is a great deal of representation of gay people in television these days, but hardly ever as incidental; it is usually central to the plot. So, gay people in a 'normalised', background sense are largely absent from TV drama.

Representational codes

A good example of a television drama that is rich with representational codes is *Life on Mars*. The entire text relies on a sense of 'authenticity'—the clothes, props, settings, music and (most importantly of all) dialogue represent Northern England in the 1970s in a way that is accurate and familiar/nostalgic. Crucially, the entire drama depends on the juxtaposition (the marked, effective contrast) between Sam Tyler's view of the

Activity 2.2

In a group (ideally as a whole class) collect and share a range of birthday cards designed for 'Mum', 'Dad' and gendered new baby cards. Hold a group discussion on nature/nurture—do these cards just represent or actually help to create ideas about gender differences?

Now listen several times to 'Geezers Need Excitement' by The Streets (from the album 'Eight Storeys'). The narrative of this song (like all of The Streets material) is operatic in form, as it follows its central character, Mike Skinner, on a night out which involves drugs, clubbing, fast food, moral dilemmas about infidelity (and double standards in that area) and the ever-present undercurrent of violence.

Now the interesting part—each student needs to cross-gender by taking on the role of female (if they are male) and vice versa. You should then note down every reference to your new gender during the song.

After you have listened several times, get into pairs (male/female) to share your responses and discuss the representation of each gender in the song.

The purpose of this exercise is to get you thinking, through an interesting and unusual example for Media Studies, about how gender is represented in a range of ways every day. This is actually easier to do if you 'borrow' a gender as it makes things clearer and less complicated in relation to your own identity.

world (taken from the twenty-first century) and the policing methods and dominant ideology (world view, common sense) of the 1970s characters.

Without the audience's complicity in understanding this contrast and accepting the 1970s representation as accurate, the text is meaningless. Take the following example: When one of the police officers is injured by a bomb blast and returns to work too early, Tyler observes his state and remarks to the 'unreconstructed' Gene Hunt that 'he's got PTSD' (post-traumatic stress disorder). Hunt replies 'this man's a hero and you're accusing him of having the clap!' For this to work, we have to accept these contrasting representations and, fundamentally, that police work today is conducted with sensitivity to such new diagnoses, whereas a 1970s police officer would have no understanding of such language. With those codes in place, the audience then has a variety of possible responses to make—maybe we might reflect that things were simpler, more straightforward and thus better in those days and that life

Activity 2.3

Take an episode of *Life on Mars* and, as you view, make a note of every police activity or practice that would not be considered appropriate, or would not be legal, in the present.
   Next, for each instance of this 'outdated' police activity, categorise it into one of three types:

1. Ethical
2. Technological
3. Cultural

The first list will be moments in the drama when the police do or say things which, by our contemporary standards, would be viewed as unethical, unfair, politically incorrect or unjust.
   The second list will be moments in the drama when the police do things a certain way that would now be replaced by another method as a result of technology advancing.
   The third list will be moments in the drama when the cultural context is specific to the 1970s and, therefore, the things the police are saying or doing would only make sense in that time period, not today.
   This activity, which is a form of content analysis, will give you a clear sense of the way that the 'verisimilitude' and authenticity of *Life on Mars* is carefully constructed.

is too 'politically correct' now. Or we might share Tyler's view that the methods of the 1970s are old fashioned, bigoted and unethical.

Representation in crisis

Although you will be working with the concept of representation for this part of your OCR Media course, it is useful to explore the claim made by some media academics that representation is a concept in crisis. This claim arises from a rather obvious aspect of the effects of digital technology. As it becomes cheaper, easier and quicker for people to make videos and upload them to the internet for an 'imagined audience', then is it the case that the representation *of* people *by* the media is increasingly replaced by people *representing* themselves?
   Consider the example of YouTube. Research in Barcelona by Gonzalez, Martinez and Fernandez (2007) found that in secondary schools in the city, students

Activity 2.3

Practical learning about representation

Although the AS course you are studying separates practical work (in the Foundation Production) from theoretical work (Key Concepts), it is easier to learn the theory if you take a practical approach to it. In the case of TV drama and representation, it makes sense to produce some sequences for your own drama. This activity is based on the work of Burn and Durran (2007) and students at Parkside Community College in Cambridge.

In a group of four or five, conduct an 'idea shower' on the subject of TV hospital drama. What are the main elements of this genre that you might expect to occur in any programme with this label? What are the main ingredients that produce various forms of 'pleasure' for the viewing audience?

Next, watch an episode of *Casualty* and list examples of typical characters, typical narratives and typical themes, as well as the iconography (setting, costumes and props).

After sharing these ideas and observations, create an idea for a new hospital drama set in your local area. Invent a title and create the main characters and situations your drama will represent.

Return to *Casualty* and study a short sequence (about 30 seconds) that does not take place in the hospital—this should be a sequence of your choice but one that is fairly typical of the programme, for example an accident or its immediate aftermath. Analyse the sequence in terms of camera shots and positioning, point of view, editing, sound and dialogue, costume, setting and performances.

Construct (film and edit) a sequence for your new drama that represents a similar situation but uses your new characters, settings and themes.

Show your sequence to the rest of your group and compare it with other students' work.

were regularly engaged in the production and uploading of video to YouTube, and that they had developed a range of discourses (ways of thinking and talking) about each other's work. Three groups had emerged—a group of students who only uploaded videos for each other to see; a 'playful' group who were uploading for a potential audience but were not concerned about the impact either way; and a third group of v-loggers who were actively pursuing a critical audience online, looking for a broader community of viewers. And it emerged from the group that being successful in 'playback' (people watching your videos and making comments) could acquire popularity with your peers, in the same way as being good looking, fashionable, good at sport or a musician. Video uploaders with lots of playback were treated as minor celebrities. This way of using the media is very different to the idea of youth being represented in, for example, *Skins* or *Hollyoaks*, and you might find it interesting to consider this as you study television drama.

Chapter 2.1
Television Drama

Despite stories of its demise in the wake of American imports, British television drama still attracts huge viewing audiences. Many of these shows are watched collectively as one-off peak-time broadcasts and this may provide some evidence that we are not yet consuming all of our media, creating our own viewing schedules or turning to YouTube and other aspects of web 2.0 for all of our media.

In 2006 *Coronation Street* averaged 12.2 million viewers, *Lewis* attracted 11.11 million, *Midsomer Murders* achieved 8.71 million and *Doctor Who* held the attention of 9.28 million viewers. However, these figures do show a significant downward trend in audience ratings for British TV drama, and a combination of less investment and more competition has led some critics to worry for the future. This 2006 blog posting from Media teacher, Steve Connolly, is a helpful introduction to these issues:

Drama series' have great potential to produce ongoing revenue through sales to other countries and channels as well as things like DVD sales. Perhaps more importantly though, 'proper' TV Drama brings prestige to institutions that attempt to make it. Traditionally, this usually meant the BBC. Take for example the BBC's recent production of *Bleak House*. A heavyweight Victorian novel, a stellar cast and a budget that wouldn't have looked out of place on a good size Hollywood movie—all ingredients that still pretty much guarantee a big hit, albeit with some adaptations to the normal format of period drama and some liberal stylistic borrowings from soap opera and American TV. Viewing figures for *Bleak House* averaged between 6 and 7 million, which was pretty good for any show in the 8–10pm slot and this figure was pretty much replicated by Tony Jordan's *Life on Mars*. Such a figure would represent about 25–30% of the audience share in an average week; something that suggests that the genre is still pretty strong at a time when more than two-thirds of the population of Britain have access to more than thirty TV channels.

And yet, there is a feeling that British TV drama is not what it was. Modern TV Dramas are often seen as sacrificing substance for style—*Hustle, Spooks* and *Life on Mars* all have a very slick, cinematic look about them. This argument is played out regularly in the British press, usually when a good piece of TV Drama is first broadcast, but I'm not sure I really see it as an argument at all. British TV Drama has always been strong; during the 1980s for every masterpiece there was a concomitant turkey. *Life on Mars* and *Spooks* might well have the look of a video game about them in places but they also address issues that are prescient in the 21st century in an accessible way: parenthood, crime, race, religion, identity.

One thing is certain though, British TV Drama is no longer the big beast that it was. In America, HBO has made a name for producing high concept drama series which harness intelligent, perceptive writing to expensive production values. The resulting products are drama series (usually between 12 and 22 episodes in length) which are breathtaking in their scale and scope; so much so in fact they become a series of movies both in the way they are written and the way they are filmed.

Source: http://mediaschool.blogspot.com/2006/06/international-landscape-of-tv-drama.html
(Accessed 10 July 2007)

Connolly concludes that while British TV drama is now something of a poor relation in comparison to the American producer HBO (most famously with *The Sopranos*), it is still in a fairly healthy state so reports of its demise are exaggerated at this stage.

While it might be of interest for the OCR Key Concepts unit, it is not necessary to study the history of television drama or its broader range of generic features. What we need to do here is become expert on how short drama sequences employ a variety of technical and symbolic elements at a micro level to create representations at the macro level.

Table 2 BARB Television ratings for week commencing 1 July 2007

	Programme	Millions
1	CONCERT FOR DIANA (SUN 2010)	12.22
2	EASTENDERS (MON 1959)	9.31
3	BBC NEWS (SUN 2230)	9.24
4	DOCTOR WHO (SAT 1905)	8.61
5	EASTENDERS (TUE 1929)	8.21
6	EASTENDERS (THU 1931)	8.08
7	EASTENDERS (FRI 2000)	7.97
8	CONCERT FOR DIANA (SUN 1530)	7.39
9	CASUALTY (SAT 2013)	6.98
10	TEN O'CLOCK NEWS (MON 2200)	6.23
11	BBC NEWS (SAT 2227)	6.04
12	TEN O'CLOCK NEWS (FRI 2200)	5.78
13	TEN O'CLOCK NEWS (TUE 2200)	5.57
14	TEN O'CLOCK NEWS (THU 2200)	5.45
15	NEW TRICKS (MON 2101)	5.39
16	HOLBY CITY (THU 2003)	5.07
17	SIX O'CLOCK NEWS (MON 1800)	4.85
18	TEN O'CLOCK NEWS (WED 2200)	4.79
19	TRUE DARE KISS (THU 2101)	4.67
20	SIX O'CLOCK NEWS (TUE 1800)	4.62
21	THE INSPECTOR LYNLEY MYSTERIES (FRI 2031)	4.60
22	THE WEAKEST LINK (SAT 1814)	4.46
23	SIX O'CLOCK NEWS (WED 1800)	4.42
24	HOLBY BLUE (TUE 2000)	4.36
25	SIX O'CLOCK NEWS (FRI 1800)	4.33
26	SIX O'CLOCK NEWS (THU 1800)	4.29
27	FRIDAY NIGHT WITH JONATHAN ROSS (FRI 2238)	4.23
28	JEKYLL (SAT 2103)	3.78
29	SAVING PLANET EARTH (TUE 1859)	3.49
30	SAVING PLANET EARTH (WED 1859)	3.45

Source: http://www.barb.co.uk/viewingsummary/weekreports (Accessed 13 July 2007)

Activity 2.4

Using the BARB ratings figures shown in Table 2, extract all the BBC programmes that you think can be categorised as drama.

Then, using the internet, research the ratings for imported US drama programmes on terrestrial channels and subscription channels.

With this data to inform you, return to the blog posting by Connolly and post a comment on his blog telling him if you agree.

The technical and symbolic elements that we need to study are as follows:

Camera shots: establishing shot, master shot, close-up, mid-shot, long shot, wide shot, two-shot, aerial shot, point of view shot, over the shoulder shot.

Camera angles: high angle, low angle, canted angle.

Camera movement: pan, tilt, track, dolly, crane, steadicam, hand-held, zoom, reverse zoom.

Camera composition: framing, rule of thirds, depth of field, deep and shallow focus, focus pulls.

Editing: transition of image and sound, continuity and non-continuity systems, cutting, shot/reverse shot, eyeline match, graphic match, action match, jump cut, crosscutting, parallel editing, cutaway, insert, dissolve, fade-in, fade-out, wipe, superimposition, long take, short take, slow motion, ellipsis and expansion of time, post-production, visual effects.

Sound: diegetic, non-diegetic, synchronous/asynchronous, sound effects, sound motif, sound bridge, dialogue, voiceover, mode of address/direct address, sound mixing, sound perspective, soundtrack, score, incidental music, themes and stings, ambient sound.

Mise-en-Scène: production design, location, studio, set design, costume and make-up, properties, lighting, colour design.

Clearly it is very difficult to learn how to analyse all of these things at once. You will have to do this in the exam, but it makes more sense during the study period to share the load, and Activity 2.5 provides a structure for this.

Background to TV Drama

As your job here is to expertly analyse a short sequence rather than a whole programme or series, it is not necessary to study television drama in terms of its breadth, history, funding or critical reception. However, you will probably be better equipped to offer a speedy response to a clip from an informed perspective if you are aware of some contextual detail.

This is a huge area, for sure. A long-standing science fiction drama series with a young audience like *Doctor Who* might seem

Activity 2.5

Divide your class into groups of three and each person take a number 1–3.

Number 1s will study camera (angle and movement), number 2s will take on editing (pace, nature of transitions) and number 3s will decode sound (dialogue, effects, ambience).

Watch a TV drama sequence twice just for comprehension—you cannot analyse a drama unless you are already situated by the narrative—you need to understand what is happening in time and space first.

Next, make notes during four more viewings, just on your particular element.

After these viewings, get into groups with other students with the same number so you can share ideas and each end up with a comprehensive list of examples. The emphasis here is on why—why this type of edit, why this sound effect, why this camera angle?

You need to get to grips with the choices made in production—this is what we call 'deconstruction'. When you all have a full list, get into new groups—each group must have at least one of each number (i.e. a 1, 2 and a 3)—this is the 'jigsaw' effect which results in everyone having, directly or indirectly, shared their ideas with everyone else.

When you return to your original starting point, you will each have every example of every element—you simply couldn't have done all of this on your own in a short space of time.

to share little in common with either the soap opera *Coronation Street* or a one-off drama documentary like *Hamburg Cell* (which was based on the post 9–11 anti-terror investigations) or a period drama like *Rome*. And these are just a few examples—the breadth of television drama casts a much wider net than this suggests.

There is no expectation that students will learn about TV drama as a genre or a form. What *is* expected though is an understanding of how serious fictional television engages its viewers by representing real world events, themes, people and places through a series of technical and symbolic devices, as outlined in the list in the introduction to this section. There are, however, a set of sub-genres or dramatic types that have different conventions:

- teen dramas (which depend entirely on the target audience empathising with a range of authentic characters and age-specific situations and anxieties)
- soap operas (which never end, convey a sense of real time and depend entirely on us accepting them as 'socially realist')
- costume dramas (which are often intertextually linked to 'classic' novels or plays and offer a set of pleasures that are very different to dramas set in our own world contexts and times)
- medical/hospital dramas (which interplay our vicarious pleasure at witnessing trauma and suffering on the part of patients and relatives with a set of staff narratives that deploy soap opera conventions)

- police/crime dramas (which work in the same way as medical/hospital dramas but we can substitute the health context for representation of criminals and victims)
- docu-dramas (which are set apart from the others by their attempts to dramatise significant real events which usually have either human interest, celebrity focus or political significance).

Each of these types has its own set of conventions, its typical scheduling patterns, its target audiences, its narrative formulae and its history/expectations. Let's spend some time looking in detail at each of these forms of TV drama.

Teen dramas

This sub-genre in itself is fairly broad, as a comparison of *Grange Hill, Hollyoaks* and *Skins* will demonstrate. Generally these series are concerned with striking an entertaining balance between social issues that are of concern to the target age group (such as pregnancy, date rape, alcohol and drug abuse, sexuality, youth crime and relationships) and creating an attractive, representational range of recognisable character types. When analysing them, it is useful to consider how they serve to represent teenagers to the adult culture as well as to themselves.

Case Study 2.1

The '*Skins* Party'

Consider the 'moral panic' and hostility to *Skins* that arose when a teenager from Northern England posted an open invite to a '*Skins* party' on MySpace, using the subtitle from an episode 'Let's trash the average family-sized house disco party' (see Figure 17). More than 200 people attended and over £20,000 worth of damage was caused deliberately.

As the MySpace example here shows, *Skins* has been very successful in engaging its target audience and either representing life as it is or life as the audience might like it to become. Derided by critics for its stereotypical characters and storylines, the programme (broadcast on E4 and made by the same production company responsible for *Shameless*) has been controversial for allegedly representing teenagers as more transgressive and 'out of control' than is realistic. Featuring a gay character, a character who cheats on his girlfriend and another who sleeps with a teacher, and storylines involving a Muslim character experimenting with drugs, car theft, eating disorders, suicide and a heroin overdose, the central motif of the series is the recurrence of high octane, drug-fuelled parties. It is this narrative element that has outraged older viewers (we might call this group the 'parent culture') and delighted teenage viewers in equal measure. Analysing the '*Skins* party' in terms of representation, the question to ask (as of all media texts) is whether the programme is merely representing accurately, for better or worse, the world as it is (i.e. teenagers are like this and the programme is accurate) or whether it is constructing a version of teenage life which may lead to more drug taking and antisocial behaviour. If the latter it becomes a question of how much responsibility you think programme makers have for the potential outcomes of the material they broadcast.

Figure 17 *Skins:* the inspiration for a controversial party organised on MySpace (*Source*: Channel 4)

Hollyoaks, while less 'shocking' also represents a range of 'real life' social issues pertinent to the teenage audience. Because of the sensitivity of many of the storylines, and the youthful nature of the audience, a full time researcher is employed for the programme, who acts as a mediator between the scriptwriting team and the audience during production. Scriptwriter Ian Pike describes (in an interview in *Media Magazine*) the appeal of *Hollyoaks* in this way:

> *Hollyoaks* is totally unique. It goes out five nights a week, is filmed considerably faster and on a much smaller budget, yet still picks up awards alongside *Coronation Street* and *Eastenders*. It is targeted at young people and goes out at 6.30pm, but it is one of the most successful homegrown programmes on Channel 4. And going on the feedback we receive, it can also make a difference to people's lives. Covering male rape and self-harming in the way we did undoubtedly helped teenagers who'd been through similar experiences. What makes us completely different though is

the humour. We often cut from something very heavy and thought-provoking to something utterly silly and light-hearted in a way that no one else does. Life is like that. In any street one family may be in the middle of a terrible crisis while their neighbours are laughing and I think we reflect that.

(Coker, 2004: 47)

Grange Hill, a long-running series first broadcast in the 1970s, when popular debate about the comprehensive school and its mixed ability teaching ethos was being called into question, was one of the first controversial teen dramas. Again, the question of its controversy hinged on the debate over whether a drama should depict in interesting ways a sense of 'reality' that is already there; in this case 'the way kids are' in inner city comprehensive schools. Alternatively, should the programme makers have a responsibility to promote a more positive view—or, put another way, should programme makers worry about kids copying the negative behaviour of less well-behaved characters?

In the 1980s, the most controversial storyline featured Zammo, a previously well balanced pupil who became a heroin addict. The cast subsequently recorded a song—'Just Say No'—which led to an appearance on *Top of the Pops*. The thirtieth series was recently broadcast on CBBC. Figure 18 shows a plot synopsis from the first episode of this series, with the key issues represented in bold type.

Case Study 5.1

Find an episode of *Hollyoaks* and choose a section of the programme that does what the above quote from Ian Pike says—moves from a serious, thought-provoking storyline to something more lighthearted. Then 'zoom in' on a 3–5 minute sequence that bridges the two storylines (ideally two minutes of the more serious element followed by two minutes of the 'lighter' material).

Watch the extract several times and assess how the sequence manages this bridge between the heavy and light.

First produce a storyboard of the precise transition section—the last shot of the first sequence and the first shot of the second.

Then produce a note-form assessment of how the preferred response is set up in each case by the following micro elements:

Camera: shots, angles, movement, composition.
Editing: within each section and crucially, between them, to make the 'bridge'.
Sound: dialogue, music, effects, atmospheric establishing sound—*Hollyoaks*, unlike more conventional soaps, uses non-diegetic sound—so analyse how this works alongside diegetic sound.
Mise en Scène: how is this different for the two contrasting storylines; how is mood and atmosphere created in each case through lighting, colour, performance and other aspects?

Key Term

Diegetic/Non-diegetic sound

Diegetic sound is that which is part of the text's internal world and thus is made by or heard by the characters as well as the audience. Examples are dialogue, sound effects such as explosions that appear to relate to the action on screen and music that is played as background to a scene, on a radio or stereo.

Non-diegetic sound is added for the audience only, such as atmospheric music or a voiceover.

Figure 18 Plot synopsis from Episode 1, Series 30, of *Grange Hill*
(Source: http://www.grangehill.net)
(Accessed 19 June 2007)

After struggling to get Tigger out the door on time, Togger is made late by little sister—and new Year 7—Lucy, who hasn't even changed into her uniform! Thanks to her, they have to sneak into school via the back way. En route, Lucy is intrigued by a **traveller's settlement** which has surfaced from nowhere.

The new term gets off to a bumpy start quite literally for Kathy, who's having a **driving lesson** and crashes into the school gates. She reveals she's under **pressure from her parents** to drive—a skill she'll need if, as her parents hope, she gets a place at **Oxbridge**. Baz and Holly celebrate **a year together**, but Holly admits she was annoyed by Donnie's lingering presence over the summer. Donnie presses Baz for intimate details, but he remains tight-lipped. Tigger and Ed jovially pounce on Alex but they knock him over complete with the smoothies he was planning to sell on his stall!

New first years size up the school. Jenny confides in Jake about constantly being compared to sisters Tanya and Karen, and Bryn finds himself pushed around by the **bullies**. A scuffle breaks out between Jenny, Lucy and Tigger; Tanya and Togger dive in to defend their siblings. Togger and Tanya are pushed into **each other's arms**, which they rather enjoy—Abel notices their chemistry!

Emma hides in the toilets. She manages to dodge Tanya at first but eventually Tanya corners her in the cubicle and is horrified to discover Emma's face **battered and bruised**. Emma reveals her **mum was responsible**—she blames Emma for her break-up with Robin and they ended up coming to blows. Emma feels a little better when she mentions her forthcoming birthday.

Jeremy asks Abel for advice on the best way to attract Emma. Abel suggests he send a text – but when he does, Emma replies with a firm rebuff. Andrea can't believe it when Chloe tells her **she fancies Max** – but he ignores her when she says hi.

Alex **sets up his smoothie stall**. Max and Mooey demand their supply of refreshments and when he refuses, they trash the stall. Taylor tries to intervene but Max coolly reminds him that as a staff member he can no longer 'sort him out'. . .McDonnell arrives and is not impressed by Taylor's lack of action. Sammy hates seeing Alex picked on and wants to help, but Chloe is quick to warn her against it. She continues her pursuit of Max as he leaves the crime scene.

The day ends and Kathy is shocked when her driving instructor is waiting for her in the playground. Man of little words Ali rescues Bryn from the bullies, while Lucy and Jenny square up again. . .Togger and Tanya realise it's going to be a long year!

Grange Hill, like all long-running TV dramas, can be viewed as a 'social document', representing a range of social changes. Here, television critic Charlie Brooker describes the balance of change and tradition in the programme, and makes some comparisons to other programmes in doing so:

> To these weary eyes, most of the kids look identical to one another but that's probably got more to do with my age than their faces, which seem to blur into one creaseless, eyebag-free wash of young flesh after ten minutes. Nevertheless a few stand out, traditional Grange Hill archetypes: the evil one (who's selling cigarettes to the little kids), the pair of scheming lovable chancers (this week trying their hand at busking), the 'weird' kid (apparently autistic), the male and female heart-throbs (you never get over your first *Grange Hill* crush), and the kids with the problems at home (a boy with a dad in prison and two girls whose parents are splitting up). Some other traditions hold firm: the teachers are just quirky enough to appear eccentric without being sinister, and the sixth-formers remain the most crashingly tedious, self-righteous shop dummies on earth.
>
> The changes then—starting with the pace, which has been upped considerably (lots of short, snappy scenes) and the camerawork, which is more stylized and energetic than ever before. Almost every sequence seems to end with a visual punch line; a sudden jump to an overhead shot, or an arrangement of pupils so symmetrical you could be forgiven for thinking you'd stumbled across an unreleased Peter Greenaway film. It works—it draws you in and keeps you entertained.
>
> (Brooker, 2005: 50)

Brooker covers a wide range of representational elements here—the use of comprehensive school stereotypes; the representation of a disability (although this is his assumption rather than an explicit, stated portrayal); the nature of some characters as 'pin ups' for the audience; the representation of youth more generally (from his ageing perspective); the representation of teachers (which you might contrast with the newer Channel 4 series) and the portrayal of domestic issues and their impact on school-age children. He then goes on to describe the ways in which the stylistic conventions of the programme have changed with new expectations from the audience, while the representational themes and characters remain constant.

Teen dramas are unlike the rest of our examples as they do not set out to appeal to such a broad audience. Phil Redmond, writer of *Grange Hill* and *Hollyoaks* as well as a host of other dramas over a long period of time, describes the 'niche' audience idea here:

> *Hollyoaks* has shown us and *Grange Hill* before that—that there are things in life that look, feel and sound different at different stages in life. There is definitely a mid-20s threshold that most people have to step over into full maturity, just as the 50-somethings have to start re-evaluating their lives when the kids have gone. It is a bit like looking at both ends of the social spectrum—20-somethings settling down to have kids and 50-somethings facing life when they've moved on. Also—in a multi-platform age—fragmentation of the audience will continue and audiences will not be so high. Programmes that can attract niche audiences will be in demand—and will be where all the fun will be!

(Grahame, 2003: 5)

Figure 19 Grange Hill—representing reality or a bad influence?
(*Source*: Lime Pictures)

Activity 2.7

Taking the example above as a template, watch an episode of *Grange Hill* or any other teen drama and produce a similar plot synopsis with the key issues represented in bold. Then conduct a content analysis to calculate the percentage of the episode devoted to each of the three categories below. We have given you examples from the *Grange Hill* episode to get you started:

Serious social issues relating to teenagers: bullying, domestic violence, treatment of travellers.

Everyday aspects of teenage life: learning to drive.

Teenage relationships: parental pressures and romances.

When you have worked out the percentages, either hold a face to face discussion with other students or set up a blog to compare views on this question—how relevant is this teen drama to your life?

If you are an older student taking AS Media, then you may wish to cast your mind back to your teenage days to do this!

Soap operas

The soap opera format can be an area of study in its own right, and once again the important interplay is between the micro and macro elements of textual analysis. Soap opera has a range of conventions that make it distinct from other forms of television drama, and these conventions add up to an overall representation of domestic 'real life' that tries to be both recognisable to the public as 'everyday' and at the same time melodramatic and exciting.

Soap opera employs some distinctive conventions:

- the constant illusion of real time
- precise continuity
- tease devices and cliff hangers
- combinations of action (information for the viewer) and enigma (questions raised for the viewer)
- the dominance of two-shots and over-the-shoulder shots of conversations (over 90 per cent of soaps are devoted to conversations between pairs of people) (see Figure 20)
- establishing shots (of locations) and tableaux (groups of people composed dramatically)
- coverage of current social issues
- meeting places that allow for gossip to circulate
- narrative flow and a nostalgic and perhaps outdated depiction of community
- interweaving storylines in each episode
- partial closure of storylines
- music used as motif (for example, the drums at the end of *Eastenders*)
- the dominance of diegetic sound (with the exception of *Hollyoaks*)
- highly symbolic costumes and set designs (for example the choice of curtains in a family's house reinforces to the audience what 'type' of people they are)
- a 'kitchen sink' *mise en scène* (naturalistic, domestic, personal).

How this balance of drama and realism is struck is the focus of our analysis. Here are some key questions to ask of soap opera extracts:

- How is the representation of particular groups of people within the broader focus on *ordinary communities and families* mediated through the specific televisual language of this kind of text in comparison to other forms of television drama?
- How does the verisimilitude achieved by the *illusion of ongoing real time* establish a greater sense of realism than other texts?
- In what ways are soap operas *topical and sometimes controversial*

in their treatments of current affairs/social issues? Related to this, what is the responsibility of a soap opera producer? Is it to reflect society 'as it is' or 'as it should be'?

- What is the *balance of realism and drama* in particular soaps? This balance is very important to the remit of a soap opera—it must cling to a very specific verisimilitude (see the opening credits of *Coronation Street*) which may be outdated, or at least nostalgic and romantic, at the same time as competing for ratings with other soaps through the development of exciting, ongoing and climaxing storylines.

The representation of family life in soaps is often the subject of debate. On 17 October 2002, *The Daily Mail* published 'Scarred by Soaps' (by Steve Doughty, Social Affairs correspondent), in response to the National Family and Parenting Institute's research. The article explained that the findings of this research were that children are encouraged by soaps to believe that family breakdown is the norm and that soaps fail to promote moral values. On the same day, John Carvel (Social Affairs editor) summarised the same research in *The Guardian*, but concentrated mostly on the research's evidence that parents regularly discuss soap opera storylines with their children.

More so than for other forms of television drama, soaps rely on intertextual and/or extratextual meanings. Tabloid newspapers routinely confuse actor/character and drama/reality at the time of popular storylines. This creates a kind of second-hand representation. In addition, soap trailers are becoming increasingly sophisticated. All the British soaps have used film noir and thriller conventions in their promotional campaigns recently and there are a number of magazines offering a range of additional meanings for the audience.

In terms of popularity, we need to consider whether the reason for the longevity of the pleasure offered by these texts is to do with representation or not. In other words, is the pleasure of soap opera to do with the recognition of the everyday in these programmes, or are they 'just' good drama? And ultimately the *social document versus junk TV* debate is important—is it possible to learn about our history from old episodes of soaps, or are these programmes a form of addictive and distracting entertainment to keep 'the masses' happy (people refer to this as 'dumbing down' but if you decide to study this idea, you must engage with it as a debate in which there are no right answers)?

Period dramas

Not all period dramas are literary adaptations, but these account for a substantial part of the sub-genre and for many audience

Figure 20 Soap opera is dominated by two shots of characters in dialogue.
(*Source*: ITV Granada)

members, a key pleasure is to be gained from this way of consuming 'classic' fiction. As a Media student, you might wish to challenge this idea that some writing is of more cultural value than other fiction. Period drama is famously expensive to produce. Think about the costs-to-income ratio of producing a programme such as *Big Brother* compared to *Bleak House*, for example. The former uses unpaid members of the public, takes place in one relatively cheap location and in return is viewed by millions every day, on various platforms and earning huge amounts of money from sponsorship, phone rates and standard advertising. This kind of television is highly formatted and very easy and cheap to produce and sell.

Period drama is hugely expensive to produce, given the demands for authenticity and the high fees earned by the kinds of acting personnel expected by the audience. Everything about a costume drama has to give the appearance of 'quality' and that is never cheap. *Bleak House* (see Figure 21) is reported to have cost

£8 million but this is now considered a worthwhile investment due to the popularity of the series, as explained here by Points (2007).

> **What was distinctive about *Bleak House* was the way it successfully captured new and younger audiences. It is therefore a good example of how broadcasters and producers approach a conventional genre in order to make it accessible to a contemporary audience. The production incorporated all the fundamental conventions of period drama (clearly defined characters and the meticulously recreated *mise en scène*) which audiences expect and relish. But it also employed more unconventionally contemporary camerawork and editing, the accelerated narrative pace of series drama, soap-like presentation and scheduling and a broad range of well-known television actors from a variety of different genres.**
>
> (Points, 2007: 68)

Typically, due to their relatively high production values, we can say that period dramas tend to be more 'filmic' in quality. Those that are based on literature will represent people and issues largely in keeping with the original novel or play, but one of the interesting things about this sub-genre is its 'intermedial' dimension—how the television interpretation offers a different 'spin' on the representational devices. In some cases the time period context might be shifted or some of the characters might be changed to give a different set of potential meanings.

It goes without saying that a costume drama set in earlier times, whether based on literature or not, will be understood and interpreted by a contemporary audience through a sense of how those times were different. This is a form of representation based on a distancing process—how life in those days was different to life today—and a consideration of which aspects were better and which were worse. And this will be largely related to the individual viewers' own set of social, cultural and political beliefs and life experiences. So when we analyse any sequence from a period drama we are deconstructing not only the representations on screen but going further to consider how these representations might be of interest to viewers when interpreted from a contemporary point of view.

Carter (2005) argues that period drama needs to have 'contemporary impact'. This might seem like stating the obvious at first, but let's explore how this works. Carter outlines a range of possible approaches drama can take to make this impact. One of these is to return to themes that have already been dramatised

Figure 21 *Bleak House:* a modern spin on a 'classic' story?
(*Source*: Mike Hogan/BBC)

and produce new connections with modern times (for example *Elizabeth I* and its focus on her attempt to balance private and public lives). Another is to foreground a writer's specific, individual interpretation of a historical period, which can of course lead to controversy among historians who may take issue with the representations broadcast (but this might still be good publicity). Another strategy (which is increasingly common as such dramas are reported to cost £1.2 million an hour to produce) is to appeal to an international market. This is fairly easy to do since British history and heritage is of great interest worldwide (though appealing to the cultural tourist audience as well as, or instead of, the home population might affect the representation). Carter sums up the agenda for producers of period TV dramas like this:

Producing successful historical dramas depends on many factors but, ultimately, comes down to two things: how well the producers balance the need for dramatic licence against

Activity 2.8

This activity will help you prepare for the Key Concepts exam and also enhance your video pre-production skills.

If you are not studying English Literature yourself, find a Media student who is, and then choose a 'classic' from the course that has not been made into a TV drama in recent years. Produce a storyboard for the launch trailer and as you are doing so make production notes on:

- Key characters
- Key narratives
- *Mise en scène* and authenticity (this will be most important)
- Style (to appeal to a contemporary audience)
- 'Spin'

Detailed storyboarding is essential to a successful video shoot. It isn't just about organising things in advance so you can save time on the day of filming, it is more than that. The storyboarding process by its nature (using boxes to represent the camera/screen) puts you in the frame of mind of the audience. In this example the storyboard situates you as the viewer of a literary adaptation—how will each frame look, sound and 'feel' to the audience member who has read the book and to the viewer who hasn't?

historical accuracy, and assembling a production team sympathetic to the producer and writer's vision. The biggest challenge to achieving either, however, is identifying an appropriate subject to dramatise and then settling on the right approach.

(Carter, 2005: 22)

All this is fundamentally different to analysing a drama which purports to represent life as it is today. To complicate matters further, take the example of *Life on Mars*—discussed here as an intermedial, post modern police/crime drama. This programme, while not a literary adaptation, is also a period drama, depicting the 1970s as a recognisable historical period. It is distinguished from *Bleak House* by the insertion of a contemporary character that has travelled 'back in time', but it does share conventions with the period drama as it relies on us accepting the authenticity of its *mise en scène*.

Hospital dramas

Like many examples of crime drama, hospital dramas balance two different narrative themes—public health and the treatment of illness on the one hand, and workplace interactions and

Activity 2.9

Use the internet to research a writer and a producer of period drama over recent years.

Produce a short case study in a format of your choice, outlining the following for an audience of your peers:

- Dramas produced
- Approaches taken
- Critical responses
- Historians' responses.

Some reasonably clever use of Google should enable you to source this information in a short space of time, but you will then need to view some of the dramas produced by your chosen individuals to see if you agree with the range of online information, which will of course be subjective.

relationships on the other. This second strand shares many conventions with soap opera and in some cases the hospital context is incidental to this aspect of the drama.

Hospital dramas feature a range of character types that are sometimes referred to as stereotypes. These characters offer different versions of a number of occupational roles and ideas about the public. These roles include medical managers, surgeons, consultants and doctors, nurses, porters and cleaners, paramedics and ambulance crews, the police, social workers, parents, children, the elderly and religious groups. This is not a comprehensive list by any means but these are recurring 'types' in this form of drama. The genre has become so well established that a new crop of programmes offering various kinds of parody or 'retake' on the format have been successful recently, with *No Angels* and *Green Wing* being the most popular. Whereas *Green Wing* offers a surreal comic response to the conventions, *No Angels* is less clearly comedic but, like *Teachers*, differs from the norm in that the characters do not display consistent vocational drive for their chosen career. Instead, the practice of nursing acts as a backdrop for a drama about contemporary female identity and relationships. We should note that the programme takes its title from the more traditional *Angels* series from the 1970s, and thus clearly sets out a riposte to the representation of nurses as 'worthy'.

Crime dramas

There are two kinds of TV crime drama, with important distinctions between them. One-off crime dramas tend to focus on the kinds of crimes that create the most anxiety among the viewing public (murder and serial killing in particular). They are distinguished by which aspects of law enforcement they focus on, for example a police inspector, a team of detectives, a psychologist or a lawyer. Long-running TV crime dramas will have a variety of sub-plots over time that help build up more sustained audience interest in the relationships between characters (for example Tyler and Cartwright in *Life on Mars*).

Each crime drama will have its own unique representational aspects that are not directly related to the crime being investigated. For example, in *Prime Suspect* the character of Inspector Tennison sets up representations of gender and the experience she has of being a successful detective in a male dominated culture. The scriptwriters include a range of personal narratives for Tennison alongside the detective work, usually involving failed relationships so that her character takes on the traits of many male detective characters from TV drama—driven and high achieving in the public world, disastrous in private life.

Activity 2.10

View one episode of a hospital drama and one episode of a soap opera. List all the similarities in terms of conventions, and then group these similarities into micro and macro examples. Micro examples are to do with specific aspects of camera work, editing, *mise en scène* and sound. Macro examples are broader representational themes.

With this information at your disposal, get in a group of ten students and arrange the group in a circle or horseshoe shape.

Each person in the group then begins an essay with the sentence 'To make hospital drama less like soap opera, I would. . .' When each person has completed this first sentence they pass their essay to the person on their right.

Each person then writes the next sentence and passes on the essay. After eight sentences all participants must begin their two concluding statements. After ten sentences each person will receive back their original piece of paper.

Now you all have a collaborative essay with all of your collective ideas in response to one question.

Lewis, the most popular TV drama of 2006, portrays the detective as a lonely bereaved figure in the evenings, while the hero of *A Touch of Frost* (another hugely popular drama, with 40 per cent of the viewing share in 2006) frequently fails to 'close the deal' on a number of potential relationships. In institutional terms, these three examples also help us understand the debate about the quality of contemporary British TV drama in relation to the increasing success of American import shows on our screens. *Prime Suspect*, *Lewis*, *A Touch of Frost* and *Cracker* are all attempts by ITV to 'rebrand' previously successful crime shows rather than invest in new drama productions.

Spooks is a long-running crime drama produced by Kudos and broadcast by the BBC. It is highly topical in terms of representation as it takes as its major theme the prevention of terrorism, in the context of 'MI5 not 9 to 5', as the publicity for the programme states. Achieving 10 million viewers, *Spooks* is broadcast at 9 p.m. Although the BBC is famously a public service institution (which means it does not generate money from advertising) it is a mistake to think of the BBC as an institution that is not commercially astute. *Spooks* makes revenue from DVD sales, board games, an interactive website, a mobile phone service offering games and episodes and, most significantly, from the exporting of the programme to the USA (with a new name—MI5).

Seen by many critics as attempting to compete with *24*, the programme is highly stylised in terms of its editing, use of split screens and the constant presence of technology, to mirror the high-tech context of contemporary intelligence operations and of terrorism since 9/11. The BBC has also been criticised (as it does not carry advertising) for the range of product placements on screen throughout the series.

Points (2007) analyses one episode at length and finds a range of binary oppositions—good and evil, Western and Arab, British and Iraqi, ordinary life and the terrorist threat, violence committed by MI5 and violence committed by terrorists, decisions made by the British Government and those made by Al Qaeda and sanctioned versus unsanctioned actions. But Points concludes that despite these oppositions, which are typical of TV drama with its need to simplify and dramatise recognisable or topical themes, the programme is constructed in such a way to allow a range of responses.

> **Although the binary structure is quite apparent, interestingly the drama does question the US and British action in Iraq (innocent Western lives apparently more valued than innocent Iraqi lives), allowing audiences some licence to adopt negotiated or oppositional interpretations. This can of course lead to a contradiction; audiences may desire the successful release of Fiona and the killing of the Iraqi terrorist, Ahmed, while still adopting a position which sees the war in Iraq as wrong (those for example, who protested against US and British action). The narrative resolution of these oppositions demonstrated their essentially conservative, ideological significance.**
>
> (Points, 2007: 77)

Taking this idea of oppositions further, Dunne (2006) suggests that media representations of crime normally set up five key binaries:

1 Crime/the police
2 Criminals/the criminal justice system
3 Lawyers versus courts
4 Social workers versus the police
5 Victims versus the public.

Each programme can be analysed using this system of oppositions and we can thus get a sense of how each programme represents crime and law and order differently. Dunne suggests this is changing and that the representation of crime is never neutral:

We are often shown that good cops are allowed to break the rules in order to put away the villains. In TV fiction the police are nearly always portrayed as the good guys with only a very occasional 'bad apple'. In *The Bill*, the use of the camera is key in this representation; there is almost never a scene without a police protagonist present. The audience is not only invited, but actually has no option other than to see the world from a police perspective—often literally, with liberal use of first person point of view shots. But there is evidence of change. During the 80s and 90s there were some infamous miscarriages of justice and since then the media's willingness to question police versions of 'the truth' has been greater. In dramas, even police-centric ones such as *The Bill*, a more critical line about policing is now more frequently explored. And with series such as *Between the Lines*, *Ghost Squad* and *Waking the Dead* there is a growing realisation that the police can—and sometimes do—get it wrong.

(Dunne, 2007: 47)

This tension between police-centric drama and the desire to represent the police as flawed is highly significant in *Life on Mars*. In this drama, not only is there a police presence in every scene, there is the presence of the main character too, as it would not be possible to have any action without him, due to the ongoing uncertainty over whether the reality depicted is a figment of his comatose imagination. Despite Tyler's constant frustration and occasional horror at the methods employed by Gene Hunt, in the end he chooses to stay in the 1970s. The drama presents this decision as being made in response to a particularly soul-less, slick and corporate senior level police meeting that Sam attends when back in the twenty-first century. How are we to read this decision—that despite the dubious nature of police tactics and the miscarriages of justice we now know about from that era, those times, free from 'political correctness', were more honest? Clearly there are many readings of the series' conclusion but the interplay between Sam's twenty-first century methods and the way he has to 'get the job done' in the 1970s provides some interesting representational issues, when placed in comparison to *The Bill*.

Shared Conventions

You have now spent some time considering different types of television drama. However, for this part of your AS studies it is essential to identify the conventions which all of these forms share, at the level of a sequence, which are as follows:

Characters who offer 'shorthand' representations of real types of people (or stereotypes).

Narrative which is visually presented and demands high levels of active audience understanding (of what is assumed to happen in between edits—the difference between plot and story).

Mise en scène (costume, props, lighting, locations, elements of performance—these things add up to an instantly recognisable atmosphere which is 'authentic' for the events, themes and people that are being represented in the drama).

Camerawork that ensures continuity and creates drama through visual conventions.

Dialogue, sound and music which create a balance between verisimilitude (the believable logic of the text's world which appears real) and drama (dialogue which might be less 'polished' in the real world, music which tells the audience that we should feel scared, happy, tense, romantic, sad or amused).

Identifying these conventions is not especially difficult, but if you don't watch much television drama at the moment, it would be a good idea to plan a significant diet of it over the course of your AS studies. You will see a lot of sequences in lessons as you prepare for the exam, but the more familiar you are with this kind of televisual pleasure in its broadcast and viewing context, the better. This will allow you to answer these key questions in relation to any TV drama:

- Which sub-genre does it represent?
- How is its narrative structure typical of this sub-genre?
- How does the *mise en scène* create verisimilitude?
- What visual codes are used as representational devices?
- How do sound, dialogue and music balance realism with drama?
- Does the programme/series employ intermedial references?
- Overall, who and what are represented and how?
- What range of audience responses are possible?

Case Study Extracts

The six case study examples that follow offer a model for your own approach to the unseen sequence you will be shown in the Key Concepts exam. It's worth restating again that television drama covers a huge breadth, which it is not possible to span in six examples. But here the intention is to offer six types of television drama and to focus on a sequence from each which is a similar length to what you will encounter in the exam. The conceptual focus is on representation and these examples demonstrate how to connect micro textual analysis/media literacy to macro themes and representations.

Because in the exam you may view a drama you know little about, we will only spend a small amount of time here on the context for each.

The six extracts are from:

- *Life on Mars*
- *Rome*
- *Skins*
- *Coronation Street*
- *The Hamburg Cell*
- *Doctor Who*.

These six sequences will be analysed in relation to how they represent people, places, times and themes. The deconstruction here will be brief and it will focus on one specific aspect of representation. You can then use this as a starting point for a fuller analysis of the extract in the context of the programme/series as a whole (but remember, the exam only requires analysis of the short extract at the 'micro' level in the main). The extracts are from contrasting sub-genres: *Coronation Street* is a soap opera and *Skins* is a teen drama. *Life on Mars* can be described as a post modern police/crime drama but also a period drama. *Rome* is a period drama which offers a new spin on historical events. *Hamburg Cell* is a one-off docu-drama and *Doctor Who* is a science fiction drama.

The extracts are also different in their conventions—*The Hamburg Cell* has 90 minutes to offer a satisfactory self-contained narrative, while *Life on Mars* constructs a self-contained narrative for each particular episode but has established characters, an ongoing enigma, various ongoing subplots and future episodes in store. *Coronation Street* has had over forty years to establish itself, broadcasts several times a week and never ends, so by nature its themes and narratives are ongoing and interwoven. *Doctor Who* is able to dispense with some aspects of continuity and realism due to its fantasy context but nevertheless establishes verisimilitude and a textual logic at the same time as using the long-running series format and the various narrative strands that this allows. *Rome* must put an interesting 'spin' on familiar historical events over the course of the series.

Case Study 2.2

Life on Mars

Context: Every episode of this two-series drama begins with the voice of the main character reminding us: 'My name is Sam Tyler. I had an accident and woke up in 1973. Am I mad? In a coma? Or back in time?' As this sequence will demonstrate, the essential ingredient for the show's success is the audience knowing what Sam knows while the rest of the cast do not—what happens in the future.

The episode in question is Series 2, Episode 3: 'Car Bomb'. During the episode, an Irishman has been wrongly accused by DCI Gene Hunt (Tyler's boss) of planting the bomb. The extract, which begins after 51 minutes and runs for three minutes, begins with the police officers giving the innocent Irish character, Patrick O'Brien, a lift home.

Heavy rock music from the 1970s plays as the camera zooms slowly through a line of washing hanging out to dry in the grey Manchester weather, while Gene Hunt's brown Ford Cortina (a key piece of iconography as this car has come to signify the 1970s) crashes carelessly into a bin on the pavement in a street of terraced houses—a stereotypically Northern scene.

The two policemen disembark from the front seats and Tyler releases O'Brien from the back. We view this from a medium long shot with passers by watching the action. Through a combination of two shots, three shots and tableaux shots, we next witness a grudging apology from Hunt, clearly elicited by Tyler. Then to a head and shoulder shot of O'Brien's badly beaten face as he makes a defiant speech in response about the plight of Irish men living in England who are denied the means to honest employment and constantly suspected of terrorism. 'You know what, big man, I'm sick of shovelling shit.' As we return to a two shot, it is clear that Tyler is sympathetic and guilty. Hunt wears a cynical frown. These two contrasting facial expressions are important aspects of performance—non-verbal communication that serves as a motif through the series in order to continually map out the differences between the two men. Hunt then snorts—'He hasn't just got a chip on his shoulder, more like the whole chippy.' For this shot, Tyler is in the foreground, back to Hunt. Tyler's long stare is then anchored by a weary 'Yeah, well, I wonder why'. This tired, exasperated expression is worn by Tyler for most of the series, again serving to reinforce the frustration he experiences trying to live in a world which is literally years behind in its thinking. To reinforce this even further, this still camera portrait of the two men is punctuated by an Asian man walking through the shot carrying a television. When challenged by Hunt, he proudly explains that he is moving into his new house. The camera pans to the exterior of the house, where his wife waits in a sari. Back to the neatly composed foreground/background two shot, with Hunt in the background announcing 'Bit parky to be out in just a nightie.' Again, Tyler's expression of dismay returns in the foreground. Throughout this part of the extract, the *mise en scène* is natural, dreary but quintessentially 1970s and Northern— terraced houses, grey skies, brown clothes and long hair. Rock music from the decade acts as a sound bridge from the previous scene and into the next one, which takes place in a smoky pub.

Tyler is framed in the doorway of the pub, ghost-like, shrouded by smoke. This ghostly appearance is another visual motif that recurs, as whether or not Tyler is actually alive is an enigma, a back-story to the drama. A round of applause breaks out and the camera moves to a tableaux shot and then a series of two shots as we see who is clapping—the rest of the team. Drinks are bought and we move to a mid shot of the characters drinking at a table, 1970s 'pint pots' everywhere. The female police officer, Cartwright, is being praised for her work, leading to another character saying 'steady on boss, you'll be having her running the country next' to which Cartwright speculates that a female prime minister might be a good idea. Tyler, of course, knows the future and says 'I've a feeling you might regret saying that one day', which is, as usual, met by perplexed expressions. As this is the 1970s, and sexism is rife in the police force, a comment about Cartwright's underwear quickly follows. Throughout this scene, the *mise en scène* is constructed through smoke, pub noise, the iconography of the types of glasses being used and the visual elements of the setting—a Rastafarian barman, a red telephone and a jukebox on the wall.

At the macro level the representational meaning of the extract as a whole is entirely dependent on the audience recognising the distinction between the viewing time (2007) and the story time (1970s). The idea of a female PM being strange, the treatment of Irish men, the exotic nature of Asian clothing and the collision between Hunt's 'no nonsense' style of policing and Tyler's sensitivity are all reliant on the audience bringing a great deal of cultural knowledge to the drama.

Case Study 2.3

Rome

Context: this expensive HBO/BBC production takes the 'handed down' historical events of the Roman Empire and offers a new perspective/spin on them (see Figure 22). Several characters and storylines are not recognisable from the historical narratives we are familiar with—see the comments from Carter (2005) earlier in this chapter on the importance of putting a 'contemporary spin' on period drama.

The episode in question is Season 2, Episode 4: *Testudo et Lepus* (The Tortoise and the Hare). The Roman Army are in Northern Greece. The extract appears 25 minutes into the episode and lasts for five minutes. The action begins in a courtyard with recognisably Roman pillars. Music with Eastern, Arabic, Egyptian and 'old world' connotations provides the soundtrack.

We see a seated Roman soldier (Agrippa) who shortly afterwards is joined by a female character (Octavia). As she sits she asks the cynical question—'Long day? It must be tiring work killing innocent people, even defenceless ones.' As the dialogue continues, with the two characters seated discussing the morality of the Roman military activities (the soldier defending the cause, Octavia mockingly stating 'all for the good of the Republic'), two shots and over-the-shoulder shots are used with continuity principles (the 360 degree rule and eyeline match) observed throughout. Then the discussion moves to more romantic concerns—whether or not Agrippa's feelings are genuine. As he says the line—'I've been torturing myself these past months', we switch to a close up for emotional impact. The dialogue now is in relation to the 'forbidden' nature of the relationship, a 'Romeo and Juliet' narrative theme emerging. There follows a pattern of two-second head and shoulder shots, cutting between the two speakers/listeners, followed by a single shot of the couple kissing, with the focus on the background where an empty corridor between the pillars implies that the space will shortly be filled, thus presenting the threat of imminent discovery and suggesting that the kiss is illicit. Knowledge of drama conventions is required for the audience to 'read' this implication, of course. The diegetic sound of footsteps breaks the embrace and as the soldier leaps from the screen to the right, another soldier (Maecenas) enters the frame by arriving in the corridor from around a corner. The depth of focus remains on Octavia as he approaches. As a conversation between the three characters ensues, on the surface about taxes but filled with inference, non verbal communication is highly significant—the couple nervous and awkward, the new arrival amused and curious. As the two male characters depart the scene, the camera moves to a close up on Octavia who wears a smile, clearly excited by the 'risk'.

Next we cut to a very different location—a mob is discussing a power struggle over the rule of Rome, in a dark, shadowy underground cave, and we enter this scene through a zoom into a closed gate above the setting. The diegetic sound of the mob talking over one another loudly is used as a non-diegetic, or at least semi-diegetic bridge over the zoom, to create immediate and striking contrast with the calm *mise en scène* of the courtyard scene. Octavia is of a different social class and the *mise en scène* reflects this contrast with the mob. The natural low key candle-lit aesthetic is accompanied by characters in grey ragged clothes and unshaven features. No women are present, meaning that the only female representation in this extract is attractive and 'forbidden'.

As various male characters discuss taxation and who should rule Rome, we cut to an overhead shot through the gates we entered the scene at, thus the space, dynamics and 'underworld' context of the scene is re-established. As the characters come into conflict, always shouting, we move to a series of close ups and two shots of characters offering one sentence at a time, followed by head and shoulder shots of each speaker as they in turn offer extended dialogue, and finally to a still head and shoulder shot of one speaker who makes a longer speech. Here, a grammar of editing is observed, with the rhythm changing as we become more familiar with the events. The extended speech is made by a character directly challenging the previous statement by a Rabbi, by asking 'Why let any of them rule? This is our land! You are traitors to your own kind!' When asked to name his group, he shouts dramatically 'We are the Wrath of Israel.' As the Rabbi enters the frame to form a two shot, he spits in his face and bedlam ensues. As the characters start to fight, first the camera stays in the midst of the action and then we return to the overhead zoom out, once again re-establishing the hostility of the environment.

The contrast between the two scenes in this extract is marked. There are three 'movements': First, the couple talk, kiss and are almost discovered. This is entirely fictional and a series of period drama romance conventions are observed. The *mise en scène* is regal, romantic and quiet dialogue dominates. Second, we witness a political argument in a darker, underground location with conflict, frustration and disempowerment reflected by the shadowy *mise en scène* and harsh candlelight (large flames moving in the wind as opposed to calming, romantic candlelight). Finally we move to a fight sequence, with action genre conventions. At a macro level the representational contrast subsequently created here is between social class, the empowered and the dispossessed and between the fictional romance and the political conflict based on 'known' history.

Figure 22 *Rome*—a very expensive drama to make.
(*Source*: Photo by © HBO/Everett/Rex Features)

Case Study 2.4

Skins

Context: *Skins* is a series broadcast on Channel 4 which has been the subject of some controversy, due to its representation of youth culture, particularly the hedonistic aspects of it. Some critics argue that it actually influences its audience to behave in antisocial ways—see the section on teen drama for more detail on this 'moral panic'.

The extract analysed here is from the episode broadcast on Channel 4 on 4 September 2007. The main storyline is Jal's preparations for the Young Musician of the Year competition. The extract begins 40 minutes into the episode, and starts with a shot of a closed, red, office door.

As we view the red door, we hear off-screen diegetic dialogue ('come in') from a female voice and see the door open and Jal enter the frame looking anxious. We are seeing her from the point of view of the office's occupant, who is still not seen, but the camera looks up slightly at Jal, suggesting that the woman who summoned her in is seated. We cut to a shot of the head teacher behind her desk, who mispronounces Jal's name and asks her to sit down. Jal is then kept waiting in silence while the head teacher completes paperwork; we observe this through an over-the-shoulder shot so the front of the frame is filled by the back of the head teacher's head, but the main focus is on the facial expression worn by Jal—anxious, frustrated, annoyed. The *mise en scène* is highly formal and tense. The office is instantly recognisable as that of a head teacher, providing the viewer has the cultural knowledge and experience to identify it as such. Another (male) teacher enters the room and we then hear a patronising speech from the head teacher, with Jal silent. We cut between head and shoulder shots of the speaker and over-the-shoulder shots of the listener, the camera always still. The lighting is simply that of an office—artificial, administrative, neutral and bland. Jal's performance is significant throughout—she grows in annoyance when hearing the line 'we want to celebrate this amazing achievement for a girl of your background'. The head teacher's non verbal communication is equally crucial to the representational outcomes of the scene—a smug smile and earnest expression showing her to be completely unaware of the assumptions she is making, which are tantamount to racism. Another statement which is rich with topical cultural satire is the head teacher's reference to 'working towards sustainable excellence under the "everything's getting better initiative", it's for people like you'. This will resonate with anyone who takes a cynical view of the New Labour Government's practice of 'initiative overload' and also with young people who feel patronised and alienated by educational professionals. The smug smile of the speaker is, through simple hard-cut editing, juxtaposed with the horrified reaction of Jal, who is required to take part in several TV interviews to discuss her musical talents, for which she is given a checklist of things to say which will promote the school. As Jal speaks for the first time ('thanks for the advice', said sarcastically), we have another head and shoulder shot of the head teacher, whose smug smile again connotes her misunderstanding of Jal's reaction. To further amplify the sense of a generation gap, the male teacher suddenly announces 'kick it, let's rock' and the camera lingers on the disgusted reaction from Jal.

The entire sequence uses a still camera, no non-diegetic sound, economic editing and a simple structure of head and shoulder and over-the-shoulder shots. The camera and editing are unobtrusive, in observer mode, allowing us to focus entirely on the dialogue and, more importantly, on the non verbal communication of the characters and the contrasts between them. The key representational theme here, at the macro level, is that the teaching profession are cynical and an embarrassment. The audience for *Skins* clearly is significant here. Although all media meaning is polysemic and every audience member will view a text through their own cultural lens, we might agree that a teen audience is more likely to share this perception of the 'parent culture'.

Next we cut to a bedroom where Jal and a friend are seated watching Jal's TV performance, through which she enacts revenge by responding to every question with 'no'. We witness this from a two shot from behind the two girls, with the backs of their heads in the foreground and the TV in the background—thus the girls' watching is of more importance than the content of the programme itself. Then we cut to a mid shot of the two characters on the sofa discussing what clothes Jal will wear for the competition and then to a mid shot of Jal's friend finding clothes in the wardrobe for Jal to wear. Jal is anxious and disinterested but her friend is adamant that she should take the advice—'you play clarinet and I look shaggable, it's talent, girl, pure talent'. Again, the scene sets up contrast—the black classical musician is a challenge to stereotyping but Jal is torn between her music, her friends and her age to some extent. Her friend contrasts with her in this sequence to set up a representational tension around femininity and sexuality, themes which may, like the loathing of patronising teachers, strike a nerve with the primary audience. Jal's friend is not simply a 'slut' representation; instead she could be seen as a post-feminist 'playful' construction, taking an ironic spin on her sexual attraction.

Because the two scenes here are all about setting up representational contrast, the most important elements of this are dialogue and non-verbal communication. The camera is always still, the lighting always neutral, the *mise en scène* highly familiar and 'everyday' and the editing economical and unobtrusive. These are classic realist drama conventions, and the director makes no attempt to use the technical elements of the production for symbolic ends.

Case Study 2.5

Coronation Street

Context: *Coronation Street*, set in the fictional northern town of Weatherfield and filmed at Granada in Manchester, has been running on ITV for almost fifty years! (The public can even visit the actual street and have a pint in the 'Rovers Return'.) The section on soap opera in this chapter outlines the key conventions of the soap opera genre and the extract selected here for analysis is a rich example as it features several of them.

The extract is from the episode broadcast on 17 September 2007. It begins two minutes into the programme and lasts for three minutes. It features an exterior location (the street itself) and an interior location (the Duckworths' kitchen). The scene before the extract concerns Sarah, a mother who was a teenager when her child was born, discussing her wedding plans. This storyline returns immediately after the extract and thus offers a framing.

We begin with a man and woman leaving a house, framed in a still long shot followed by a two shot of them in conversation, which turns into a slow reverse track as they walk across the street talking. The man is 'camp' and is discussing a male partner and the woman is pregnant, though this is not visibly apparent—we are informed of this through the dialogue.

The fact of these two characters sharing a house could be seen as a representation of contemporary social life and some might say the breakdown of the traditional family unit. The conversation is about the woman's morning sickness and the man's hangover in regard to a planned date that evening—'It's hard to kiss with confidence int it when you can feel your hot-pot rising', which is accompanied by a camp gesture to represent the movement of the hot-pot. Camp gay characters and strong females have for a long time been archetypes of the show, leading some commentators to describe soap opera as a predominately female genre. The reference to hot-pot is a classic 'Corrie' convention in itself, as patrons of the 'Rovers Return' pub have been eating Betty's hot-pot for decades, so we can see this as a textual motif. The familiarity reinforced here is certainly a key soap convention.

As the two characters depart the screen on opposite sides, a long-standing character, Sally, exits the newsagents with a newspaper under her arm and is immediately surrounded by women on their way to work in the factory. The newspaper reminds the audience of the time of day—most soap episodes try to establish a sense of real, continuing time and usually the episode starts in the morning with images that reinforce that (milk bottles, breakfasts, people in pyjamas, newspapers). Gossip, another soap convention, is exchanged, the subject of which is another character, Ashley, who is sleeping on Sally's sofa. Sally puts a stop to this with 'Well I don't know and even if I did I wouldn't tell you cos it's Ashley's business int it?' which is followed by 'You're no fun are you?' from a friend. This serves to re-establish gossip as the norm and Sally's integrity as unusual.

As the four women disperse in a mid shot, another female character, Hayley, enters the frame behind in a slow pan from right to left and is joined by another factory worker, who in a reverse track two shot, asks her about her state of mind. Hayley's response is rich with irony. 'Not myself? That's the trouble int it, that's always been my trouble.' The audience know that Hayley is a transsexual which means that 'not being herself' means much more than the phrase normally transmits. Again, this is a stock convention of soap opera—deep prior knowledge of characters which bring different meanings to the things they say.

As Hayley and her acquaintance walk off screen a male character enters the frame, running, from right to left and the camera pans slightly quicker to establish the urgency. He catches up with the postman outside the Duckworths' house and sifts through the post, until smiling when he finds what he is looking for he stuffs one envelope into his pocket and enters the house. This character is the grandson of the long-running Duckworths and the audience knows that Tyrone, the adopted son of the family has correctly accused him of taking post, but the grandson has managed to convince the Duckworths that this accusation was ill-founded. As we enter the house, the camera lingers on a full English breakfast and burnt toast, a familiar image in this household. The layout of the kitchen is one of the longest-running pieces of iconography in British television history and this representation of domestic working class life is entrenched in our media knowledge. As Jack complains about his toast, his wife Vera declares 'give over you miserable swine' while behind her, in the head and shoulder shot, Tyrone approaches with tea. This rapport between the Duckworths has been a convention of the programme for as long as Betty's hot-pot. The grandson sits and a conversation leads to a grudging apology from Tyrone, who the audience knows should not be apologising—this is classic dramatic irony and is a narrative device that soap opera shares with Shakespeare, despite the more highbrow reputation of the bard! The camera switches from a tableaux shot of the family at breakfast to a two shot of Tyrone and his rival and then to a head and shoulder shot of Jack reading his racing paper and shaking his head—another very familiar image. We then cut to the hairdressing salon, where we return to Sarah discussing her wedding, a circular narrative approach.

The narrative economy of this extract is typical of the soap genre. In three minutes we experience four storylines, three of which are connected by the movement of characters in the street. Sarah discusses her wedding then we cut to the street where each of the storylines—the night before/morning sickness, Hayley's state of mind and the Duckworths' post—are connected by a character from the next section moving through the frame as the previous 'movement' ends. Thus the editing is unobtrusive and the choreography/scriptwriting is more instrumental. Hard cuts dominate, but bridging by script is the most important device.

In terms of representation at the macro level, in three minutes we encounter many women, a gay man, a pregnant woman, a husband sleeping on a sofa, a transsexual and a variety of ages and ethnicity. The common focus is domestic relationships—the public sphere is absent here. The *mise en scène* constructs a classic realist depiction of northern working class life: terraced houses and an exaggerated sense of community where people are literally running into one another constantly. The interior scene in the Duckworths' house is the best known stereotype of working class family life available, from the legacy of social realist drama known as 'kitchen sink'.

Case Study 2.6

The Hamburg Cell

Context: This drama was a one-off terrestrial broadcast offering a fictional dramatisation of the radicalisation and training (in an Al Qaeda cell in Germany) of a group of men who carried out the terrorist attacks on September 11 (see Figure 23).

The extract begins 18 minutes into the drama and is easily located by the appearance of lower case text on screen saying, 'hamburg, some months later'. It is a three-minute sequence. First we see a yellow Volkswagen Camper Van driving over a flyover with a backdrop of grey, rainy, miserable, industrial Hamburg. These are connotations, so we can say they are constructed through *mise en scène*. Soundtrack music plays, providing inharmonious but frenetic tension (but underlying rather than foregrounded and overbearing)—creating connotations of nervous energy.

Figure 23 *The Hamburg Cell*: intense *mise en scène* locks us into the scene.
(*Source*: Channel 4)

Next we see mid shots of characters getting out of the van at what appears to be a meeting hall or warehouse and there is a plethora of dialogue in Arabic language, until the camera rests on a two shot of two main characters discussing a third party. Key dialogue here is 'Is he a God-fearing Muslim?' and 'He is learning to put God at the centre of his life'. During this interchange the editing moves us from a two shot to an over-the-shoulder shot, a key drama convention. As another character arrives to take a box from one of the speakers, it becomes apparent (or implied) that this person is the subject of the dialogue and hence a narrative bridge is easily created.

We move into a hall where one man is speaking (mid shots and close ups) and men are listening and responding non-verbally (three shots, two shots and close ups—the facial responses are serious, intense, concerned expressions and then nods and expressions of approval and intent). As we edit to a close up of the speaker, lower case text appears on screen—'mohammed haydar zammer'. It is likely now that prior cultural knowledge of the events leading up to September 11 will lead the audience to assume that this man is a 'radicalising' Muslim cleric. A slow pan from left to right is used as he speaks, inter-cut (always simple hard cuts) with other men's reactions every few seconds, with his dialogue always acting as a sound bridge. He recounts an atrocity he has witnessed—'I heard the screams and I heard the crack of pistols', and then as he says 'bang' the realist conventions are partly shattered by the intrusion of a 'real' gunshot sound and grainy images with the look of real footage of a murder victim. As the dialogue becomes more intense—'I saw Muslim houses on fire, I smelt the smell, like meat', the editing crescendos with more rapid cuts from the speaker to the listeners, who are now nodding and murmuring in agreement. Always the cleric's dialogue is heard. The *mise en scène* is dark and serious; the characters' appearance shortcutting the representations—dark, western clothes, leather jackets and beards. The atmosphere created by the economy of the scene—close ups, mid shots, mostly looking at faces, is intense, dramatic and disturbing.

To accentuate this further, we cut to conversations taking place around the room, after the speaker has finished. Three different groups of men are listening to a new speaker in each case, with dialogue referring to the evils of America, the persecution and humiliation of Muslims worldwide, Jews as an enemy and the West's hatred of Islam. The editing moves us (hard cuts) from one dialogue snippet in one group to another, always with a small ensemble shot so we can see responses as well as the speaker. As the editing quickens and the dialogue overlaps from group to group, a sense of compulsion and persuasion builds. The point of view of the potential radical is established as vulnerable; there is a sense of the persuasive dialogue being irresistible, seductive and disturbing in equal measure.

The key representational features of this extract are to do with gender, age and ethnicity. Women are completely absent. Muslim men are depicted as angry, seeking vengeance, highly articulate and serious. Within this, older men are speakers and younger men are listeners, so there is a real sense of the younger men being vulnerable and the elders manipulative. However, this reading is dependent on knowledge of the outcomes of this radicalisation. The intensity is amplified by the audience knowing where the story ends and responding to this scene with a sense of helplessness.

At a macro level it is clear that the drama seeks to 'explain' September 11 through a focus on the radicalisation of young Muslim men in 'cells' around the world. This particular scene is rich in its representation of the speakers: Persuasive, older men use a variety of emotive and discursive techniques, while the listeners—concerned, angry young men—are seemingly frustrated and seeking an opportunity for action. The representations are partly stereotypical, especially in terms of appearance, with the 'excuse' of being based on real events, and the directorial techniques—intense dialogue, low key lighting, dialogue sound bridges, mid shots and close ups and editing that quickens as the speeches reach their climax—serve to 'lock us into the scene'. It is difficult to resist the feeling that the listeners will inevitably be persuaded, such is the intensity created by the *mise en scène*.

Case Study 2.7

Doctor Who

Context: *Doctor Who* certainly appeals to a wide audience (around 8 million on average) with its pleasures being derived at many levels. First broadcast in 1963, taken off the air in 1989 and returning in 2005, it is now viewed by a young audience for the first time and also by original viewers, who are now adults. Because of this multi-layered context, at times the programme takes a 'post modern' approach, parodying itself and referring back to previous versions.

This episode is from Series 2 and is titled 'Tooth and Claw'. It begins three minutes and fifty four seconds in, and on the DVD version this is Scene 2: 'Queen Victoria'. We are in the Tardis, looking up at the Doctor and Rose, who appear to be on the ceiling laughing manically. As the camera cuts to their level, we realise we were above them as they completed their time travel journey, landing with a bump. The *mise en scène* inside the Tardis is familiar to viewers and under normal circumstances might be described as 'futuristic', but really there is a kind of 'retro-futurism' to it, compared to the more high-tech imagery of contemporary science fiction. This is a post modern element—we are given a nostalgic form of futurism! The Doctor announces—'1979, a great year!' and then goes on to list a series of events—'China invades Vietnam, The Muppet Movie—I love that film, Margaret Thatcher' [pulls a face]—the older audience will understand these connotations differently.

As they exit the Tardis we see a two shot as the Doctor looks bemused, followed by a hard cut to a group of Scottish soldiers on horse back on moor land, pointing guns at the space where continuity dictates the Doctor and Rose are standing outside the Tardis. '1879' says the Doctor, with a wry smile. 'Are we in Scotland?' Amused, Rose then puts on a ludicrous Scottish accent, retaining the humour and playfulness of the scene. We experience this interaction through head and shoulder shots of the two characters and the soldier in command, whose non-verbal communication is significant—irritated and bemused by the time travellers.

As the soldier asks the Doctor to identify himself we see a point of view shot, literally looking down the barrel of the gun. The Doctor remains playful and offers an amusing intertextual reference for the younger viewers—'I am from the township of Balamory.' This interchange is interrupted by a well-spoken English female voice directing the soldier to let them 'approach the carriage'. Cut to a tableaux shot of a black carriage, with black horses and a butler dressed in black, set against the cold, grey skies and barren moor land. This image is slightly eerie, with some horror conventions observed in the *mise en scène*, and is typical of the series which combines comedy, thriller and horror conventions as well as fantasy and science fiction. 'Approach the carriage and give due deference' barks the soldier, again from a point of view shot, from below, giving authority to the image. As the Doctor and Rose do so, we see this from a slow track behind them, and at this point Rose's modern clothes offer a stark contrast to the *mise en scène*—a pink T shirt and blue denim dungarees mark her out as from the future much more than the Doctor's slightly old fashioned attire.

We see Queen Victoria in a head and shoulder shot performing an expressionless stare. Then to a two shot of her visitors, again greatly amused by the meeting. Music is heard, non-diegetic and connoting a dream-like ambience with some regal chime qualities also. The characters discuss an assassination plot, with the editing economically and unobtrusively switching from medium close up of the Queen to two shot with the soldier with the gun now in the frame behind the Doctor and his assistant. The Queen's performance is important—stern but with a twinkle in her eye, the Doctor still playful and witty. After she instructs the procession to 'Drive on' in the expected clipped tones, we switch to a slow track of the Doctor and Rose walking behind the carriage, still joking.

Doctor: 'We just met Queen Victoria, what a laugh.'
Rose: 'She was just sitting there.'
Doctor: 'Like a stamp.'
Rose: 'We are not amused. I bet you five quid I'm gonna make her say it.' [The younger audience may or may not be aware of this historical catchphrase.]

At the macro level, the representation here is entirely post modern. Jeremy Points calls this 'conspicuous constructedness' (2007, p.82). Time is placed on its side—we are in the past with a stereotype from history playing up to her future image and the main characters playfully responding. Rose is an empowered female, yet there is subtle flirtation with the Doctor. The treatment of history is on one level educational, hence the centrality of the series to a renewal of the BBC's public service remit. In the accidental arrival in 1879 instead of 1979, the science fiction convention of time travel is treated light heartedly, and the way the programme uses intertextual elements, such as the Balamory reference, can be described as a form of 'post modern pastiche'.

Activity 2.11

Exam practice

In the Key Concepts exam you will need to take the kind of approach to micro/macro analysis that has been modelled in this chapter. The representational focus may be on gender, locality, occupation, age, social class or a particular set of events, theme or time period. To prepare for this, you will need to go through the process described below.

Ensure you have a clear understanding of how representation works in TV drama and in particular types of TV drama, such as teen drama, hospital drama, crime drama, soap opera or period drama. This will help you analyse the unseen extract in context. Ideally, prepare one or two quoted definitions of representation to apply to the extract.

Practise the micro/macro analysis on a range of four to five minute extracts from a range of types of drama. Use the format modelled in the six case study examples above. First work as a group using the 'jigsawing' approach mentioned earlier in this chapter, where each member of the group takes one micro element and everyone shares the outcomes. As you move closer to the exam, practise reducing the number in the group so everyone takes two elements, then work in a pair and finally on your own. Phasing in your analysis in this way is sensible because you are taking on more material as you become more expert in 'spotting' the conventions.

Finally, there is no substitute for holding a 'mock' exam. This isn't difficult to do—begin by getting together in a small study group. Now find 15–20 four- to five-minute extracts between you (this is easy, as TV drama has a constantly high profile), which you think are typical of the formats they represent and share them so you each get to analyse them all.

At this point, you must watch each one in exam conditions for this to be effective, limiting yourself to four screenings and thirty minutes altogether to watch and make notes. At this stage, do not attempt to answer an exam question, just get used to making notes and comparing your notes with others in your study group—what did you spot that they missed and vice versa?

Finally, practise with three extracts and go the whole distance, which means four screenings, thirty minutes for watching and note-taking and then forty-five minutes to answer this question:

How does this TV drama sequence employ the following technical areas in order to establish representations?

- Camera angle, shot, movement and composition
- *Mise en scène*
- Editing
- Sound.

Link to A2: Doctor Who and hyper-diegesis

The AS TV Drama topic only requires analysis of an on-screen extract from a programme like *Doctor Who*. But if you study this programme in more depth, you will be well prepared for some of the Critical Perspectives topics that you might choose for A2 Media. *Doctor Who* is described by Hills (2002) as an example of 'hyper-diegesis' which means that the diegetic world of the TV programme is a small element of the whole imagined world of the story, in the minds of fans. Fans make use of a wide range of media in relation to *Doctor Who*, from magazines to 'Tardisodes' on the internet, which are digital stories that fill in gaps and add extensions to television episodes. This 360-degree culture that surrounds the programme is described by fans as a 'Whoniverse' and if you study either Post Modern Media, Media in the Online Age or We Media and Democracy, the way that these additional media experiences compensate fans for the 'incompletely furnished' nature of the TV programme would be a rich case study for your research.

Ethnography

The OCR Key Concepts exam does not require you to speculate on the countless different viewing contexts in which a TV drama sequence is actually interpreted. So to some extent you have to take for granted what the technical and symbolic elements of the extract amount to in terms of representational meaning. However, you might also refer to the limitations of this approach, and one way of approaching this is to consider the *ethnography* of media consumption. Ethnographic research methods are concerned with resisting large-scale assumptions about groups of people viewing television and also with avoiding artificial 'effects' experiments where people view television in laboratories. What they offer instead is described here by Tubb:

> Ethnography attends to the everyday contexts, practices and relations within which television consumption is situated. With its focus on specific practices within local contexts, ethnography calls attention to the material conditions which construct specific kinds of viewing and in which audiences construct specific meanings from their engagement with television.

(Miller (ed.), 2002: 87)

Ethnographic media research is often concerned with social class contexts but it isn't exclusive in that focus. So you might consider the ethnographic context of your own viewing of a TV drama extract in an AS exam, the specific material conditions of such a viewing context and how different this is to your usual viewing practices.

Chapter 2.2
Radio Drama

Radio drama is similar in breadth to its television counterpart, but in broadcast outlets it is more limited, with two BBC stations— Radio 4 and Radio 7—dominating provision in the UK.

Radio 4 offers the long-running radio soap, *The Archers*, analysed below, and a range of other dramas, plays and audio broadcasts of fiction. Radio 7 averages ten different radio dramas a week, some one-off broadcasts, some serials and some radio soaps. Both stations have a website which will allow you to listen to episodes and pause and rewind for analytical purposes.

But radio drama is not restricted to these two BBC stations, and radio drama continues to play a broad and important role in the creative and cultural media in the UK, contrary to the assumption that the form is endangered by television, film and the internet. And whilst it may be tempting to undermine the production values of radio drama by suggesting that no images equate to less creative work, radio drama producers remind us that it is in some ways more difficult to construct a meaningful and engaging narrative that demands more sustained concentration. In addition, the writer of radio drama is liberated from the constraints of the film or television set as the mise en scène is constructed in the imagination of the listener. This comment from the radio dramatist Craig Warner takes this idea further:

> **A radio play can move through any dimension of time and to any location . . . can voice metaphysical, surrealist and**

subconscious motivations and images. The radio dramatist needs a creative intimacy with the listener to conjure a unique world in his or her imagination. Radio is very good at dramatising the contrast between what people say and . . . think. Indeed, radio drama has been called the "theatre of the mind". "Interior thought" is a convention . . . special to the radio medium; the listener is instantly transported inside the head of a character and can hear those secret, private thoughts that are often left unsaid. The medium liberates the scope of imaginative recall, providing a perfect opportunity to explore consciousness and dramatise all the voices that motivate different aspects of experience . . . radio drama can also give animals a voice, invest inanimate objects with character and give emotion to all aspects of nature.

(Warner, 2003, http://www.writernet.co.uk/professional_ development/radio_drama/what_makes_radio_drama_different.ph tml - accessed 6.1.8)

It is important, then, for your work in the Key Concepts unit, to establish an approach to Radio Drama that does not reinforce a 'deficit model' of the media form, but instead is attentive to the rich possibilities afforded by freedom from the limitations of visual presence. As you analyse radio drama extracts in preparation for the unheard exam task, you must be 'bearing witness' to the ways in which the listener needs to construct the meaning and this may be, as Warner suggests, actually harder work than simply watching the moving image.

In the exam you will analyse a previously unheard extract, so a thorough knowledge of the history of radio drama or established understanding of particular narratives in specific programmes will only be of contextual value. What is more important, however, is an ability to recognise and deconstruct the following conventions, and how they are related in terms of representation:

Speech: how is character established and narrative developed through the dialogue (what is said) and performance (how it is said)?

Music: how do diegetic music (which the characters can hear) and non-diegetic music (heard only by the audience) add to the atmosphere, realism, verisimilitude and dramatic effect?

Sound effects: how is the realism of the drama enhanced by these?

Editing: how is the 'flow' of the drama aided by the grammar of the edit, and how does editing create particular effects to enhance the representational aspects of the broadcast?

While radio drama is to be studied in its own right here, and we must resist the temptation to think of it as television without pictures, it is important to consider the ways in which producers are working with different tools. Tim Crook offers this explanation:

> **Worlds are not created by dramatic dialogue alone. There is attitude and atmosphere. This is determined by detail and relevant detail. It could be in a sound effect. It could be in the writing. It could be in the music. It could be in everything. But the result is that the fifth dimension of radio writing—the imagination of the listener—is stimulated to become a picture palace of the mind.**

Source: www.irdp.co.uk/scripts
(Accessed 24 September 2007)

Section 2 of this book began with a lengthy discussion around the concept of representation, and it is this aspect of 'textuality' that is at the foreground of our analysis of radio drama. The four elements described above are the micro details that combine to form particular representations at the macro level. It is this equation—how the representation is the sum of the technical and symbolic parts—that is the key to success in this part of your AS Media course. Before we turn to some specific examples of radio drama, let's establish some key questions to ask about any extract:

- What are the different voices doing and how do they relate to each other? We can call these conflicting voices in an extract *discourses*.
- If there is a narrator, how does this element serve to 'anchor' (pin down) the meaning of the characters' dialogue?
- How do dialogue and the various other sound elements other than speech create a context, setting, time period and atmosphere?
- In terms of narrative, what phase does the extract represent— what balance of action and enigma is offered?
- In simple terms, what is the drama? Some form of struggle is probably evident as this is what makes it dramatic. How does the struggle set up empathy/concern/intrigue?

As with all texts, we have to ask who the representation includes and excludes.

- Does Crook's golden rule apply? This rule states that every word must serve dramatic purpose and move forward narrative and characterisation. Nothing must be superfluous to this.
- Does the extract follow the other radio drama maxim—that the material should always be arranged through interplay between tension–humour–tension–humour?
- What is the relationship between dramatic/theatrical dialogue and natural (everyday) dialogue?

Case Study 2.8

The Archers

Context: This episode was broadcast on Sunday, 23 September 2007 and was accessed on the same day through *The Archers* website at www.bbc.co.uk/radio4/archers.
The website also offers this plot synopsis:

Second thoughts

Shula and Alan are discussing the knotty problem of replacing the pews. Shula says she'll press on with the village survey and arrange a meeting with the diocese. Alan's missing Amy, so Shula asks him to the Bull at lunchtime. They meet Kenton and Kathy, who have gone there to take Kathy's mind off the rape case. But Alan's comments about Amy being a young girl out on her own in the world touch a nerve. Kathy makes an excuse and leaves.

Meanwhile Fallon admits her feelings for Ed to Kirsty. Kirsty thinks Fallon's got to say something, and offers to talk to Ed herself. Fallon thinks it's better if she does it on her own.

Kenton offers to miss lunch at Glebe Cottage and stay at home with Kathy, but she says she just wants to sleep. Earlier she had torn up the card the police had given her, having decided that she can't change things, and she still has Jamie to think about. But when she gets home she pieces it back together and dials the number. She tells them she wants to report a rape.

The episode begins with the famous theme music. As we enter the fictional world of Ambridge, the first sound we hear is Kathy refusing an offer of tea and toast by a sympathetic male character, Kenton. But no matter what he offers, Kathy says 'that's not going to make me stop thinking about that poor girl, is it?' and hence the drama, tension and emotion are reinforced. Regular listeners will be aware of what she is referring to, which is not only a current rape case but also a previous experience of her own. All of Kathy's dialogue is accompanied by dramatic sighing, a signifier of exasperation and despair—'the longer I put it off the worse it will be!'—while Kenton's tone is cajoling and comforting. As she asks for the police card her voice becomes faster, more frantic but at the same time more direct and purposeful. At this point the audience and Kenton believe she is about to call the police, but instead we hear a tearing sound, and 'there, done, I never want to see it again'. It may be stating the obvious, but the listener assumes it is the card that has been torn up. This is only so obvious because of timing and the clarity of the sound effect and the dialogue preceding it. After the crescendo of the scene—'I can't change it!' in a higher pitched voice—we hear a second of silence to indicate an edit to another scene.

A much more light hearted discussion about pews takes place between a male and female character, who appear to be in a public space, which we assume to be a church, given the subject matter of their conversation. The triviality of where to store chairs balances the gravity of the rape case storyline, as does the domestic scenario of 'empty nest syndrome' which is also discussed.

The characters agree to a meal at the pub, and after another moment of silence, this bridges a move to a pub scene, with diegetic pop music from The Kaiser Chiefs in the background while two females exchange gossip about a possible relationship or unrequited attachment. Again, the classic soap opera conventions of interweaving narratives, domestic drama and gossip pervade.

Kenton and Kathy join other characters in the pub, which we discover from a clear welcome— 'Kenton, Kathy, are you joining us?' Kathy responds to a question about the pews but is interrupted by Kenton who is, it seems, protecting her from such trivia. An outgoing vicar is discussed (more gossip), while diegetic pub noise reinforces the lunchtime pub context. Humour dominates, in relation to the pew. Then back to the chat about the desired romance and back to Kathy, who is clearly not listening to the discussion about vicars (we know this as every time she is questioned, she has to ask what the question was).

As the discussion moves on to grown up children enjoying Fresher's Week at university, the crucial real time extra-textuality of soap opera is provided—it is Fresher's Week in the 'real world' as well, as the audience know. The listeners are likely to be, in many cases, older parents, and the characters' amusement when they imagine a grown up daughter telling them to 'chill out' is likely to resonate with this audience but embarrass younger listeners. The subject of this humour is Amy, and when her father describes his anxiety over being vulnerable away from home, Kathy suddenly interrupts, claiming a sudden headache, and insists on Kenton taking her home immediately, thus reminding us of the connection between the conversation and what is on her mind. As the audience is aware of this but the characters in the scene are not, this is an example of dramatic irony, a much used soap convention.

At the macro level, the representational elements in this extract are age-related, with 'empty nest syndrome' at the centre of this. Alongside this familiar anxiety, the balance in Ambridge between high drama (a rape case) and trivial village life (the pews) is maintained; a balance that complies with our radio drama rule—drama, tension, humour—and also the conventions of all soap opera—realism, trivia, domestic life and high drama.

Case Study 2.9

Afternoon Play: '*Alf Said I was Great*' by Colin Shindler

Context: This play was broadcast on Radio 7 on Friday, 21 September at 2.15 p.m. and accessed through the Radio 7 website. Afternoon plays are a long running feature of BBC public service radio provision and are self-contained narratives, in this case 45 minutes long, which is fairly typical. The narrative here concerns an ex footballer called Len Farley, who is talking to his son, also a player, about the differences between the professional game in the two generations.

This extract begins eight minutes and 30 seconds in. It is immediately obvious from the tone and pitch of each speaker who is the father and who is the son. As the father talks about his reasons for not being picked for England, the son repeats back lines he has clearly heard before in a weary, slightly sarcastic tone. How we know this dynamic is, of course, due entirely to the cultural conventions of speech and discourse and also our familiarity with the father/son relationship—notions of 'the good old days' bound up with degrees of masculinity, disempowerment and envy and/or respect. Northern accents are heard, with the son's much softer, and as the argument develops (over great England teams and the father's claim that the victorious 1966 team was not the best), the father's dialect becomes more pronounced—'I watch that bunch of overpaid prima donnas today—Owen, Beckham, Rooney' in resentful tones, while the son sighs, again indicating he has heard this before. As the argument reaches crescendo, we hear the father ask for a sick bowl, suggesting the discussion takes place at a hospital bed, adding poignancy. The son's protestations, that Rio Ferdinand is not as lazy as his father thinks, are drowned out by the sound of vomiting. Some complex sound arrangements follow—as the father is sick, the sound of crowd noise bridges an edit to a sound archive of a commentator describing a player called Farley—'what a game this boy Farley is having'. The 'clipped', old fashioned BBC tones of the commentator connote to us that Farley senior is the subject of this description, hence the assumption that this is archival material (in the fictional world of the drama), and certainly non-diegetic.

After this sound clip, we hear the son discussing his diet with a female nurse in the canteen. We know this as we hear ambient diegetic sound and the nurse mentions it early on: 'I thought you would be above eating in a canteen'—this has two functions, both narrative (establishing where we are) and representational (reminding us of how the public view footballers as rich, famous and pampered). Some flirtation also reinforces the stereotypical representation of footballers. Asked how his Dad is feeling, he describes feeling like he doesn't know him. Then he goes on to repeat his father's story of nearly making the World Cup team, but goes on to describe some anecdotes of neglect and interference and a feeling of having 'lived in the shadows'.

The *Match of the Day* theme plays (intertextual reference) and we realise this is the player's phone, which he answers to his agent and a discussion about a transfer ensues, which we hear only from one side, of course. Then back to more dialogue about the patient—'My Dad was a good honest pro; he's barely got enough to pay the gas bill.' The younger player's story is punctuated by the nurse's responses—'oh, no, that's terrible', etc. As she tries to persuade him to stay until the Doctor arrives, it becomes clear that there is bad news, but he is distracted by a forthcoming property deal which he enthusiastically describes in financial terms. The audience at this point is situated alongside the nurse, concerned at the apparent lack of understanding of how serious things might be and feeling distaste at the talk of money.

The representation at the macro level in this extract is clear and not subtle. The older footballer is stubborn and strong-minded and resentful of the playboy lifestyles of today's footballers, including that of his own son. The son respects his father but hasn't told him so, and is bored of his repeated discourse about the differences between then and now. The nurse represents the audience, seeking reconciliation between them, upset by the father's poverty and displeased by the son's gratuitous financial focus at a time like this.

As she tries to make him realise the gravity of the situation, he recounts stories of how tough his Dad is, accompanied by imitations and anecdotes, including one about playing on with a broken leg. The decision of the scriptwriter to have the son speak with a softer accent allows for this imitation to happen without confusing the listener. We leave the scene with the son saying 'He's tough, my Dad. Whatever that Doctor tells him, he'll be fine.' As the audience realises this won't be the case, we are left uneasy. This is dramatic irony, the audience feeling they know something that a character is denying, and feeling apprehension about where this will lead. The function of the anecdotes is to punctuate the serious drama and tension with humour, a standard convention of radio drama.

Case Study 2.10

Westway

Context: *Westway* is a radio soap set in a medical practice in West London. The extract described here is from the episode broadcast on 20 September 2007 at 1.00 p.m. and accessed on the BBC Radio 7 website.

The extract begins two minutes and 15 seconds into the episode. We hear the sound of 'bustle' in the background as a door knocks, a female character says 'come in' and a door is opened. These noises are pronounced and clear, and the door opening is probably a sound effect. Dialogue follows regarding one character's forthcoming HIV check up. A patient, Olga, who has HIV, is discussed and an enigma is left hanging—something further to discuss about possible treatment 'which might buy her some time'. It is clear from the ensuing conversation that both characters, who are speaking with 'received pronunciation', are medical staff.

A moment of silence indicates the edit to a new scene, where two male characters discuss filing and one character's recent absence. This conversation is interrupted by a phone call, which one of the speakers takes and a romantic discussion ensues—'Hi baby'. This dialogue fades into the background as the other character, Ned, a clerical staff member, speaking with a more regional dialect, strikes up a conversation with Joy and then other staff. We hear about tension in the restaurant and a series of unexpected deliveries for Zoe, while Olga is discussed in regard to a recent fit of anger in the restaurant. The soap opera convention of gossip between characters moving dialogue forward is evident here.

Next we return to the female staff discussing Olga and an enigma is used. As the conversation moves to information from Olga's immigration lawyer, the audience is left waiting for the outcome—'He gave me some advice about Olga's situation which I think you might like to hear.' This scene takes place with total silence in the background, indicating that we have moved into an office with a closed door.

This is followed by a second of silence before we return to another more crowded scene (again with generic 'bustle' in the background) in which it becomes apparent that two characters, Shaun and Zoe, are an item, which is not public knowledge. Shaun is pretending there is a problem with Zoe's software which necessitates his frequent visits, but this is exposed by another character who looks at her computer. This is a humorous scene, where the other characters pretend not to know this but they (and the audience) do. Tone of voice, performance and exaggerated emotion are important here so the audience can pick up on the narrative.

Following this, we hear a scene in a restaurant, which is made obvious by the sound of cups and saucers and diegetic music. The owner of the restaurant speaks in a Jamaican accent and is asked if Olga will return, to which he says, 'No, she won't be back.'

At the macro level, this extract offers a topical representation of multicultural London; a key social issue is foregrounded (HIV as the 'forgotten disease' has been the subject of renewed media attention recently) balanced with a humorous storyline about two staff members in a romantic situation. As such, it observes the convention of tension–humour–tension–humour discussed previously.

A very important feature of this clip is the fact that Olga is in many ways the central character—she has HIV, an immigration lawyer has some advice for her GP and she has recently angrily departed the restaurant where she works—but she herself is absent. Every word of the dialogue is crucial, there is no small talk. And there are four spaces in which the drama takes place: in a quiet office, in a generic more crowded area, in a restaurant and at Zoe's desk. This is only clear to the audience as a result of complex sound arrangements so we can differentiate between different levels of contextual atmosphere but also link the dialogue to the ambience quickly. If these rules were not observed, continuity would be broken.

Activity 2.12

Exam practice

In the Key Concepts exam you will need to take the kind of approach to micro/macro analysis that has been modelled in this chapter. The representational focus may be on gender, locality, occupation, age, social class or a particular set of events, theme or time period. To prepare for this, you will need to go through the process described below.

Practise the micro/macro analysis on a range of four to five minute extracts from a range of types of drama. Use the format modelled in the three case study examples above. First work as a group using the 'jigsawing' approach mentioned earlier in this chapter, where each member of the group takes one micro element and everyone shares the outcomes. As you move closer to the exam, practise reducing the number in the group so everyone takes two elements, then work in a pair and finally on your own. Phasing in your analysis in this way is sensible because you are taking on more material as you become more expert in 'spotting' the conventions.

Finally, there is no substitute for holding a 'mock' exam. This isn't difficult to do—begin by getting together in a small study group. Now find 15–20 four- to five-minute extracts between you, which you think are typical of the formats they represent and share them so you each get to analyse them all.

At this point, you must listen to each one in exam conditions for this to be effective, limiting yourself to five hearings and thirty minutes altogether to listen and make notes. At this stage, do not attempt to answer an exam question, just get used to making notes and comparing your notes with others in your study group—what did you spot that they missed and vice versa?

Finally, practise with three extracts and go the whole distance, which means five hearings, thirty minutes for listening and note-taking and then forty-five minutes to answer this question:

How does this radio drama sequence employ the following technical areas in order to establish representations?
● Speech
● Music
● Sound effects
● Editing.

Case Study Extracts

The three extracts (Case Study 2.8, 2.9 and 2.10) that follow are all accessed through the BBC websites for the respective stations, each of which has a 'listen again' facility which allows you to pause and rewind. It is recommended that you use this service for your own practice analyses. Other ways of accessing extracts are to download podcasts of radio drama, buy CDs of drama series or use the old fashioned method of recording to a tape—you may need to ask your parents about this one!

Section 3
Institutions and Audiences

The part of the AS Media course that looks at institutions and audiences is the most 'factual'. You will need to know how particular media industries operate and how audiences are formed. To some extent it is still possible to talk of the 'film industry' or the 'magazine industry'. However, media convergence means that today a lot of TV programmes, films and music exist across a range of media and are the products of several industries, with the result that the industries themselves are converging. The way the audience for *Doctor Who* engage with it as a media product is a good example, as shown by the case study below.

The 'job description' for a successful Media Studies student at AS includes five inter-related skills:

1 Creative realisation of media (making interesting and engaging practical work)
2 Micro level deconstruction of media (in TV or Radio)
3 Macro level analysis (representation)

Doctor Who

Doctor Who is a good example of an intermedial text. It is relevant across all of the OCR AS specification; indeed it would be possible to develop an extended case study on it and cover every unit to some extent! *Doctor Who* is first and foremost a TV show, but it can be watched on terrestrial broadcast, on BBC digital channels and on Sky and Virgin 'on demand', as well as on purchased DVDs. So far we are only talking about TV or DVD viewing. However, BBC7 also broadcast *Doctor Who* as a radio drama, the *Doctor Who* website offers a range of online pleasures related to the show and there is a popular BBC magazine, *Doctor Who Adventures* that accompanies the programme, as well as a wide range of books based on episodes. There are *Doctor Who* videogames for every platform and a search for *Doctor Who* on YouTube will lead you to 84,400 uploads. Of these, some are clips from programmes, some are related TV and film clips and some are user-generated films based on aspects of *Doctor Who*.

The question to address, then, is simply whether *Doctor Who* is a TV show with a range of associated 'spin offs' and related, but secondary media texts and experiences available, or whether *Doctor Who* 'fandom' is an intermedial experience.

4 Understanding how media institutions currently operate
5 Ability to explore ideas about how audiences use media.

The last of these is the most complex of course, and in this section we will engage with two very different approaches to understanding the contemporary media. We will cover a factual knowledge base for each media industry, along with an investigation of how each industry converges with the others in the online digital environment. In addition, we will look at a range of theoretical approaches to studying media audiences, and at this point you will be required to form your own view of how best to relate media audiences to the practices of institutions—this is where it gets interesting.

Institutions

Anticipated for almost as long as the second coming, the digital media era is finally upon us and that much misused word 'convergence' has become meaningful. Newspapers are talking about video journalism; broadcasters are talking downloads and web companies? Well, if you've got a blog, a site or, Holy Grail, a community, then your job is to look smug and talk hard cash. From Murdoch's deal to buy MySpace to the selling of YouTube for more than a billion dollars after 18 months of trading, we are slap back in the middle of the second dot.com boom. Don't even mention Google, whose founders, Sergey Brin and Larry Page, must be crossing off the days till it's time to become full time philanthropists and cancel third world debt.

(Gibson, 2007: 7)

Media Studies is all about the contemporary, so while it is useful to have a sense of the history of, say, the film industry in Britain (so we know how successful the industry is at present relative to other time periods, perhaps), we are really much more concerned with how the different forms of media—film, music, newspapers, radio, magazines and videogames—are currently being produced and distributed and how this is changing. The key agent of change is convergence, which is why you are not expected to learn about specific media industries. This is because it makes little sense these days to talk about the film industry without referring to other media industries, especially internet distribution. The word *institution* refers to the companies and organisations that provide media content, whether for profit, public service or another motive. This involves an understanding of media as business, the relationship between media providers and the public and media as a form of power. One thing is for certain—it makes little sense to talk about 'the media' as a single entity any more, as though it is a collective force with a shared agenda.

Link to A2

We need to talk about media institutions in the plural and to recognise that it is possible, through such distribution networks as MySpace and YouTube, to be a producer and distributor of content some of the time, and a consumer of media produced by powerful corporations the rest of the time. This interplay is sometimes described as 'post modern', and if you progress to A2 you may encounter this critical perspective in more detail, looking at a range of texts and forms of media that have been labelled post modern.

For AS, we will be concerned with how media institutions producing and distributing material in each of the five sectors operate within a context of *ownership*, *convergence*, *technologies* and *globalisation*. And we will be very interested in how things are changing. If you are the average age of an AS Media student your eyes probably glaze over when your Media teacher talks about her analogue past ('there were only three channels', 'music was on vinyl', 'the Walkman changed everything' and probably a notion that things used to be 'better' in some way as well). You can't be expected to feel the pace of change as you will have grown up with online media as the norm, but for this part of your studies you do need to acquire a sense of how rapidly institutions and audiences are being transformed by digital technology:

> The question that needs to be answered is: do new media forms produce both distinctively different content and 'audiences' when compared with their predecessors? The answer to this question is a qualified yes.

> (Marshall, 2004: 3)

Careers

To understand the workings of media institutions it is useful to be aware of the changing nature of employment and careers in the various media industries. Skillset, the national training organisation for media, published some data in 2003 that gives us a sense of the 'state of play' in recent years. Just under two-thirds of people working in the media are younger than 35, and in the last ten years two-thirds of new entrants to media sectors have been female. Two-thirds of people working in the media have a degree, and a quarter of those have a degree in Media, so don't listen to people who tell you doing Media Studies won't get you a job in a related field. In financial terms, working in the media is far less lucrative than you might think, with only 46 per cent earning over £30,000 a year.

What does all this tell us in relation to the AS focus on institutions and audiences? Well, the figures here reveal more than just the fact that older people are absent and the media is a world dominated by young women working long hours for a modest income. In terms of media representation, we might conclude that the people providing our information resources across the vast spectrum of popular media culture mainly come from one or two demographic groups. It is unlikely that the entire cross-section of our society will be equally represented by the media we are provided with.

Convergence

Convergence describes two phenomena: First, technologies coming together, for example, a mobile phone you can use as a still and moving image camera, download and watch moving images on, use as an MP3 player and recorder and access the internet with. Second, media industries are diversifying so they produce and distribute across several media—for example, a newspaper with an online version and audio podcasts or the coming together of videogames with films. Gavin Luhrs (2006) describes some of the implications of convergence for television as we know it:

> Channel 4 has offered episodes from the first series of *Lost* for free download; it seems even television channels are turning to platforms other than television to reach their audience. Another implication for television is distribution via other platforms, in particular the rise of internet-based 'channels'. Gamespot.com is a website devoted to videogames and is proving that although television programmes about gaming don't work, videos about gaming can; a subtle difference perhaps, especially considering much of the video content on Gamespot.com is structured 'programmes' of reviews or coverage of events. Is the website becoming a gaming channel without the need for a television? A more high-profile example of the internet-based television channel is Google Video. As well as home users, existing television channels are offering content via the service, again suggesting that the future of television broadcasting isn't necessarily tied to the television set as we know it.

(Luhrs, 2006: 44)

There is no television option in the Institutions and Audiences component of OCR's Key Concepts unit, because you have the option to study television drama in the other section. But this doesn't necessarily mean that television will not be relevant for your case study work, as the examples cited by Luhrs demonstrate. We no longer live in a media world where television, videogames, films, newspapers, radio, magazines and music exist separately. For this reason it is essential that you study the impact of convergence on the media sector you work with for this part of your course—the focus here is on the *contemporary* nature of the media form you choose to become expert in.

Audiences

Audience is a huge area of Media Studies with many variants and competing approaches, so it is important

Case Study 3.2

News Corporation

Despite the ways (described above) in which the media may be becoming less 'linear' and elite producers may be letting go of some power over content (but not distribution, if they can help it), it remains true that a number of super-rich media moguls own a tremendous amount of the media we have access to. One of these is the Australian tycoon Rupert Murdoch, who began owning media institutions in the early 1950s. Since then his News Corporation has come to acquire a vast array of newspapers, TV channels, radio stations, film companies and websites. In the UK he owns BSkyB, 18 per cent of ITV (and he is interested in Channel 5), *The Sun*, *News of the World* and *The Times*. Globally he dominates the press, owns the Fox Broadcasting Company and Twentieth Century Fox, and most recently he purchased MySpace.

News Corporation has a gross annual income of approximately $20 billion and employs around 40,000 people worldwide. The music industry is the only sector of the mass media that Murdoch's company does not have a major stake in, although the acquisition of MySpace may be a move towards this.

Murdoch's huge 'media empire' is the subject of much concern. Some people think that the de-regulation of media ownership in the UK, begun by Margaret Thatcher when she was Prime Minister and continued by Tony Blair and Gordon Brown under New Labour, has allowed Murdoch to become so powerful that he now has influence over the way political events in particular are reported. For three different accounts of Murdoch's power, see the film *Outfoxed*, the extracts of Alistair Campbell's recent diary *The Blair Years*, which chronicle Murdoch's relationship with the then Prime Minister, and Anthony Sampson's *Who Owns this Place*, a book about power in contemporary Britain—who has it and how it is exercised.

to be precise about our focus in this section, which is on the relationship between audience and institution. Ferguson (2003) distinguishes between audience theory (thinking about how audiences are constructed) and audience research (trying to provide evidence for how audiences respond to media). Research is best understood as trying to provide supporting evidence for a theory. A big part of this is the 'effects model' of audience behaviour through which countless attempts have been made to 'prove' the harmful effects of violent media, usually in artificial laboratory conditions. This tends to show little concern for the obvious fact that if you play a violent game for ten hours and then hit a punch bag it doesn't really prove you will want to hit a real live human being when you get outside! For this part of your Media AS you are more concerned with audience theory, as you will be exploring the ways that audiences are created/constructed for each media sector—film, music, newspapers, radio, magazines and videogames.

You will need to analyse the more complex nature of new media audiences and how digital media distribution and consumption has allowed consumers to become producers or at least interactors, and thus far more active users of media. This is more difficult than simply saying 'the videogame industry targets teenage males'. Gauntlett (2007a) goes as far as to say that new media erodes the boundary between producer and audience to the extent that it makes little sense to talk about media *audiences* at all anymore—he calls this rethink 'Media Studies 2.0'.

> Conventional research methods are replaced—or at least supplemented—by new methods which recognise and make use of people's own creativity, and brush aside the outmoded notions of 'receiver' audiences and elite 'producers'.
>
> (Gauntlett, 2007a: 4)

The next activity is designed to get you thinking about institutions and audiences at a general level, before

Activity 3.1

The questions below will help to establish how much you already know about institutions and audiences, so no answers are provided.

1. List five media sectors and one leading profit making company for each sector.
2. Name two independent music labels.
3. Why is some music downloading illegal and some legal?
4. Who owns the British Board of Film Classification?
5. Name three organisations that own British newspapers.
6. Why does the BBC have no adverts?
7. What is OFCOM?
8. What is MP4?
9. Why does the sound regularly disappear on the live *Big Brother* feed?
10. Who owns Channel 5?
11. What happened as a result of the Hutton Report?
12. From what do magazine publishers make most of their money?
13. Who owns your regional ITV channel?
14. How do websites that offer content for free make money?
15. Who responds to viewers' complaints about adverts?
16. Which is the biggest film industry in the world?
17. Who decides on age classifications for videogames?
18. Which media company do you pay the most money to?
19. What is an RSS feed?
20. Who are BARB and what do they do?

It really doesn't matter if you couldn't answer any of these questions, and it would be surprising if you could answer more than half. The activity is intended to establish a sense of why institutions matter and what you need to be thinking about in terms of the knowledge base you are going to build for this unit.

you focus on your chosen media sector. It will help you discover how much you know, or don't know, about where your media comes from.

The Concept Formally Known as the Audience

This phrase is now commonly used by media professionals to describe the ways in which people engage with media, and it shows how contested the idea of audience is in the digital era. The ways in which convergence, user-created content and social networking have transformed the audience are often thought about in terms of audience 'fragmentation'. This means that the decline of the broadcasting schedule, rolling news and internet information and media downloaded in various ways 'breaks up' the potential audience group for any media form. On the other hand, Csigo (2007) sees this trend as a 'duality'—convergence leads to the old fashioned mass audience falling apart in some ways (into lifestyle segments and niche audiences) but 'falling together' in other ways (multi-platform media, television extending out into other media). In this climate media institutions are desperately trying to provide 360-degree branding for their products—to surround us with them across all the various converged media forms that we come into contact with—a good example of this is *Big Brother*.

Csigo suggests that media institutions are no longer interested in keeping the audience together, but in 'triggering engagement' in people. Converging media, then, can lead to both control by media producers and resistance by the consumers, who now get to produce their own media. For media institutions, this imposes key changes: the media world changes from a 'value chain' (cultural products made and distributed to audiences) to a social network (a complex system where producers and audiences are mixed up). Another way of describing this is the shift from 'push media' (where producers push media at us and we receive and consume it) to 'pull media' (whereby we decide what we want to do with the media and access it in ways that suit us). The key term that is often used to describe the proliferation of people making and distributing their own video is the *long tail*. John Naughton describes the changes we have touched on here as a new 'ecosystem', which, in comparison to 'old media' is:

> . . . richer, more diverse and immeasurably more complex because of the number of content producers, the density of the interactions between them and their products, the speed with which actors in this space can communicate with one another and the pace of development made possible by ubiquitous networking.

(*Source*: http://reutersinstitute.politics.ox.ac.uk/about/discussion/blogging.html)
(Accessed 2 September 2007)

Digital Media

The OCR AS specification requires you to choose one of five media areas, and this section of the book offers a range of material, case studies and ideas for further study for each of them. We have already established that, whichever media area you select for your research, you are going to have to consider the relationship between that sector and the others, in the broader context of media convergence. It is productive to first spend a little time exploring some of the new digital media activities that make this convergence possible and accelerate it.

When previously 'do-it-yourself' media creations such as YouTube and MySpace were purchased by very big media players (News Corporation bought MySpace; Google bought YouTube), immediately the cavalier approach to copyright ceased and the sites became more visibly 'corporate'. For example, much illegally posted material has been removed from YouTube and MySpace is now using the Gracenote software made famous by iTunes to clear copyright and intellectual property at the point of download.

If it seems strange that the big corporations are keen to either take over or form partnerships with websites that threaten them by distributing material for free, then a consideration of the advertising revenue raised by such sites clears things up. UK internet advertising generates around £2 billion a year, which is more than 50 per cent of the money made from TV ads. This figure has increased greatly in the course of 2007 and the reason for this is that more UK homes are now equipped with broadband. This results in an increase in time spent online compared to other media (such as TV) and this has in turn created a huge increase in money invested in online adverts—a fairly simple equation. Currently, Google 'clean up' around 45 per cent of all the revenue from online ads in the UK. Convert that to a global figure and it is easy to see how attractive the acquisition was to Murdoch.

Web 2.0 or 1.5?

The phrase 'web 2.0' describes a new phase of the internet, which allows us to create material, distribute it to one another (and thus share it) and perhaps move closer to the democratic 'spirit' of the internet that its inventor, Tim Berners-Lee, had in mind. Two other developments that co-exist with web 2.0 add to its impact. The first is the availability of a Creative Commons licence for DIY media uploaders (see www.creativecommons.org for full details), which allows people to make money from sharing content as opposed to selling it to individuals—a pretty revolutionary concept. The second is the development of open source software for editing and manipulating content for peer distribution. Examples are Firefox, Audacity and Moodle. Gavin Luhrs (2007) describes the implications of these innovations for Media students:

> These three areas (web 2.0, Creative Commons and open source) are part of a growing trend in media away from established institutions and 'expert' content, towards user-generated content and the power of communities, in this context usually virtual communities. You can't have failed to come across the story of how Arctic Monkeys used MySpace to take over the world. Even though it's not strictly true, MySpace did help to generate a tremendous amount of interest in the band amongst users, illustrating the power New Media has to reach audiences. It also demonstrates why traditional media institutions feel threatened by new media: if they don't keep up they will die. Why else did News Corp buy MySpace, or MTV offer screen time to user-created content, or The Guardian set up so many blogs and talkboards to encourage audience participation?
>
> (Luhrs, 2007: 15)

Luhrs' view resonates with the Media Studies 2.0 ideas from Gauntlett that we considered earlier, so there is certainly a shared view that we need to look at media production, distribution and consumption in new ways. This is clearly a positive, enabling development for ordinary people who find themselves with relatively cheap, instant access to media production and distribution—a camera phone or webcam and a broadband connection can make you an overnight sensation on YouTube—but we need to take a 'reality check' with regard to two issues. First, the most popular web 2.0 sites are owned by huge companies and so every moment of democratic 'We Media' social networking makes money for the big corporations (the same ones that were making billions from web 1.0, in fact, only now they are getting even richer). Second, consider these statistics from Hitwise (2007):

- Only 0.16 per cent of YouTube visitors upload video
- 0.2 per cent of Flickr visitors upload photos
- Wikipedia, the most web 2.0 site imaginable given that the online encyclopaedia is written by its readers, only gets edited/expanded by 4.59 per cent of users.

These figures make it clear that most of us are still just using the web 2.0 sites to read, watch, play and listen (not to create and upload), which is how we were using 'old media'. For these reasons might we be more sensible to think of where we are now as 'web 1.5'?

Google

The following information from Google Finance explains how Google make so much money from what might on the surface appear to be a free service.

Google maintains an index of websites and other content, and makes this information freely available to anyone with an internet connection. Its automated search technology enables people to obtain nearly instant access to relevant information from its online index. Google generates revenue by delivering online advertising. Businesses use its AdWords program to promote their products and services with targeted advertising. In addition, the third-party Websites that comprise the Google Network use the Company's AdSense program to deliver relevant advertisements that generate revenue. In August 2006, it acquired Neven Vision, an online photo-search company. On October 10, 2006, it acquired the online video company, YouTube. In October 2006, it also acquired JotSpot. JotSpot applications are delivered as Web-based services. In March 2007, the Company acquired Adscape Media Inc., a company that makes technology to deliver advertising over the internet for placement within videogames.

(*Source*: http://finance.google.com/finance?q=Google)
(Accessed 31 August 2007)

YouTube

YouTube is possibly the most revolutionary example of web 2.0. For many people it has become the first port of call when seeking video material, and along with MySpace, it enables indie/amateur film-makers and musicians to distribute their material to a vast audience. Media Studies students have also taken advantage of YouTube to widely disseminate their production work. A feature that is especially useful to media students (particularly for the Foundation Portfolio's electronic evaluation element) is the way that users can post comments on a video.

YouTube, like Flickr and Del.icio.us, offers 'social tagging', which means that the users categorise and classify the content (as opposed to this being done by the website or through software). YouTube is an interesting mix of 'We Media' DIY uploads, with some notable examples of ordinary people achieving global recognition for their videos or creating a 'moral panic'. For example, at the time of writing the uploading of videos made by teenage gang members brandishing guns is causing serious concern in the aftermath of fatal shootings of children, and the perhaps less serious 'happy slappy' culture was made possible by YouTube. In addition, uploads of existing commercial material act as 'below the line' advertising.

MySpace

Most MySpace users are between 16 and 25, which, considered alongside the staggering number of profiles in existence, helps us realise why Rupert Murdoch wanted to buy the site. This age group is one that advertisers are always desperate to reach, as they are the major audience for a host of entertainment-related products and services. You may already know this, but in case you don't, MySpace allows you to create an online profile, upload a range of content (images, music, video) to your MySpace blog and create a (social) network of friends by invitation. MySpace has become a 'hub' for a variety of commercial enterprise, much of it the independent distribution of music by bands without a record deal. It is now possible to sell music via Paypal through MySpace, so we currently have the slightly ironic state of play whereby small bands and independent film makers can use a website owned by News Corporation (the most major of all the major media institutions) to bypass the mainstream music and film industries. MySpace now has its own music label, and many existing bands with long established recording contracts now release some of their music on the site.

Steve O'Hear describes this complex arrangement and the implications for media ownership in this way:

> The content published on MySpace by its users varies from personal diary entries and discussions about the latest film or television episode, to the publication of original creative works such as digital photography and artwork or poetry. Of particular interest to News Corporation is that prior to its purchase, the top four discussion areas on MySpace were for content owned by NewsCorp itself: Family Guy, The OC, The Simpsons and Napoleon Dynamite. Whatever the fate of MySpace, it's clear that media companies (both new entrants and established players) are starting to see the value of user-generated content and the advertising revenue that can be made from it. Murdoch may be right in his view that the 'MySpace generation' of digital natives wants to consume and produce media on their own terms, but if he has his way it will still be the one god-like figure from above who will be the one to profit.

(O'Hear, 2006: 36)

Second Life

Books take about six months to go from being written to being published, a very old fashioned media form you might think, certainly when compared to the instant flow of information afforded by 'blogosphere'. How is this relevant to Second Life? Well, it is almost certainly the case that by the time you read this Second Life will have been acquired by a major media company, for the reasons that Gibson suggests here:

> The big movers in internet content, MySpace and YouTube, have been bought out. Next, if only judging by its phenomenal public profile, is Second Life, the virtual world in which its million inhabitants play games, dress up as more glamorous versions of themselves, flirt and shop. The simulated land has hosted concerts by established artists and is home to various 'virtual stores' started by big name brands. The rules set down by its founders are key to its success; first, that all its users own the copyright to anything they build or create within Second Life. Second, the money that is used for trading 'in world' has an exchange with US dollars. It is, therefore, possible to spend one's working life there as well as recreational hours, and make an income.

(Gibson, 2007: 234)

Second Life (see Figure 24) is discussed here rather than in the videogames section because the jury is out as to whether it is a game, a Massive Multiplayer Online Role Play Game, or actually a world, a place, a life. It isn't a game in one sense because it is possible to live there without much happening, with no real objectives and nothing to win. But in terms of media institutions it is pioneering in the same way as YouTube, MySpace and Google for the simple reason that it has created an entirely new way of making money from a 'free' form of media consumption.

Figure 24 Second Life: allows visitors to make money and convert Linden dollars to real currency. (*Source*: AFP/Getty Images)

Production Link

For your Foundation Portfolio work, you need to present an electronic account of your research and planning, production in progress and critical evaluation of the work itself. The Foundation Portfolio section of this book offers a set of critical questions for each of the production briefs, but the way in which you present this reflective account of the process through electronic media will also be important. Depending on the institution you are studying at, and/or the resources you may have at home, the web 2.0 examples described above all offer rich opportunities for uploading your work stage by stage, and both commenting on the process yourself and inviting comments from viewers/listeners along the way. MySpace and Moodle offer this for all media; Youtube for video; for radio you can use Audacity and then podcast in Moodle or MySpace; and if you can get your work on Second Life, then there are no limits!

Chapter 3.1
Film

To succeed in this section of the Key Media Concepts exam you need to develop a case study on a particular studio or production company. This institution must be located in a contemporary film industry and it must produce and/or distribute films to the UK. The focus will be on how this institution relates to:

Production: making films
Distribution: promoting films and getting them into cinemas and out on DVD/UMD, as well as any spin offs/related media products
Consumption: people paying at the cinema, renting or buying DVDs/UMDs and downloading and purchasing related products.

This section of the book will provide an overview of contemporary film production, distribution and consumption in relation to UK audiences, three case studies on specific films, and three institutional case study starting points, one of which you may wish to pursue further for this unit.

Whichever case study you choose, at some point you will have to debate how we categorise a British film. British cinema has always enjoyed an ambiguous relationship with America. On the one hand, British cinema has a tremendous advantage over other European national film for the simple reason that America is geographically huge and Americans speak English. Couple this with the fact that many people across the world speak English as a second language, and there is potentially a huge audience for British films as a result of this linguistic access. But the flipside of this coin is obvious. American films have the same advantage and the American studios have enormous capital at their disposal. They produce more films, those films are more expensively created and they can afford to take more risks, knowing that one success will pay for nine failures at the box office. So while British film producers periodically experience boom periods (we are in one now) and have the possibility of attracting a large global audience, in Britain we are generally consuming an ever more American diet of film. And because of the popularity of Hollywood films in the UK, the distribution of films into our cinemas and DVDs into our shops is dominated by US companies, who are clearly going to put their money and resources into pushing their own products.

Film Distribution

Consider these two competing views of who holds the most power in terms of influencing what films get made and seen:

> If you break it down and look at it as a business then the audience has the greatest power. It's the audience that tells you what they like. So if the audience likes a particular superstar, then Hollywood is forced to use the superstar and that star then becomes extremely powerful.

> In a world where money spent on the budget of a film often sees 50 per cent going on promotion as opposed to what you actually see on screen, the idea that we have a world where the consumer can exercise authority is absurd. This industry is like any other. Of course it has to sell things, but it doesn't rely on waiting, listening, responding to what audiences want and then delivering that to them. It relies on knowing which parts of the world and the media need its products and will pay for them.

The first statement is from Tony Angellotti, from within Hollywood, and the second is from Toby Miller, an academic, both quoted in an article by Helen Dugdale (2006, p. 52). They can't both be right and you therefore need to come to an informed judgement on this dynamic. In reality, the question is much broader and is really to do with the nature of capitalism as a way of organising society! Put simply, does 'market forces' competition give the consumer more power and choice and thus influence what gets made for us to buy? Or does it actually convince us that what we want is what is being made for us? In the case of film marketing, it is a complex issue. Do millions of people go to see *Pirates of the Caribbean 2* in the first week of release because it is such a great film, or because it is so well marketed? Or both? Well, as *Big Brother* has it, you decide!

Film distribution describes everything that happens in between production (making the film) and exhibition (people watching the film in cinemas or on DVD/UMD, on television, via the internet or on a plane, or anywhere else). Far from being a straightforward state of affairs, distribution involves all of the deals done to get films shown (many films never get seen) and, just as importantly, promoted. This promotion involves paid for 'above the line' advertising, which will be funded as part of the project, such as trailers, posters, billboards and various spin-offs which are of mutual benefit to the film and another commercial agency, for example a McDonalds 'Happy Meal' with a film theme. It also includes related merchandising and 'below the line' publicity which is not paid for, but again generates mutual interest. For example, an interview with a star in a newspaper or magazine and reviews (the former will generally be positive, but the latter is, of course, the great unknown for film producers).

It is crucial not to see film distribution as a 'helpful' stage in the life of a film whereby distributors treat all films equally and ensure fair play in getting films to the public's attention. The key players, the big companies who control much of the industry, control distribution of their own products, and of others. Effectively films are loaned out to cinemas for a finite period and release deals are done that secure access to a certain number of screens at a time. In the UK film market, an increase in the quantity of screens showing films has not led to an increase in the number of films shown.

Production Link

If you choose the film production brief for your Foundation Portfolio, you will need to establish a clear sense of the potential audience for your film. This element of pre-production research and planning influences the production of the titles and opening sequence, but also by considering your audience you will be thinking ahead to how the whole film would be distributed.

Activity 3.2

This is a straightforward piece of content analysis that can lead to interesting data.

Collect cinema listings for five multi-screen cinemas in a specific region. This can be done via the internet so you are at no disadvantage if you live in a rural area rather than a big town or city—simply select a big city on the web and go from there.

1 Over one weekend, how many separate screenings are there?
2 How many films in total are being exhibited?
3 How many films are being screened several times at the same cinema?
4 Of these, how many are being screened at more than one cinema at the same time?
5 Express the number of unique screenings as a percentage of the total screenings.
6 Express the total number of films in relation to the total number of screenings.
7 What conclusions can you draw about film distribution in the UK?

Five major distributors dominate the UK film industry: United International Pictures, Warner Brothers, Buena Vista, Twentieth Century Fox and Sony. Roughly nine of every ten films seem in the UK are viewed as a result of these distributors. In most cases these distributors are directly linked to the Hollywood production companies who make the films. They deal with exhibitors who are no longer (as used to be the case) owned by the same Hollywood companies, but who do, for reasons of profit, prioritise Hollywood films over others. Usually the blockbuster films we are familiar with are distributed via 'blanket release', so even if a small UK independent company manages to get its product into cinemas, it is usually competing for attention with one or more films that take on the status of an 'event'. One of the outcomes of the distribution arrangement outlined above is that half of the films released in Britain do not reach the whole country.

Perhaps surprisingly, given we live in the digital age, one of the obvious problems smaller companies face is a rather old fashioned one. Every film shown in a cinema is a separate 'print' of the film, projected via a reel. The major companies can afford to produce far more prints than the smaller companies, knowing the expensive outlay of funds at this stage will be worth it in relation to box office returns. A small company producing a less commercial product cannot afford to do that, so people who do want to see more 'alternative' films often have to wait until their local independent cinema has a print, and often there is little choice over where and when to see it. The UK Film Council is addressing this problem via its Digital Screen Network—the deal is that cinemas receiving financial support to equip themselves with digital facilities (thus avoiding the issue of prints) will in return be expected to show more films from independent distributors.

Classification

A crucial aspect of film distribution is film classification, which is not the same as censorship. The British Board of Film Classification produces a set of guidelines which are easily obtained for your reference from the organisation's website (www.bbfc.co.uk). The BBFC is not a separate entity from the film industry or a government department. It is a self-regulatory body, as it is made up of film industry representatives. But despite this, this is the one area of film distribution over which the makers and promoters of a specific film have limited control. It is possible for a film to be targeted and promoted for a particular audience group such as 15 and over, only for the BBFC to impose an 18 certificate, although this is rare.

The BBFC's guidelines state that there are three main considerations for any film:

1 Legal (material may break the law—there are several laws to do with obscenity, equality, incitement and the protection of children)
2 Protective (material is scrutinised for its potential to cause 'harm' though this is a huge area for debate—who decides who needs protecting from what?)
3 Societal (material is reviewed with broader public opinion in mind with particular regard to language).

The second and third considerations are more significant in stipulating an age classification for a film. It is important to recognise that the BBFC make recommendations, but it is possible for local authorities not to comply and either allow films to be exhibited to a wider age range than the BBFC recommends, or to deny younger viewers access in the locality, or even to ban a film from release in the area. This hardly ever happens, but a famous example was the decision of Westminster Council to ban the screening of David Cronenberg's *Crash*, which was given an 18 certificate elsewhere.

The BBFC's relationship with Government is known as a 'Gentleman's Understanding' which means that Parliament observes from a distance and the BBFC regulates itself in accordance with the political climate established by the Government (stricter or more liberal depending on who is in power). During the New Labour Blair/Brown era, the BBFC has been more relaxed about material for the 18 certificate, but 'tougher' when considering material for younger children.

For your AS studies of film, it is important to be aware of classification as an element in 'gate keeping' the distribution process. The classifications, as published in the BBFC guidelines, are as follows:

U: Universal (suitable for all).

PG: Parental Guidance (general viewing, but some scenes may be unsuitable for young children).

12 and 12A: Suitable for 12 years and older. No one younger than 12 may see a 12A film in a cinema unless accompanied by an adult. No one younger than 12 may rent or buy a 12 rated video or DVD. Responsibility for allowing under 12s to view lies with the accompanying or supervising adult.

15: Suitable only for 15 years and over. No one younger than 15 may see a 15 film in a cinema. No one younger than 15 may rent or buy a 15 rated video or DVD.

18: Suitable only for adults. No one younger than 18 may see an 18 film in a cinema. No one younger than 18 may rent or buy an 18 rated video or DVD.

R18: To be shown only in specially licensed cinemas, or supplied only in licensed sex shops, and to adults of not less than 18 years.

(*Source*: BBFC guidelines: 8–9)

The introduction of the 12A classification demonstrates that the BBFC have become more stringent with children's viewing, but the introduction of the R18 legalises forms of pornography that were previously banned completely.

Activity 3.3

In order to assess how effective film classification is, ask yourself these questions:

Have you watched films classified as 18 when you were below this age?

Does classification work for home viewing (DVD, TV broadcast, online, YouTube)?

Can parents/guardians/supervising adults be trusted to monitor what children are viewing? Should they have this responsibility?

In a liberal society, the balance between state intervention and citizen responsibility is crucial, and the current BBFC guidelines demonstrate an emphasis (in keeping with New Labour ideology) on citizens making 'responsible choices'. You will form your own critical judgement on this approach.

Link to A2

If you progress to A2 you may study a range of contemporary media regulation and the surrounding debates and critical perspectives in more detail. In the case of film censorship and classification, this might include 'who decides who should be protected and from what?'

Defining British film

There are various different 'official' ways of categorising British film. The British Film Institute (BFI—not to be confused with the British Film Industry, which has the same initials) divides films into the following categories:

Category A: films made with British money, personnel and resources.

Category B: films co-funded with money from Britain and from foreign investment, but the majority of finance, cultural content and personnel are British.

Category C: films with mostly foreign (but non USA) investment and a small British input, either financially or creatively.

Category D: films made in the UK with (usually) British cultural content, but financed fully or partly by American companies.

Category E: American films with some British involvement.

It is fairly obvious that Britain can claim a great number of films under the D and E descriptions, a decent number in categories B and C and very few that have been successful as category A films. There are few well known 'purely British' films. And this equation becomes even more complicated when we start to explore the notion of where the money comes from. For example, if a film is made by a British film company, but that company is owned by a larger American group, is the production financed in the UK? And what is the significance of distribution? If a film is 'purely British' at the production stage but it is distributed in this country by an American company (who then claw back a chunk of the box office profits), is this film really a success story for the British Film Industry? For your case study, you will need to ask these questions and explore the way the studio/company operates both in 'old fashioned' production and distribution contexts and in the current online distribution and intermedial 'spin off' climate.

The Current Boom

UK film production experienced a crisis in 2005 and early 2006. Investment in the making of films dropped, largely due to the rate of the English pound against the American dollar and the availability of low cost studios in Eastern Europe. But later in 2006 and since, investment has returned, and this is related to a new Government policy of tax relief. This allows producers to be exempt from certain tax payments. Previously there had been a compulsion for films to be mainly shot in the UK for them to qualify for the avoidance of tax, but in March 2006 this was revised to allow for more overseas filming, an attractive amendment for investors. This is a great example of the importance of politics in understanding the media. It is impossible to critically assess the relationship between British films and audiences by only thinking about cultural reasons why British cinema is more or less successful in relation to Hollywood blockbusters. 'Behind the scenes' there are financial, political and *institutional* reasons why films do or don't get made and released and seen by a potential audience.

A recent good example of Hollywood's dominance is the record-breaking box office performance of *Pirates of the Caribbean 2*, seen by industry commentators as a victory of blanket marketing. Cynics suggest that a film of this scale does not need to be critically well received, as the efforts and dollars put into promoting the film so lavishly will guarantee an audience on the opening few nights and subsequent 'buy first, review later' DVD sales. In this case over £50 million was made at the UK box office, and 1.5 million copies of the DVD were purchased in the ten days after release. A study of the ways in which the big Hollywood studios time the release of films is another area of key institutional knowledge for a Media student. The timing of releases in relation to the Oscars, school holidays, the spring/summer blockbuster period and DVD releases at Christmas is strategic, and any British release attempting to get attention amidst this marketing stealth will be at the mercy of this.

Television company co-funding

British films experienced a boom year later in 2006, largely due to a renaissance of television companies' involvement in production and distribution. The BBC and Channel 4 have both invested far more in film than at any time since the 1980s. If the television licence fee increases, as is planned, then the BBC will have more money to invest in domestic film production, another example of cross-media political/institutional events being hugely important in cultural developments. BBC films are co-funded with an overseas investor, usually American. The most successful of these in 2006 was *The Queen*, produced without major Hollywood finance, *The History Boys*, adapted from the quintessentially English Alan Bennett's play and *The Wind that Shakes the Barley* from social realist political director Ken Loach (usually cited by critics as the absolute antithesis of all things commercial and Hollywood). All grossed over £3 million at the box office in the UK and went on to attract international audiences. Clearly *The Queen*, despite its indigenous qualities, can be seen as following the well worn path of making films about English culture with an eye to the US audience, previously achieved by films such as *Notting Hill* and *Bend it Like Beckham*. Additionally, there is the complexity of funding to consider. *The History Boys* was distributed by Twentieth Century Fox UK, who spent over £2 million on marketing. A cynical response to claims that Alan Bennett's material had against all the odds broken through to a mainstream audience would be to suggest that this was more a success of Hollywood style marketing than a victory for 'old school' drama. But you will form your own view on this. One thing is for certain, though: the policy in the 1990s of British film makers trying to imitate the Hollywood genre approach (most notably with the proliferation of gangster films in the wake of the success of *Lock Stock and Two Smoking Barrels*) is now seen by the industry and its commentators as fatal, as this statement from Ian George, managing director of Twentieth Century Fox UK, demonstrates:

> **The films that have succeeded have not tried to ape Hollywood. They have been typically British subjects, done in an entertaining, confident way.**

> (In Grant, 2007: 24)

The institutional relationship between TV and Film is always changing, but at the moment it is in a healthy state. As well as the films mentioned above, TV companies have recently funded *Red Road, The Road to Guantanamo, The Last King of Scotland, This is England* and *Ghosts*. Let's consider two examples from this list in more detail, in the context of these two descriptions of the current climate from Nick Roddick and Nick James:

> **In the UK the tradition has been less protective of film culture (than other countries) and more concerned with commercial viability. The policy has been to back those films that have a 'reasonable' chance of producing a return on their production investment. Arguably, this is a contradiction in terms, because if a film has a reasonable chance of making a profit there should be enough potential producers willing to risk their capital. Nowadays, television plays an**

important part in the process, investing real money in the real marketplace while remaining cushioned from the direct economic constraints of failure by the nature of TV accounting. The 'return' on the investment is represented by the broadcast rights to the film, money that would otherwise have to be spent to acquire some two hours of programming.

(Roddick, 2007: 22)

It may be down to a collection of coincidences that reflecting life in the UK is back in fashion among the green lighters of the television companies and funding bodies. It had seemed a career-lethal choice to pitch such ideas in the days before the UK government closed off its easily defraudable tax-break schemes in 2004. Before then producers seemed more interested in Miramax-style novel-

Case Study 3.3

The Last King of Scotland

The Last King of Scotland is described by Film Four's Tessa Ross (in Roddick, 2007: 24) as the film the company should be most proud of, because it was directed and written by 'home grown' talent (Kevin Macdonald and Peter Morgan respectively), has subject matter that is challenging, political and hard-hitting (the reign of Ide Amin in Uganda) and was the result of a partnership with an American major (Fox Searchlight). So for Ross, this film seems to represent the current 'success story' of British film and the newly found ability of producers to attract American investment for less commercially obvious projects.

The film was produced by eight companies in collaboration (DNA Films, Fox Searchlight Pictures, FilmFour, Cowboy Films, Scottish Screen, Slate Films, Tatfilm and the UK Film Council) and distributed by three (various forms of Fox Searchlight in the USA, Japan, Holland, Singapore, Argentina and Germany, Channel Four Films in the UK and Fox-Warner in Switzerland). The writers, cast and crew were British and American. As these details and the views of the Head of Film at one of the production companies demonstrate, this is a good example of a co-funded British film with British cultural content. Despite the Ugandan setting and political context, the film portrays the fictional story of a Scottish visitor to Uganda who is taken in by the dictator running the country, but is based on real events, hence the title. Despite the claims made for the film as a British success story, however, this extract from a review in the *San Francisco Chronicle* sees things rather differently:

Now that Hollywood belatedly has gotten around to Amin, he shares screen time with a fictional character, something the self-aggrandizing general surely would have found galling. But the brilliance of 'The Last King of Scotland'—an immediate contender for Oscar consideration and a spot on critics' top 10 lists—is the way it shows his dangerous allure through the eyes of an innocent.

(Ruthe Stein, *San Francisco Chronicle*, 6 October 2006)

based international prestige films of the *Chocolat* and *Captain Corelli's Mandolin* variety. Then again, it's hard to say for sure if the UK-based successes of 2006 are projects put together before the tax crunch or ones made in recognition that in financially adverse conditions we might as well look at ourselves again.

(James, 2007: 16)

Case Study 3.4

This is England

This is England is directed by the Midlands director, Shane Meadows (see Figure 25). The plot couldn't be more 'indigenous', but this is not the England of *The Queen*, *Notting Hill* or *Pride and Prejudice*. Instead the 1970s Skinhead movement, its uneasy relationship with West Indian culture (from respect for which it grew) and its distortion by the racist National Front forms the backdrop for a story about the adolescent life of a bereaved boy.

Meadows previously had varied box office and critical success with a range of other films all based on domestic life and relationships in the Midlands, including *Twenty Four Seven*, *A Room for Romeo Brass*, *Once Upon a Time in the Midlands* and *Dead Man's Shoes*. In his films the presence or absence of fathers and older male authority figures and the effects of such on young working class men are depicted with a mixture of comedy and sometimes disturbing drama. Another major difference between Meadows' output and the more commercially 'instant' British films from Working Title and similar companies, is the importance of cultural reference points—clothes, music, dialect—that only a viewer with a cultural familiarity with provincial urban life in the times depicted would recognise.

This is England was produced as a result of collaboration between no less than seven companies—Big Arty Productions, EM Media, FilmFour, Optimum Releasing, Screen Yorkshire, the UK Film Council and Warp Films. It was distributed by six organisations—IFC Films, Netflix, Red Envelope Entertainment and IFC First Take in the USA, Madman Entertainment in Australia and Optimum Releasing in the UK.

The critical response to *This is England* has largely been to celebrate a perceived 'return' to a kind of cultural reflective film-making that was threatened by extinction in the context of Hollywood's dominance and the Government's preference for funding films with an eye on the US market, as this comment from Nick James, editor of the BFI's *Sight and Sound* magazine shows:

I forgot, when watching Shane Meadows' moving evocation of skinhead youth *This is England* at the London Film Festival, how culturally specific its opening montage might seem: it goes from Roland Rat to Margaret Thatcher to the Falklands War to *Knight Rider* on television. What will people outside of Northern Europe make of the regalia of 1980s skinheads from the Midlands? Hopefully they will be intrigued. *This Is England* made me realise, too, that some British films are at last doing exactly what *Sight and Sound* has campaigned for; reflecting aspects of British life again and maybe suffering the consequences of being harder to sell abroad.

(James, 2006: 16)

Figure 25 *This is England*: reflecting British life but less attractive abroad?
(*Source*: FILM 4/OPTIMUM RELEASING/SCREEN YORKSHIRE/UK FILM COUNCIL)

The Impact of Technology

As with all media, any attempt to ignore the fast approaching world of legal film downloading is seen as 'swimming against the tide'. Piracy is a major concern of all film distributors, with Hollywood investigators claming a 10 per cent increase each year in revenue lost to illegal distribution. In the UK the Film Council's report *Film Theft in the UK* (2004) claimed that only Austria and Germany have a higher degree of DVD piracy.

The industry's recommendations include a strategy for responding to internet distribution opportunities, and for working with other media and communications industries. Ultimately the

Case Study 3.5

London to Brighton

London to Brighton, released at the end of 2006, follows a long tradition of 'social realist' British films that, like the films of Gary Oldman, Shane Meadows and more established directors such as Ken Loach and Mike Leigh, reflect on the less palatable but arguably more important aspects of contemporary, divided and uneasy British social life (see Figure 26).

Clearly the film has British cultural content, depicting two females attempting to escape to the coast in fear of revenge after involvement with a gangster and a pimp. The locations are those often described as the 'underbelly' of London. The producers raised the initial budget through a group of private investors, and eventually it cost £80,000 to shoot and edit the film. Several scenes were then shown to the UK Film Council, who subsequently provided £185,000 to complete post production and create all the materials needed by a production company. The cast was made up (by necessity) of unknown actors and the style of filming was determined not only by the aesthetic desire to be 'gritty' but also by resources.

The final production credits are shared by Steel Mill Pictures www.steelmillpictures.co.uk and Wellington Films www.wellingtonfilms.co.uk. *London to Brighton* was distributed by Vertigo Films www.vertigofilms.co.uk in the UK, MK2 Diffusion www.londontobrighton-lefilm.com in France, Paradiso www.paradisofilms.nl in Benelux and Noble Entertainment http://www.nobleentertainment.com/pub/ in Scandinavia, to name but a few territories. The film won several awards at film festivals and was critically well received. The outcome is an interesting example of what is sometimes called 'guerrilla' film-making, and time will tell whether Williams' strategy will act as a blueprint for other aspiring directors on a shoestring budget. The official website is www.l2b-themovie.co.uk.

Case Study 3.6

Working Title Films

Working Title Films has the appearance of being an independent production company, but it is owned by Universal Pictures, who distribute its films. The most notable successes from Working Title are *Four Weddings and a Funeral*, *Bridget Jones's Diary* and *High Fidelity*, as well as the Coen Brothers' films *The Hudsucker Proxy*, *Fargo*, *The Big Lebowski* and *O Brother, Where Art Thou?* Working Title has a smaller subsidiary company, WT2, which makes small-budget films.

An example of a recent major title from Working Title is *Atonement* (see Figure 27). Unlike many films produced by British companies, *Atonement*'s sole production credits are held by Working Title. However, as a subsidiary of Universal, whether the film 'counts' as a British film is a matter for debate. The film was distributed by eight companies: Finnkino Oy in Finland, Focus Features in the USA, Hoyts Distribution in Australia, Studio Canal in France, Toho-Towa in Japan, United International Pictures in Argentina and Singapore, Universal Pictures International in Holland and Universal Pictures (the owners) in the UK.

The film was shot entirely in England and was adapted from a novel by British writer, Ian McEwan. The screenplay was by Christopher Hampton, also British, and the film featured a mainly British cast. However, because Working Title is owned by a major US company, it is not entirely clear whether we can treat this film as 'British', using the BFI categories on page 143.

Figure 26 *London to Brighton*: exists to critical acclaim.
(*Source*: Photograph by Amanda Smith, copyright UK Film Council/LTB Films Ltd)

report sought to remind the public that small production companies are actually hurt more by piracy than multinational conglomerates, as they cannot bear the impact with already acquired capital. Another aspect of technological change that the Film Council is concerned with is digital filming and projection. The Digital Screen Network project is the Film Council's attempt to provide cinemas with digital projection facilities, and it is hoped (but by no means guaranteed) that more small-scale independent films will get seen this way.

At the other end of the 'food chain', digital technology has made life a lot better for low budget film makers and distributors. In the case of short films, it is now possible for these to reach a potentially wide audience via a range of hosts, from the UK Film

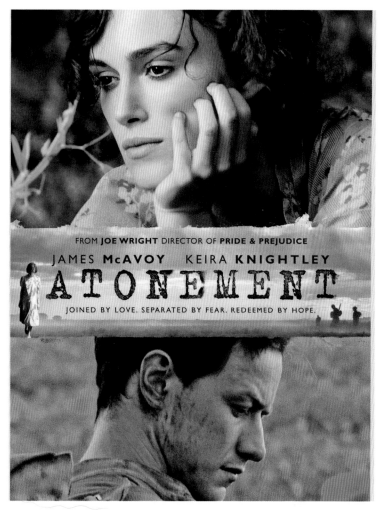

Figure 27 *Atonement*: produced by Working Title, owned by Universal.
(Source: WORKING TITLE/CANAL+/Ronald Grant Archive)

Council to The UK Media Desk, BBC Film Network and Big Film Shorts, Film London's Pulse and a host of short film festivals, all of whom have online submission.

Digital distribution

As far as the major studios and distributors are concerned, digital technology offers great potential to increase profits and dangers in equal measure. Digital distribution will certainly transform the film industry more than any previous technological change since sound. Once it becomes the norm to download film via broadband, the potential for a new form of 'blanket distribution' is obvious—not only do you no longer need

DNA Films

Andrew MacDonald's DNA Films was bolstered greatly when it secured a distribution deal with Fox Searchlight in 2001, and is thus another example of a British film success story being dependent on collaboration with an American major. Prior to the merger the company had success with *28 Days Later*. Since the deal was struck it has had a run of success with such films as *The Last King of Scotland*, *Notes on a Scandal* and *The History* Boys, all finding an audience both domestically and internationally for a focus on British cultural issues.

DNA Films is a company with a 50/50 ownership split between The Film Council and Fox, and offers a great example of how the contemporary 'boom' in British film is contextualised by both Government backing and American confidence, as a result of the tax-break policy described earlier in this chapter. DNA Films play different roles on different projects. For example, it was creative producer on new film *Sunshine*, but provided finance and distribution only for *Notes on a Scandal*. This flexibility is another feature of the contemporary film industry.

For the seven films the company has made at the time of writing, roughly a fifth of outlay has been returned, but this is expected to rise as *28 Weeks Later* was produced taking advantage of the aforementioned 20 per cent tax relief. Perhaps ironically, given his success in the film industry, MacDonald is pessimistic about the public's interest in UK film, as he states in this *Guardian* interview with Jane Martinson:

> **My theory of the British film and TV business is that if there were no more British films in the cinema, nobody would care. But if you turned off *Coronation Street* and *Match of the Day*, they'd be rioting in the street.**

(*Source*: Guardian Finance, 2007.Copyright *Guardian* News & Media Ltd 2007)

multiple prints, you can also bypass the cinemas (although the big screen offers a separate experience that is likely to remain attractive).

Digital film has the advantage of offering identical versions of the film to each viewer, and this will without doubt save billions of pounds at the distribution phase. Despite the 'hype' over piracy and the digital enabling of this illegal activity, industry commentators believe that one advantage of digital distribution will be control and security, as most piracy is the result of a cinema-goer with a hidden camera distributing a poor quality version of a film to parts of the world where it has not yet been released (because the prints are currently somewhere else). Simultaneous global distribution via the internet will put an end to this 'time gap' and thus its exploitation by pirates. One issue for debate is about the quality of digital movies. Whereas some film makers and critics argue that the 'binary reduction' of images in the digital compression process reduces the complexity of image and light, it appears that just as music in MP3 comes without the parts that the human ear cannot hear, so digital films remove the degrees of texture that most viewers wouldn't notice anyway. Randle and Culkin explain the issues here:

> The movie we see at our local multiplex may have been shown many times over and the wear and tear on it will be considerable: scratches, dust and fading—as a result of having been exposed regularly to bright light—all reduce the quality of the presentation. Even before wear and tear kicks in, what we are watching may well be a third generation copy—a process similar to making a photocopy of a photocopy, where some of the original definition is inevitably lost. Some experts believe that D-cinema will overtake the quality of the best conventional cinema within the next year or two, and at the same time address age-old industry problems. Prints are bulky and their manufacture, distribution and exhibition are labour intensive and therefore expensive. What's more, in a world increasingly concerned with the impact industry has on the environment, it is hard to justify the use of a technology (film manufacturing), which involves a highly toxic process, when a cleaner alternative is available.
>
> (Randle and Culkin, 2004: 10)

Another interesting prediction that Randle and Culkin make is to speculate that film extras (another costly necessity for the film industry) may soon be replaced by digitally generated 'synthespians'—time will tell.

To summarise, the digitalisation of film offers a range of new institutional practices. There are greater possibilities for the manipulation of the image itself, the editing process becoming more creative and composite images can be produced to incorporate digital animation. The 'one way' process of film making and consuming is threatened by the interactive 'zeitgeist,' so that the generation of media users who are immersed in online media and videogames are likely to require new forms of interactivity in the film medium.

Digital technology has reduced the costs of film making so much that DV can be seen as widening access to the 'means of production' for new creative talent. And the convergence of media through digital technology creates new opportunities for distributing and exhibiting. Marshall (2004) sums up the scene like this:

The (digital) rejuvenation of film is not limited to the grand-scale strategies of a lugubriously large industry. The digital has created new cultural economies. There is clearly a place for short film via the internet. Through different websites, the digital version of film breaks down the limitations of exhibition that have controlled what it is possible for audiences to see. Digital cameras have made it possible to have filmic qualities in the smallest of productions. Although this expansive development of film is still quite circumscribed, it demonstrates how 'film' has been more accessible and is connected to the wider new media and cultural phenomenon of the will-to-produce.

(Marshall, 2004: 87)

Activity 3.4

Cinema as an institution has survived several threats to its life. Most notably, it was predicted that television would make it extinct, but cinema survived by securing cinema releases prior to TV broadcast and because of its social, 'night out' context. Later, the VCR seemed to have put a bigger nail in the coffin, but this time cinemas redefined themselves as multiplexes, offering a broader 'leisure experience' on an American model, together with the emergence of the 'blockbuster' and its associated expensive marketing.

Despite multi-channel television offering viewers the opportunity to download films to watch at their convenience, hard drive recording, specialist film channels that are now relatively cheap to subscribe to and online rentals making the visit to the local Blockbuster unnecessary, cinema still survives (as does Blockbuster).

So the question is—will cinema always survive technological change, or is the latest technology a bigger threat because it is at the exhibition end of the chain? Whereas the changes in accessibility given above are to do with distribution, the pleasure of the filmic experience is determined greatly by the size and quality of the screen. Hollywood films in particular are still largely driven by spectacle and noise, as well as character and narrative (perhaps with an eye to the preservation of the cinema box office), and people still want to see these films on the biggest screen with the loudest sound.

Hold a focus group with ten students aged 15 to 20 (this is a key cinema audience in demographic terms) who you know to be regular cinema goers. Show them examples of big, 'next generation' HD televisions and ask them open questions in relation to the debate above.

If each participant owned one of these televisions and had access via broadband to new releases instantly via the kinds of digital distribution processes outlined above, how likely would they be to give up on the cinema?

Alternatively, you could set this up as a blog thread or a wiki.

Bollywood

Bollywood is often mistakenly described as a genre, when actually it is a film industry producing popular Indian cinema out of Bombay which rivals Hollywood for worldwide appeal. It produces an average of 800 films a year which are distributed globally. In Britain today, several cities and towns have a Bollywood cinema showing Indian films. Increasingly Hollywood studios are developing their own versions of Bollywood film and there is a proliferation of co-funding. Cinema going (and home viewing) in India and of Indian cinema in the UK is said to be more of a whole family experience than is the norm in the West. An old fashioned (in British terms) intermission is a common feature in Bollywood cinemas. Bollywood audiences in the UK can subscribe to Star Gold through digital and cable providers, or via the internet, to view Bollywood films. Eros International recently teamed up with YouTube to launch a Bollywood channel on the internet on a free subscription basis.

In terms of box office success, Gant (2007) recently reported the following trends for Bollywood films in the UK. Most films open at around forty screens, and are increasingly shown at multiplexes rather than only at Bollywood cinemas, independent or art-house venues. Of these, Cineworld holds over half of the market, and its top venues are Ilford and Wood Green in London and Bradford and Wolverhampton. The most successful Bollywood films in the UK are those that offer something different to Hollywood, such as sentimental comedies as opposed to action films. In audience terms, however, there is still a sense of ghettoisation, as Gant explains:

> **Thanks to a huge disparity in ticket prices between UK and India, the export market offers producers richer margins. But in the UK films have so far failed to cross over much beyond the Asian-ethnic audience.**
>
> (Gant, 2007: 9)

Consider this description of current access to Bollywood films and music in Birmingham, England from Somak Raychaudry:

> **There are lots of channels you can access now. Many of them are free. On Sky I get Zee and B4U music, which are essentially film music channels, and several regular channels that do Indian TV programmes—soaps, etc. And if I were to pay I could get B4U, Zee and Sony's three premium movie channels. Then there are channels for other**

Activity 3.5

Research the availability and consumption of Bollywood films in your local area. Depending on where you live, you might start with designated Bollywood cinemas, then look for Bollywood films on general release, assess the distribution of Bollywood DVDs to rent and buy in local retail outlets and research local subscription to Bollywood subscription channels.

The above outline tells you that Bollywood rivals Hollywood for global appeal and that the audience for Indian film in the UK is huge. How visible is this in your locality?

Case Study 3.8

Yash Raj Films

Here is how Yash Raj films describes and promotes itself on the company website:

The second largest film industry of the world has contributed many talents—each brilliant in its own creative field. Very few, however, have enjoyed consistency in their creative endeavours and even fewer have managed to create an organization that has become an integral part of the entertainment business in India. Yash Raj Films (YRF) has merited this unique distinction.

YRF is spearheaded by Yash Chopra—a leading light of the Indian entertainment industry for the last five decades.

YRF started out as a film-making company in 1970. In the last three decades it has grown from strength to strength and today has to its credit India's most enviable film catalogue—some films of which have been the highest grossers in the entertainment business.

YRF, over the years, has expanded to distribution of films all over the world—its own as well as films made by other well-known Indian names. YRF has also widened its horizons into Home Entertainment by marketing and distributing DVDs and VCDs of classic Indian films all over the world through its offices in UK, USA, UAE and India. YRF has been associated with producing various successful music albums and has recently launched its own Music Label—Yash Raj Music. YRF has also been involved in production of television software, ad films, music videos, and documentaries—with its enviable creative team always at the fore.

YRF has its own Post-production facilities, Design Cell, Equipment Division, Marketing Division, Internet Division, Merchandising Division—all in-house facilities, which make it one of the most coveted creative houses in the country, listed as 27th in the world, making it thereby the Number 1 film distribution house in India.

YRF has recently constructed its own state-of-the-art fully integrated Studio (YRF Studios) and a new Corporate Office at one of Mumbai's prime properties where the heart of the entertainment business beats.

YRF is India's leading Entertainment Conglomerate—veritably a 'Studio' in every sense.

(*Source*: www.yashrajfilms.com)
(Accessed 30 August 2007)

Yash Raj Films (YRF) was established by the director/producer Yash Chopra in 1970. As the above extract explains, YRF is now regarded as the prominent company in India. In the UK, YRF has distributed a host of successful blockbuster films, including *Dhoom: 2*, *Fanaa*, *Veer-Zaara*, *Salaam Namaste*, *Bunty aur Babli*, *Dil To Pagal Hai*, *Mohabbatein* and *Hum Tum*.

This case study focuses on the distribution of Yash Raj films in Birmingham, a city with such a large Indian population that 80 per cent of the crowd at the England v India cricket match at Edgbaston in August 2007 were supporting the 'away' team. The most prominent new release in the autumn of the same year, *Chak de India*, was on release at the Piccadilly Bollywood cinema in Birmingham and on general release in the city as well. This film was seen as a departure from the YRF formula to an extent, due to its focus on hockey, as this Piccadilly Cinema web review suggests:

The Yash Raj–SRK combo is back. No lush green fields here. No running around trees either. No chiffon sarees to make the ladies look their best. No melodrama, no parental opposition, no lovers defying their parents. CHAK DE INDIA, directed by Shmit Amin, charters a new territory. Yash Raj is not really known to venture into unconventional lanes, barring a KABUL EXPRESS in the recent past. CHAK DE INDIA isn't unconventional as such, but it's definitely different and awe inspiring at times. Frankly speaking, CHAK DE INDIA doesn't boast of a path-breaking script, but execution of the subject material succeeds in making you find purpose and meaning and also arouses patriotic sentiments.

There's a flip side as well. Sports-based themes, barring a few, haven't really found many takers in India, especially with the aam junta, for various reasons. Sure, hockey is the national sport of India, but cricket gets more prominence in our dailies and also on news channels. The common man also keeps tabs on the Tendulkars and Dravids, when compared to those belonging to other sports. CHAK DE INDIA is about hockey, about women's hockey to be precise, but most of us haven't given more importance to this thrilling sport for no particular reason.

(Source: www.piccadillycinemas.co.uk)
(Accessed 30 August 2007)

Given the huge popularity of Bollywood film in the UK (see the information above on the size and scale of the Indian film industry and its global reach), no study of the film industry in the UK is complete without paying attention to this sometimes ignored but very significant aspect of British film culture. Yash Raj Films is a company which offers a sound case study for further exploration.

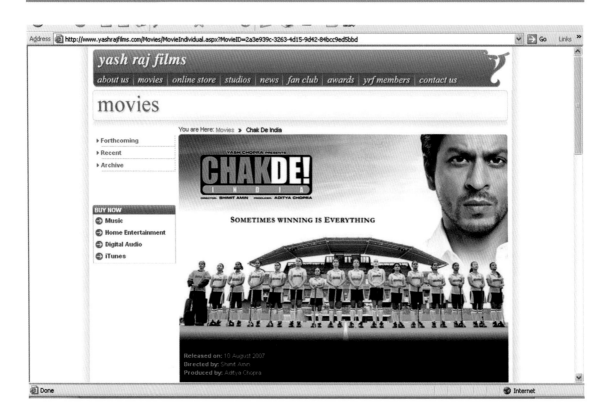

Figure 28 Yash Raj films, a major distributor
of Indian films to the UK.
(Source: Yash Raj Films Pvt Ltd)

Exam Practice Question

What impact has digital
technology had on the studio/
production company you have
studied?

languages—not strictly Bollywood—Punjabi, Gujarati and
Bengali.

The scale is amazing. I watch them often. Sometimes the
premium channels are free on weekends. The advertising on
these channels is phenomenal, which shows the extent of
the audience. Like Sunrise FM radio, for instance. I haven't
seen Chak de India yet but it's on at Star City I hear and is
highly recommended. In Birmingham it seems every major
cinema has a Bollywood movie showing.

(*Source*: email exchange, 31 August 2007)

Link to A2

For the Critical Perspectives unit at A2, you could study
British film in more depth for the Media and Collective Identity
topic.

Chapter 3.2
Music

To succeed in this section of the Key Media Concepts exam you need to develop a case study on a particular record label. This institution must be located in the contemporary music industry and it must produce and/or distribute music in the UK. The focus will be on how this institution relates to:

Production: recording music
Distribution: promoting music and getting it into shops, on the radio and downloaded for payment
Consumption: people buying CDs, downloading music, paying for live concert tickets and purchasing related products.

This section of the book provides an overview of contemporary music production, distribution and consumption in relation to UK audiences and four case study starting points, one of which you may wish to pursue further for this unit. The case studies are purposely not mainstream major labels or multinationals, since information about these is much easier to come by. Instead, your strategy for this topic should be to contrast these smaller, 'grass roots' case studies with the likes of the 'big four'—Sony/BMG, Warner Brothers, Universal and EMI—in order to get a full sense of the contemporary, changing state of play for the music industry.

The Music Industry

Stafford (2007) offers this helpful way of describing what is meant by 'the music industry':

> The music industry can be defined as the organisation of the various activities associated with performing and recording music and distributing access to those performances around the world. Because the basis of music production is accessible to everyone with a modicum of talent, the industry is both more 'open' than filmmaking and less easily 'controllable' than traditional broadcast television. This has led to a longstanding institutional difference between small and 'independent' music organisations and a large corporate 'mainstream'.

(Stafford, 2007: 17)

While the 'big four' are incredibly powerful, there is much more independent activity and success in the music industry than in other media sectors. So we have to think about the industry as being divided into two. One portion (the majors and the subsidiaries they own) is much bigger than the other (the huge number of much smaller independents, who between them make up roughly 20 per cent of the market). I addition, we now live in an online age so we must consider the importance of hardware producers and music distributors like Apple.

The Music Industry and Technology

Like most media sectors, the development of the music industry is inextricably linked to the development of technology, in this case portable hardware for recording, listening and more recently, downloading. Let's spend some time charting the various innovations that have shaped the industry. In 1980 compact disc technology emerged and in 1982 CDs were usable on a PC for the first time. By 1988 sales of the CD had overtaken vinyl and in 1990 recordable CDs became available. In 1997 we saw the emergence of MP3 and in 1999 the infamous Napster service was launched by 18-year-old student, Shawn Fanning, providing the first peer-peer software. This really was a revolution and led to legal battles over copyright, which made public the tension between the radical rebellious nature of the *content* of popular music and the corporate context in which it is sold. In particular, the metal band Metallica became highly visible as careful guardians of profits. In 2000, broadband was introduced in the UK and in 2001, Apple launched

Figure 29 The iPhone: the next stage in media convergence.
(*Source*: Courtesy of Apple)

the iPod and iTunes. By 2003 CD sales had fallen by a third, and in 2005 the iPod shuffle made downloading much cheaper and more accessible.

The iPod now sells at a rate of 3.5 million a month. We cannot understand how Apple operates without looking first at convergence—between the music industry, computing, television and telecommunications. The analogue 'switch off' in the UK will allow mobile phone companies to compete for bandwidth, with a view to enabling mass downloading onto mobile devices such as the iPhone, with iTunes acting as the software which allows the whole system to work.

Richard Branson's recent decision to sell his chain of Virgin Megastores was heralded by media commentators as a nail in the coffin of mainstream music retail. Branson's business strategy was informed by evidence that only specialist music retail can withstand the competition from iTunes, piracy and supermarket chains undercutting the traditional 'record shop'. But there is disagreement over the validity of claims that the high street music store will soon be extinct:

Activity 3.6

An example of a converged, multinational media institution *par excellence* is Sony. If you research the various ways in which Sony profits from popular music, you will get a sense of how major companies work, which you can then contrast with one of the independent labels profiled later in this section.

The Sony Corporation is a huge institution and it is divided up into several sectors, of which music is one. Sony's music wing is merged with Bertelsmann AG under the name of Sony BMG Music Entertainment. Through group research, find the answers to these questions:

1 Which subsidiary labels do Sony BMG own?
2 How are Sony vertically integrated (how do they profit from the different stages of music production, distribution and consumption)?
3 How do Sony profit from media convergence at the level of the media product (for example, a film soundtrack or music in a videogame)?

According to ERA figures, in 2006 specialists accounted for the biggest slice of the music market with 46.5% of CD album sales by value. Supermarkets had 25%, high street multiples such as Woolworths and WH Smith 12.2%, the internet 11%, mail order 2.5% and others 2.7%.

(Gibson, 2007: 35)

Vertical integration

Vertical integration has for some time been a developing feature of media ownership, but Sony and Apple have taken this to new levels. Consider Apple for a moment—it designs computer hardware, markets a range of accessories, monopolises the operating software that the user needs to use the computer (just as Microsoft does) and produces a range of software that broadens the appeal of its system—iTunes, imovie and Garageband to name but three. Another key element of Apple's strategy is the resource they have invested in their retail outlets, employment at which is competitive.

This vertical integration strategy is significant for Media students because it blurs traditional boundaries between production, distribution and consumption. iTunes is, of course, a legal downloading facility among a range of criminal alternatives. Stafford (2007) foregrounds the centrality of copyright to the development of the music industry. This, of course, is much more complex than ever before because of web 2.0 technologies, which allow people to easily share music over the internet, a practice referred to as 'file sharing'.

File sharing and the industry response

In an interview conducted for this book, Ben Andrews, independent music promoter from Birmingham, offered this extended description of the climate:

> Independent music producers and distributors operating in the climate of downloading are now using Paypal buttons on websites to pay for homemade CDRs that are sent in the post, streaming their music from their MySpace or website. In addition, they are uploading video files into YouTube, selling vinyl versions or vinyl-only releases at gigs and handmade sleeves of limited edition CDs and LPs. And organising festivals of like-minded musicians who then trade or swap or link up with galleries and visual artists for one-off performances.
>
> As anyone with a decent internet connection can get their music heard and can hear similar music to their own through

Case Study 3.9

Selectadisc

Here, Neil Burrows, manager of independent record store Selectadisc in Nottingham, provides a detailed account of the precarious position his company finds itself in.

'In a climate of increasing decline for many high street retailers, independent record shops appear alone in being hit from all angles by several different factors, making survival difficult and, for some, impossible. The proliferation of music downloads, combined with a growing perception of tracks as individual commodities as opposed to making a composite 'album', is a naturally destabilizing trend, which along with companies like Amazon offering very competitively priced, on-line purchasing opportunities, produces an obvious effect on the number of shoppers buying music from traditional record stores. This, these days, has to be taken as a fact of retail life and shops must try and adapt what they have to offer to suit what is left of their customer base. 'Indie' music shops have always been perceived as the domain of the young but increasingly this demographic is shifting to an older, yet apparently more financially settled music buyer.

However, concentrating on specific, localized competition, another more pressing profitability problem arises. Other high street traders, such as the newly reborn, HMV-owned Fopp and the supermarkets, particularly a very aggressive Tesco, insist on selling brand new product at hugely reduced retail prices, a position they can justify due to their buying power and the resultant file discounts they receive from the record companies. In order to save face and try to compete, independent retailers must match these prices or lose custom. As a result, weekly profits from healthy sales of new product, previously used to augment the stocking of a greater depth of more esoteric back-catalogue titles, the 'indies' staple, are greatly diminished. It also appears to have resulted in loss of sales of the more mainstream chart titles, again hitting the smaller shops' ability to provide something of an alternative to the choices stocked by the larger companies.

In an attempt to combat this, the record companies, to try the preserve the ever-dwindling number of independent retail outlets (who have always been prepared to stock albums by new, lesser-known artists, which it is in the companies' interest to 'break') have started offering the indie sector temporarily reduced dealer price discount campaigns, in which a selection of the older, catalogue titles are offered at budget prices. In essence this is seemingly perfect for the smaller stores but again it throws up a couple of anomalies; not only is the quality product from which indies have always thrived devalued in the eyes of consumers, in as much as they become increasingly reluctant to pay more than a certain price for older titles, the profit margins on which we work are obviously reduced, so selling more of the catalogue on which we depend has little or no net effect on takings as the mark up for retail is much smaller. The result is that, unless this product is offered at the lower prices, there becomes little point in us stocking it at the higher rate when the campaigns are not running as people become less inclined to buy at these prices, so consequently what we have to offer as deep catalogue at any given point involves significantly fewer titles.

The only way around this is to try to sweep up any overstocks and deletions from other companies who specifically deal in this type of CD. But again, although we buy these titles at sometimes ridiculously cheap prices, there are but a few on which we can make a healthy mark up, so again we find ourselves selling product which competitors may or may not have at artificially low retail prices, as the consumer is by now clearly unwilling to pay any more than three or four pounds for what they, perhaps rightly, perceive as 'old' titles, deleted or not. . .

On top of all this, indeed as a direct result of it, smaller shops can no longer afford to operate with the overheads, wage bills and stock levels they once had, redundancies ensue, with them go the knowledge and experience of key staff members, leaving the core staff effectively running harder on the spot to prevent the company going backwards. Something eventually has to give, and I think we all know by now exactly what that will be.'

Figure 30 Selectadisc: independent record stores are struggling to stay afloat. (*Source*: Selectadisc Ltd)

MySpace, this might seem to inevitably lead to a decline in sales. But there is now no need for a middle-man distributor. Obscure music that would not appear in the standard generic categories at HMV can get out there—examples are the successes of Finders Keepers and Ghost Box—these would fall into the cracks between 'film soundtrack', 'children's music', 'library sound effects', 'electronic', whatever. As regards small labels, the growing success of the subscription website emusic.com, which only sells small label music, is certainly an advantage. Because the label has no distribution costs, the artist gets a larger percentage of the money.

The technological transformation is clear—iTunes means you don't need a hard copy of the music and that the consumer can order and reorder their collection in endless overlapping play lists. But the decline of the local record shop also kills off personal one-to-one recommendation as a key factor—it has been killed by file sharing, Amazon and supermarkets. Five years ago people would come in for the latest Radiohead or Coldplay CD and that would keep them afloat, especially as people purchased other stuff when visiting. Now people just buy it from Tesco or online. The other side of this is that music is everywhere now. Glastonbury on Channel 4, special music digital channels.

From a local promoter's point of view, the music industry has become borderless. Anyone can distribute their music very easily to anyone in the world. MySpace is a giant listening booth where the consumer can sample any type of popular music and explore other people's friends' music.

Music Radio

Note: This material appears in both Chapter 2: Music and Chapter 4: Radio, highlighting its significance as an example of convergence.

The impact of the 'MP3 culture' or the 'iPod generation' on music radio is complex—they offer extraordinary challenges, making DJs and a one-dimensional play list very old fashioned—yet music radio is currently more popular than ever. The most tangible outcome of music radio's response to downloading has been to place more importance on the music itself and less on the presenters. This, as Miranda Sawyer (2007) points out in an interview for *Observer Music Monthly*, is an unexpected victory for the late John Peel. Some stations have dispensed with presenters entirely, while others have made the focus of conversation much more explicitly about the music and the credibility of the music played a key ingredient.

Activity 3.7

Soul Jazz Records

This label has established a reputation for distributing a range of music to a wide audience, often Reggae and other styles given an 'underground' tag (see Figure 31). It also distributes a wealth of older music that was not given due recognition at the time of its original release.

Use this activity as a starting point for your own case study, or develop it further for this unit. First go to the Soul Jazz website (www.souljazzrecords.co.uk) and spend some time familiarising yourself with the range of music they distribute, and how you can purchase it through the site, either as CD delivery or download. Next, research the label and some of its key signings on the internet and in the music press. Try to find answers to these research questions:

1 What kinds of music do Soul Jazz Records produce?
2 What strategies do Soul Jazz Records use to promote and distribute their music?
3 Who is the audience for Soul Jazz Records?
4 What is the relationship between Soul Jazz Records and the mainstream music industry?

If you look at the case studies on Finders Keepers and Ghost Box that appear later in this section, you will see the kinds of answers you are looking for. For this activity, however, you need to get the information for yourself.

Figure 31 Soul Jazz: giving a wide audience access to 'underground' music.
(*Source*: www.souljazzrecords.co.uk. Courtesy of Soul Jazz Records; sited created by Rudovan Scasascia; design by Adrian Self 2007.)

Link to A2

If you progress to A2 Media, your Critical Perspectives studies will provide you with the opportunity to study a range of topic areas that can further develop your understanding of how music is produced, distributed and sold in the contemporary media environment. Key examples are **Media in the Online Age**, for which you could look in more detail at downloading and compare online music with another online media form; and **Global Media**, for which you might research the emergence of global markets for music in comparison to another media form.

Finders Keepers Records

Finders Keepers is a label that describes its mission as giving music listeners access to 'a lost world of undiscovered vinyl artefacts from the annals of alternative pop history' (see Figure 32). The audience for Finders Keepers' output is mainly record collectors, DJs and producers, the latter group often using the music as a basis for their own work—sampling, mixing and reworking the previously unavailable music the label unearths for them. This is a niche audience *par excellence*, as the label's website demonstrates:

Purveyors of the bizarre and abnormal should expect Japanese choreography records, space-age Turkish protest songs, Czechoslovakian vampire soundtracks, Welsh rare-beats, bubblegum folk, drugsploitation operatics, banned British crime thrillers and celebrity Gallic Martini adverts. . .presented on CD, 7" and traditional black plastic discs in authentic packaging.

(*Source*: http://www.finderskeepersrecords.com/)
(Accessed 30 August 2007)

The way that Finders Keepers operates in the context of the contemporary music industry is explained here by Doug Shipton, who runs the label:

Place in the industry

Finders Keepers, and our sister label Twisted Nerve, are quite indicative of the smaller independent labels in the UK at the moment. Fronted by 3 people we are a cottage industry in every sense of the word, we do everything in house between ourselves and with the help of friends—licensing, mastering, artwork, marketing, press, tour managing etc. As a small outfit we do not need to departmentalise roles and functions within the label like majors and some of the larger independents do. Each of us brings a specific strength to the label to push it forward. Although it may appear that we are bound by small budgets it is also quite liberating for labels like us—without massive overheads we are able to work on titles that major labels would not consider to be cost effective by their own standards. We do not need to sell their numbers in order to turn a profit and therefore do not need to justify massive marketing budgets and production costs.

Marketing

Given our relatively small sales and therefore budget in comparison to major labels we can't really afford a marketing budget in the conventional sense, i.e. advertising, promotional merchandise and branding. Much like most independents, we feel a more grass roots/hands on approach is more effective for us—word of mouth is a very powerful tool even in this age of mass communication, simple tools such as mailing lists and messageboards allow us to spread word of releases and gigs quickly and cheaply whilst building and maintaining a loyal fanbase. Press and radio coverage are also an important means for us, much like any record label, in order to help boost exposure for the label and our artists. The internet is a great leveller for labels like us who can't afford mass marketing campaigns—adverts, etc.

Distribution

We are distributed through a company we feel is strongly geared towards the needs of independent record labels, shops and music as a whole. With record stores in general decline owing to the rise in downloads and a power shift away from independent record shops and smaller chains to the likes of HMV, Virgin, Tower and supermarkets, selling records through these outlets is getting increasingly difficult as more and more labels vie for shelf space. Although it is important for us to have a presence in these ubiquitous entities, it is equally as important to us to have a presence in smaller independent record shops. As well as dealing directly with independent stores on a wholesale basis, our distributor has a special relationship with these shops that enables them to stock our releases and compete with the larger chains.

Production

Our production needs to be monitored very carefully in order to ensure we don't tie up too much money in manufacturing. We produce minimal runs of CDs and records in order to keep costs low and repress as and when is needed so that we are not left with an abundance of stock. As a reissue label the whole process is pretty straight forward—we receive a master from the licensor which may or may not be production ready so perhaps may need cleaning up, artwork is reproduced predominantly from original sources (record covers, etc.) or is designed and put together in house, all of which is sent off to the manufacturers. We have to be careful which manufacturer we use; money constraints mean we need to find a cheap manufacturer but one that does not compromise the quality of our releases.

The Online Age

Online distribution is a multifaceted issue. Most record labels consider this to be the cheapest possible, and therefore best, way to get their releases on to people's stereos, which is true, but we cater for a more discerning market. Although we do have online distribution, we place more importance on our physical releases—CDs and vinyl—as we feel there is still a thriving number of record collectors and DJs.

(*Source*: Doug Shipton, Finders Keepers Records, September 2007)
To learn more about Finders Keepers Records, visit www.finderskeepersrecords.com

These are strange days for radio. More and more of us are listening to it, but we're not tuning into the same station. Music radio is all over the shop. You can have non-stop oldies, never-ending alternative; you can have cheesy DJ banter, or wit and knowledge. The only problem, I find, is locating a show that does everything you want.

(Sawyer, 2007: 5)

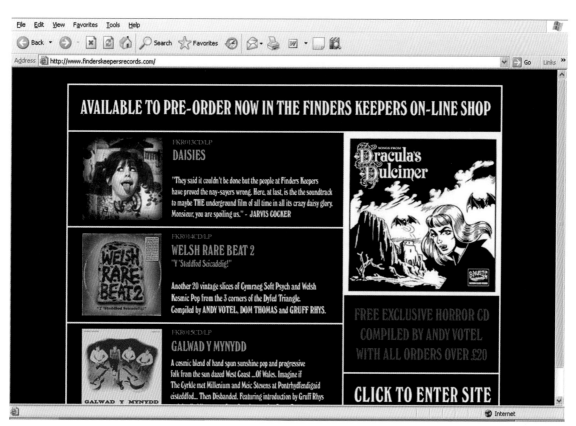

Figure 32 Finders Keepers Records: taking a
grass roots approach.
(*Source*: Finders Keepers Records)

Case Study 3.11

Ghost Box Records

Ghost Box is another independent label catering for a niche audience (Figure 33). Here, Jim Judd, co-owner of Ghost Box Records, provides an extended summary of how Ghost Box operates in the contemporary climate, with some key words in bold type.

So far we've managed to run the label very much on our own terms by bypassing traditional **distribution** and marketing channels. We sell more or less exclusively through our own webshop and Warpmart. There's also a number of stores around the world that we wholesale direct to. The big high street stores only deal with distributors but I don't expect our **audience** uses those kind of stores anyhow.

Traditionally record shops work on a sale or return basis, and most small labels generally had to put up with a really slow cashflow and the eventual return of damaged unsaleable stock. So we offer a take it or leave it cash in advance wholesale model to stores and charge them for the shipping costs too. Ultimately this means we don't get nearly as many CDs out there in shops as we would if we used distributors, but we don't have to pay **middle men** so the cut for our artists and our own profit margin for each CD is much higher. Most of our sales still come through our own **website** anyway.

As the label grows we might well have to change this and start looking for **distributors**. One of the problems is US customers who are put off our web store because of the unfavourable exchange rate. We have a lot of listeners there so we may have to bite the bullet and find a US distributor soon. I guess we're faced with a choice between going a little more **conventional** and selling lots more records and having constantly to worry about cashflow and marketing, or selling fewer records at a higher profit margin with lower overheads, while retaining complete **creative control** without the pressure of a long term business plan.

As things are though we have **100% creative and financial control**, we never risk more cash than we have on marketing or big manufacturing runs and can release whatever we like whenever we like. Both the co-founder, Julian House, and I have full time careers and we're proud to run the label on amateurish lines because we're realistic enough to know that even a hugely successful label **specialising** in weird music like this won't pay our mortgages. We do this for the pleasure of it and the little bit of extra income is a nice bonus, and I hope we retain enough control to be true to our ideas and concepts.

The label would never have come into being without the internet. We started in 2004 with the idea of setting up a website to sell CDRs of our own music on a burn and print to order basis to friends and anybody else we thought we could interest. We started dropping messages on fan forums for musicians whose listeners we felt might like our stuff and it gradually grew into a business from there. We shamelessly exploited the fact that our inhouse designer was well known for his work with Broadcast, Stereolab, Prodigy and Primal Scream.

The internet means we've never really had to spend any money at all on marketing. Early on word got around via **music and cultural bloggers**, like K-punk and Woebot, who championed our work from the start. Having hip and talented bloggers on our side meant that the word spread through the journalistic community and people started coming to us to ask for promos rather than us ever having to send loads out blind.

At the beginning we gave away quite a lot of material on our site as **free downloads**, to give people an idea of what we were putting out. We always assumed that we'd have a fairly small potential audience, many of whom would be record collectors and would prefer to buy a physical product rather than downloads. Now even though we sell downloads through iTunes and Bleep this only accounts for a small part of our sales.

We feel that certain kinds of music are greatly enhanced by the context of cover art, design and sleeve notes. Design and packaging are integral to all our releases; we're kind of developing a fictional world through our website and music and CD booklets. Nothing heavy handed we hope, but just trying to give the releases the feel of artefacts from a familiar but parallel world. It all sounds very high concept and po-faced but we've always tried to do it with a certain sense of playfulness.

MySpace seems to be helping us to widen our audience, although it's hard to know whether MySpace 'Friends' equate to people ordering CDs or downloading music. I suppose we could exploit MySpace further to keep in touch with fans and release exclusive content and news, but we find the whole environment ugly and klunky to use. The other artist and myself have also discussed the notion that **too much presence** in this kind of space detracts from the notion of the artists having a kind of weird, fictional background.

As far as we know a lot of our audience are record collectors, especially fans of library music, soundtracks and vintage electronics, so it's quite a niche market. From very early on we've maintained an **email list** so all our regular customers will get to hear about new releases. Also we always try to cultivate a good relationship with bloggers and journalists who write about the kind of things we love, so we're always fairly certain of getting **reviews** on sympathetic websites and in print in Magazines like *The Wire*.

We also have a following in the world of **art and design**. This is primarily to do with Julian's graphic design work for the label. But our label has had airplay at several gallery events and has been written about in the arts magazines like *Frieze*. As a result we wholesaled CDs to art and design stores that presumably sell them for the design content as much as the music. Again the more **artsy cultural bloggers** have been a great help in promoting this aspect of the label.

(*Source*: Interview with Jim Judd, 21 September 2007)
To learn more about Ghost Box, go to www.ghostbox.co.uk/

Figure 33 Ghost Box records: the visual appeal of design is a key selling point for this label.
(*Source*: Ghost Box Records; design Julian House, copyright Ghost Box 2004)

Exam Practice Question

How does the label you have studied reach the audience for its music?

The print brief for Foundation Portfolio requires the production of elements of a new music magazine. Your understanding of the music industry from this part of your studies will be invaluable if you apply it to answer the following questions before you begin.

1 How will the magazine find its niche in an increasingly fragmented market?
2 How will the magazine strike the balance between promotion and critique and will it offer music itself, either via a free CD, through downloads from its website or via a digital radio station linked to the title?
3 What use would your case study label make of the magazine? To make the most effective synoptic links between the units, you should produce a feature on a band or artist from the label in your magazine.

Chapter 3.3
Newspapers

To succeed in this section of the Key Media Concepts exam, you need to develop a case study on the contemporary UK newspaper market and a particular online version of a national or local newspaper. This online paper must be located in the contemporary news industry and it must be accessed in the UK. The focus will be on how newspapers and their online versions are produced, distributed and consumed in various ways.

This section of the book will provide an overview of the contemporary UK news market and two case study starting points, one of which you may wish to pursue further for this unit.

The traditional newspaper industry is threatened by two developments: technology, in the form of digital television and the internet, is turning people away from daily newspapers, and 'freebie' local newspapers undermine the community stronghold of the local paper. Both of these shifts combine to 'groom' the public in the expectation that news is not something you need to pay for. Here are two examples to start the ball rolling.

Writing in *The Media Guardian*, Alan Ruddock reviews the chances of the *London Evening Standard* surviving the rivalry of *London Life* (from Associated Newspapers) in this way:

> The Standard cannot avoid making a choice. Either it
> continues to cut its costs so far to the bone that its output
> will be indistinguishable from a freesheet, or it throws more
> money at the paper to sell itself on the quality that a
> freesheet can never match.

(Ruddock, 2007:5. Copyright Guardian News & Media Ltd 2007)

Figure 34 provides a more substantial example to illustrate the centrality of the internet to contemporary news circulation.

The UK Newspaper Market

For a number of reasons, UK newspapers are in decline with most papers experiencing either a fall in circulation or, as a result of major strategies, a 'flattening out' of sales. The internet, rolling 24 hour news, blogs and video journalism are contributory factors, and there is a widespread migration to online newspapers as a response. Technology is only partly responsible for the public's reduced lack of engagement with newspapers, though. Two other events have had a significant impact on the sales of newspapers: First, the ability of supermarkets and petrol stations to sell newspapers has led to a huge reduction in newspaper delivery from the local newsagent. As the customer increasingly picks up a paper when out and about, this may be a different paper each time, and more crucially, on some days no paper at all. Second, the distribution of free newspapers on public transport and around city centres, together with 24 hour news channels and internet news, have combined to create an expectation among the readership that news should be free.

Newspapers continue to survive, however. The Audit Bureau of Circulation (ABC) reviews newspaper sales and publishes monthly reports. Table 3 shows the average net circulation figures for some of the nationals in July 2007.

While these figures may look healthy enough, they are meagre in comparison to those achieved in the past. Adopting an 'if you can't beat them. . .' approach to the internet is a survival strategy, but even this is fraught with danger, as Stephen Brook of *The Guardian* observes:

> With the state of mild panic afflicting the British newspaper
> industry deepening, no one can claim with any certainty that
> the future looks bright; circulation continues merrily on its
> downward curve, newspapers increase cover prices, cut
> costs, sack staff and grapple with digital integration.
> Newspaper websites are yet to overtake their print

Table 3 Average net circulation figures: July 2007

The Daily Mirror (Trinity Mirror PLC)	1,424,710
The Daily Express (Express Newspapers)	735,037
The Daily Telegraph (Telegraph Group Limited)	833,430
The Guardian (Guardian Newspapers Ltd)	311,768
The Independent (Independent Newspapers Ltd)	189,797
The Daily Mail (Associated Newspapers Ltd)	2,205,172
The Sun (News International Newspapers Ltd)	2,916,821
The Times (News International Newspapers Ltd)	595,172

(*Source*: www.abc.org.uk)
(Accessed 1 September 2007)

counterparts in terms of staffing or revenues, but many certainly have in terms of readers. More importantly, they are gaining critical mass. And newspapers are sober in the realisation that, even if websites exponentially increased their advertising and unique users, every print reader lost needs between 20 to 80 replacements on the web to maintain revenues.

(Brook, 2007: 25)

News International and Associated Newspapers have both responded to the threat of free papers by launching, in London, their own freesheet, in direct competition with one another. It is predicted that the next move of News International will be to try this in a broader set of regions, which will pose a direct threat to the local newspaper industry, of course.

National Newspaper Ownership

At the time of writing, there are eight companies dominating the British newspaper market. Rupert Murdoch's News International (*The Sun, The Times, The News of the World* and the *Sunday Times*) has the largest overall share of circulation, with by far the most readers consuming *The Sun. The Daily Mirror, Sunday Mirror* and *The People* are owned by Trinity Mirror, with the historically strong *Daily Mirror* now losing out to both *The Sun* and *The Daily Mail* for readers. *The Daily Mail* and *Mail on Sunday* are owned by Viscount Rothermere (or rather his company, Daily Mail and General Trust) with a market share of around 20 per cent (readers are likely to be the same for both papers). *The Daily Express, Daily*

Mail goes surfing for millions of new readers

It may be a latecomer, but – by some measures at least – Associated's new website is making waves across the net.

by James Robinson [Business & Media section, *The Observer*, 2 Sept 2007]

Internet news pioneer Matt Drudge and the *Daily Mail* make an unlikely alliance. But the mercurial founder of influential US website the Drudge Report has played a pivotal, if unwitting, role in the overnight success of dailymail.co.uk, which last month shocked many on Fleet Street by taking second place in its first appearance in the ABCe online readership figures.

The *Mail*'s 11.8 million unique users in July put it ahead of telegraph.co.uk and Times Online, but behind Guardian Unlimited – owned by *The Observer*'s parent company, Guardian Media Group.

The measure was introduced to provide advertisers with an accurate guide to the popularity of Britain's growing newspaper websites. But the *Mail*'s rivals claim around a third of traffic was generated by referrals from the Drudge Report, which shot to prominence when it broke stories about the Monica Lewinksy affair a decade ago.

'We counted 36 *Daily Mail* stories on Drudge during July,' says Edward Roussel, the *Telegraph*'s digital editor. Publicity for the *Mail on Sunday*'s free Prince CD pushed huge numbers of users towards dailymail.co.uk, while other popular stories, including several about David and Victoria Beckham's move to LA, also played well with the US audiences. 'It's testament to the power of Drudge,' says Roussel readily concedes. 'They write stories with global appeal – terror stories and showbiz stories in particular.'

But the *Mail*'s ABCe success has reignited a fierce war of words among media owners about the way news site figures are measured. The three main ratings agencies – Nielsen NetRatings, Hitwise and ABCe – all measure slightly different things, and it was only the Mail's popularity abroad that catapulted it to second spot: UK users accounted for just 23 per cent of hits. The *Daily Telegraph* prefers to trumpet Hitwise's data, which bases its figures on UK users and defines a news site more narrowly, arguing that it is more accurate. Hitwise also happens to be the only one that consistently places telegraph.co.uk at the top of its rankings, which allows the paper to run adverts claiming it is the most popular news website in the country.

Guardian Unlimited has long published figures for advertisers to scrutinise and Tim Brooks, managing director of *Guardian* Newspapers Ltd, says: 'Everybody in the internet business knows the *Telegraph*'s claim to be the most popular news website in the UK is nonsense.'

The *Mail*'s Martin Clarke, who launched *London Lite*, Associated's free evening paper in the capital and is tipped as a possible successor to *Mail* editor Paul Dacre, is in charge of the web operation. He says UK user are far more valuable than overseas readers, despite the fact that 78 per cent of page impressions come from abroad (the equivalent figure for the *Telegraph* is around 40 per cent). 'Advertisers at the moment are most concerned with UK traffic. It's great to have international visitors and it's great the internet's such an international phenomenon, but in economic terms you can't [convert] it into revenue. It's pointless everyone judging themselves by traffic that no one can quite work out how to monetise.'

But Clarke points out the dailymail.co.uk's domestic growth has also been impressive, increasing by 14 per cent in July compared with the same month last year. Crucially, it is just not silver surfers that account for its success. 'The website is expanding the *Mail*'s demographic reach: 60 per cent of

Figure 34 James Robinson: 'Mail goes surfing for millions of new readers'.
(*Source*: *The Observer*, Business and Media section, 2 September 2007. Copyright *Guardian* News & Media Ltd 2007)

visitors are ABC1s, and over half are aged 18-24. It's the market advertisers want – affluent and young. We also have a female bias, as you'd expect given our heritage.'

The *Mail* site now boasts 2.55 million unique users in the UK, although that places it well below the *Telegraph*, *Times* and *Guardian* on most measurements … As one senior industry figure concedes: 'It's very confusing for advertisers when they see two – or indeed three – separate [analyses] being bandied around. And media owners' understandable habit of shouting about the numbers which show them in the best light doesn't help.'

What is beyond dispute, however, is that the overall market is growing and British papers are finding a new audience in the English-speaking world. After years of gloom about falling circulations, one senior industry source says that, at least, is welcome news. 'Britain doesn't lead the world at much. We should celebrate our success in this field.'

Any collective euphoria is likely to prove short-lived in a notoriously competitive industry. The *Mail*'s performance in the ABCe index alarmed rivals, which had always felt its parent Associated had been slow to innovate online. 'In isolation it's a slightly shocking figure,' Clarke concedes, but he says there has been 'solid, steady growth' since the *Mail* and its Sunday sister title started to integrate its online operation into the newsroom last spring.

Placing Clarke, who remains associate editor at the *Daily Mail*, in charge of the group's internet operation last year was a statement of intent. Although Associated has invested heavily in the digital world, buying several websites to hold onto advertising review that is migrating online, Clarke says: 'Editorially we were a bit slower. But we have always kept a watching brief and the economics of the digital world have changed.'

A new site built from scratch will launch in a few months and it will make use of video footage and user-generated content, he adds, but the *Mail*'s approach will continue to be low-key. 'We tend to just get on with the job. We don't show tourists around our news hub,' he says.

That is a thinly disguised dig at the *Telegraph*, which has invested heavily in its state-of-the art newsroom and is happy to show it off to industry executives. Clarke's assertion that Associated's 'market-leading' papers will always be given priority over the website could also be construed as a shot across the bows of his rivals: 'You don't want to distract a specialist reporter from covering a story to record a podcast that will be listened to by one man and his dog. It's important not to do things just because the technology allows you to.'

The *Telegraph*'s Roussel retorts: 'We had a global growth rate of 63 per cent year on year in the UK. If we hadn't been so evangelical we wouldn't have those figures.' But he agrees with Clarke that UK users are the only ones that count. 'That's really where the values of the business reside and that's what will pay journalists' salaries and meet the cost of newsrooms. We need to get [foreign hits] in perspective. The idea that British newspapers can take on the best US newspapers in their home market is hubristic and misplaced. We're minor brands in the US and will remain minor brands.'

Overseas readers are, at the very least, an added bonus, but the domestic market continues to grow rapidly and in a sense everyone is winning at the moment. The real battle will commence in 18 months time, when the growth of broadband penetration begins to slow down – as in the US – and the established players begin a fight to protect their online readership in a more mature market.

'We're 18 months behind the US and we will fight voraciously when that time comes,' says the same senior industry source. In the meantime, he argues, British papers should be thankful they are making an impact on a global scale – even if some of them may have Matt Drudge to thank for it.

Star, Sunday Express and *The Daily Star Sunday* are owned by Richard Desmond's Northern and Shell Company. The Telegraph Group, owned by the Barclay Brothers, own the two versions of *The Telegraph*, while *The Guardian* and *Observer* form the Guardian Media Group, owned by the Scott Trust (a different ownership format altogether) with a small share of the market. *The Independent* and its Sunday version are owned by Sir Anthony O'Reilly's Independent Newspapers.

Regional Newspaper Ownership

Ten regional publishing institutions control 90 per cent of the total market for the local press. This is a clear example of 'concentrated ownership' which has in recent years come to define the 'behind the scenes' institutional structure of the mass media, often without much public awareness. Ask yourself these questions: do you read a (paid for) local paper? If so, who owns it? You might not think it matters, but it may well have implications for the extent to which the publication reflects the community to whom it is sold. Look at these figures which were sourced from the Newspaper Society (July 2006): Trinity Mirror have roughly 20 per cent of the market, owning 234 titles. Newsquest Media Group weigh in with 219 (15 per cent share). Johnston Press have 282 and 14 per cent share, Northcliffe Newspapers are close behind with 111 (12 per cent) and Associated Newspapers have 10 per cent of the market with just 11 papers (clearly these are bigger selling titles in bigger regions). So close to 70 per cent of the regional newspaper audience is catered for by five companies.

The freesheet threat is not a new one for local papers, but the way in which *Metro* is circulated is proving to have an impact, with an average of 10,000 sales of paid for papers reportedly lost to free papers in the major cities. Unlike national newspapers, some of which are maintaining sales as a result of a host of strategies and innovations, the average net circulation of every paid for regional paper is in decline. However, the regional press is still a very lucrative media sector, just slightly less so than in the linear news era.

Press Regulation

As for all media institutions, legal and ethical regulations play a 'gatekeeper' role in the news we have access to. However, in the case of the press, editorial policy and commercial agendas are far more significant in selecting and constructing our news. Regulation is very 'light-touch' and is largely the result of self-monitoring by the newspapers. The Press Complaints

Activity 3.8

Access regional newspaper circulation figures for the companies above, either from The Newspaper Society or ABC. The figures for 2006 above represented a decline from the previous year. Two years on, what is the trend? Have the regional papers bucked the trend or has the downward curve in sales continued?

Link to A2

If you progress to A2, you may study **Contemporary Media Regulation** as one of your topics for the Critical Perspectives unit. Within this you might develop your knowledge of and response to the debates surrounding the 'free press' further. This critical area involves the status of the press in a democracy and the balance to be struck between freedom of the press to investigate events without restriction and the invasion of privacy that results. Compared to other nations, the press in the UK are relatively self-regulating and you will be asked to judge the extent to which this is satisfactory.

Commission is considered by many to be weak, and some newspapers continue the practice of 'publish and be damned', safe in the knowledge that they have far more capital resources to deploy in a legal battle than the individuals who may sue them. This way of working is described by critics as 'power without responsibility'. However, the PCC code of practice, which journalists and editors are obliged to observe, lays out guidelines with regards to accuracy, right to reply, distinguishing between fact and comment, privacy, harassment, misrepresentation, chequebook journalism, intrusion (into grief or shock), the identification of the relatives or friends of convicted criminals, the protection of children, confidentiality and (crucially) the definition of 'public interest'. This last area is very grey. Investigative journalism into potential corruption by a Government minister is clearly in the public interest. But is the constant surveillance of celebrities on the beach? Newspaper owners might argue that if enough people buy newspapers with candid images of famous people in them, then that is how 'public interest' comes to be defined. *We get the press we deserve* is the logic of this argument.

The Impact of Technology

The local press relies on its established reputation of representing a local community to resist the threats of the more globally orientated internet. In addition, national news is often 'cherry-picked' from local stories, with broadcast news following newspapers, so local news maintains a protected status to some extent. However, the internet hosts an array of free listings and public selling sites (Gumtree and Ebay being the most notable) which do pose a challenge to the role of the local rag in providing classified ads, entertainment listings, property details and job vacancies. The response to this has been widespread development, by regional papers, of small, local sites offering free listings alongside their existing paid-for classified ads.

National papers do not enjoy such a protected status among the general public, having no equivalent sense of community to cling to. The development of new media versions of their news provision has, then, been far more rapid and substantial. A key shift in 2006 was the decision by *The Times* to release news on the internet first, whereas previously there had been an agreement among newspapers to publish in printed form first. Since then, online news, blogs and podcasts have become the norm. The three case studies that follow provide a starting point for exploration of three aspects of life in the online newspaper era.

It is not only the distribution of 'citizen news' via the internet in the form of words that is destabilising conventional journalism. Mobile camera phones offer ordinary people the chance to

Case Study 3.12

The Mirror online

The Mirror's website (www.mirror.co.uk) offers a homepage with the main news splash and a set of sections which 'mirror' the structure of the paper—news, sport, showbiz, bingo and forums along the top menu and a range of other features on the left side menu. Scrolling headline text appears under the top menu and the visitor is reminded that news on the site is updated throughout the day. The two most obvious features in terms of the distinction of this site from the hard copy *Mirror* are the forums, which allow readers/visitors to respond to news stories and discuss issues, and the presence of several news videos. Video journalism is a growing feature of a newspaper's work in today's climate. The visitor can click on 'blogs' and then read and contribute to a range of ongoing discussions in response to news, entertainment, sports and showbiz content. A search facility allows non-linear selection of content. The site is dense with hyperlinks and each section of the site is constantly updated, which is, of course, the key distinguishing feature when compared to a newspaper.

To take this case study further, these are the research questions to pursue:

1 How does traffic to the site compare to newspaper sales?
2 How does the hard copy news provision compare to the online version over a 24 hour period? Pay particular attention to 'breaking news' that is reported online in between two editions of the paper.
3 How much activity is there on the blogs and forums and what difference does this make to the news provision?
4 What is added by the news videos?
5 How does the online *Mirror* news provision compare to a 24 hour rolling news TV channel (such as Sky News or BBC 24)?
6 How does the online *Mirror* news provision compare to a news site offered by a media source not related to a newspaper (e.g. BBC News)?

Guardian Podcasts

Of all newspapers, *The Guardian* has been the quickest and most prolific in responding to the internet by utilising it. The *Guardian Unlimited* website (see Figure 35) is a very different entity to the online version of *The Mirror* in the case study above. *The Guardian's* web presence is constantly referred to in the newspaper itself, as an extension of the material in the newspaper. And the site, which also has a sales aspect, offers a wide range of archive articles, online services, blogs and podcasts. The podcasts page alone, on any given day, offers links to roughly 30 current podcasts, and the visitor can also choose to access archives from previous editions, multiplying the total podcasts available at any one time.

The access route for readers/listeners to *Guardian* podcasts is outlined in this article by Neil McIntosh, which appears on the site:

How to listen to our audio and podcasts

Neil McIntosh
Thursday June 8, 2006
Guardian Unlimited

Guardian Unlimited produces hours of audio every week, across a range of subjects. The good news is that all you need to listen is the computer you are using now—no special software or gadgets required (although a broadband internet connection makes things much, much faster).

Listening on your computer

Every bit of Guardian Unlimited audio is available to play immediately through your web browser. Click on the 'listen now' link next to each piece of audio on the site—a standard setup on any PC or Mac should allow you to listen straight away via your speakers or headphones.

Subscribe free via iTunes

Some of Guardian Unlimited's audio is daily, weekly, or part of a series, and we offer these as podcasts. Podcasts are simply audio files offered via a mechanism that makes it easy to keep up with new editions.

You can find a full list of regular shows on our <u>podcast blog</u>. The easiest way to subscribe, free of charge, to our series is through Apple's <u>iTunes software</u>, and the related iTunes Music Store.

If you don't have the iTunes software for your Windows PC or Mac OSX computer, you can download it for free <u>here</u>.

You access the iTunes Music Store through the iTunes software on your PC or Mac.

If you already have the latest version of iTunes installed, then simply click on the 'subscribe free via iTunes' link where it appears. You'll be taken directly into iTunes, and the podcast page for the relevant show will load. Simply click on the 'subscribe' button to automatically download new shows for free.

If you have an iPod music player which you synch with that computer, subscribing also means the podcast will be loaded to your iPod the next time you connect it to the computer.

Subscribing as a podcast with other devices and software

For all our podcasts you'll find the podcast feed URL on the front page of this, our podcast blog. You can paste these URLs into the podcast-ready feed reader of your choice.

(*Source*: http://www.guardian.co.uk/podcasts/story/0,,1793369,00.html. Copyright *Guardian* News & Media Ltd 2007)

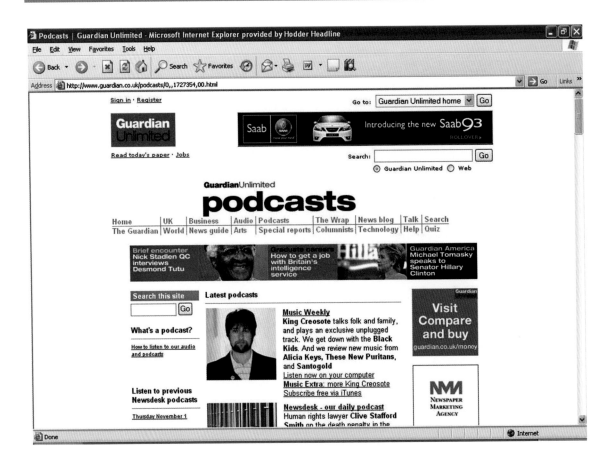

Figure 35 *Guardian* podcasts: a strategic response to 'We Media'.
(*Source*: Guardian News & Media Ltd 2007)

Exam Practice Question

'Newspapers will soon only exist online.' Referring specifically to your case study, discuss this claim.

photograph, film and, via broadband, publish eye witness footage that gives them a huge advantage over news photographers arriving at a scene considerably later. Indeed, the official news coverage, mediated as it is by politically compromised journalists, is increasingly at odds with eye witness images that tell a different story.

In conclusion, to really get to grips in your case study work on the newspaper industry it is vital that you research specific examples of threat and response. While newspapers are very vulnerable and threatened by a range of developments and trends, they are very much still alive. The industry, employment structures and distribution practices have been transformed. Online versions continue to appear, but the old fashioned newspaper still survives in its national, regional and international forms. This dynamic, of change, threat, competition and counter-strategy, is what you must explore, and at a more analytical level the question to ask is—what difference do these institutional changes make to the news itself?

IndyMedia UK

Indymedia UK (www.indymedia.org.uk) is a website founded on a 'DIY' ethos. Dan Gillmor coined the phrase 'We Media' to describe this potential 'taking over' of the media, in this case the news agenda, by ordinary citizens, and Lax (2004) cites Indymedia as an example of the democratic power of the internet. Here is an extract from Indymedia's mission statement:

> Inherent in the mainstream corporate media is a strong bias towards capitalism's power structures, and it is an important tool in propagating these structures around the globe. While the mainstream media conceal their manifold biases and alignments, we clearly state our position. Indymedia does not attempt to take an objective and impartial standpoint. Indymedia UK clearly states its subjectivity.

(*Source*: www.indymedia.org.uk)

Indymedia is an open publishing forum, where anybody is free to author and publish news reports (through a 'publish' button on the site) on issues concerned with oppositional politics and struggles for freedom. These include things like anti-war campaigning, anti-racism, ecology, education, animal liberation, social struggle and gender. The site is part of a worldwide collective. A monthly video bulletin of Indymedia's news provision is posted at www.indymedia.org.

Lax (2004) describes the simplicity of how the internet could threaten the stability of news providers more fundamentally:

> The falling costs of computer technology and internet access, and simpler authoring software, mean that it is almost as easy for a solitary individual or tiny group to put their aims and thoughts on the World Wide Web as it is for the corporate or state giants. It is also just as easy in principle for someone anywhere in the world to look at those ideas as to seek the views of News Corporation.

(*Source*: Lax, 2004: 220)

But we must be cautious—as Lax states, this is only in principle. So why is Indymedia included as a case study for the Newspapers topic? Well, it's to help us understand that newspapers are not only having to respond to other media agencies providing news that is quicker, more interactive, constantly updating, less expensive and much more environmentally friendly. They are also having to respond to a 'clawing back' of power over the news agenda by the public, through peer to peer blogs on countless websites where citizens exchange their own versions of news events or create their own news entirely, and more formally through campaigning websites like Indymedia who are actively trying to transform the news agenda for the purposes of changing the way news is circulated.

Chapter 3.4
Radio

To succeed in this section of the Key Media Concepts exam, you need to develop a case study on a particular radio station or media group operating in the contemporary radio industry and producing and/or distributing radio programmes in the UK. The focus will be on how this institution relates to:

Production: recording and broadcasting radio
Distribution: promoting content and broadcasting it on FM, LW, digitally and via TV, the internet and through podcasts
Consumption: people listening and/or downloading and subscribing.

This section of the book will provide an overview of contemporary radio production, distribution and consumption in relation to UK audiences. Two case study starting points are provided, one of which you may wish to pursue further for this unit.

Radio has been a constantly threatened and constantly evolving and transforming media form. When television arrived and threatened radio with extinction, the audio medium survived by playing to its relative strengths. For example, radio was broadcasting throughout the day and in the early hours, whereas television (until relatively recently) was an afternoon and evening medium only. In addition, radio was portable as it could be listened to at work or while the listener did something else, and this became even more important when car radios became standard. The content of radio programmes also shifted to areas less covered by television, for example talk, news and music have come to dominate, and radio accepts its status of 'background' media—one not requiring full attention. Increasingly the radio became interactive by giving listeners more and more air time on phone-in programmes, which now dominate some stations.

Public Service Broadcasting

Public Service Broadcasting (PSB) in the UK is normally associated with the BBC, but in fact the four other terrestrial channels and radio broadcasters have a public service remit as well. The idea dates back to an early Director General of the BBC, Lord Reith, who stipulated that the BBC should, in equal measure, inform, educate and entertain. Because the BBC are funded by taxation—the public paying for the station through the licence fee—they are obliged to stick to this responsibility and they cannot accept money from advertisers. The view is that money from advertising compels a broadcaster to achieve higher ratings and that this influences decisions over what programmes get made and broadcast. By funding itself in this way, the BBC are not reliant necessarily on huge audiences, which means they can afford to make programmes for a wider spectrum of people and programmes that may be less obviously 'entertaining' and instead more educational and informative.

The debate over the future of PSB really comes down to this question: In the digital, de-regulated, open market media world, should a broadcaster give the public what they want, or what they ought to want? But even this simple question is made more complex by the idea of 'pull media', whereby the public are no longer being given everything—instead they are taking and using and increasingly making media for themselves.

The Impact of Technology

All media have been transformed by digital technology, and radio is no exception. By 2010 the Digital Radio Development Bureau forecast that half the population will be reached by this new version of the old 'wireless'. As digital radios become cheaper and more people switch on to digital radio through the television and over the internet, this figure will grow. At present, however, digital radio has an ironic lack of portability when compared with

Conduct a small scale research exercise in your local region, to gauge the take up of digital radio and who is winning the battle for listeners. Select a sample that you feel represents a cross section of society (young, middle aged, senior, both genders, mix of ethnicity and people from different areas within the region that you feel represent the social mix).

Produce a simple questionnaire that will be clear, quick to complete and user-friendly. Make sure you work ethically—do not ask direct questions about age or salary. The survey needs to produce some simple, quantitative data—how many people have a DAB radio? Of those that do, what do they listen to on it? How much of it is digital only broadcasting and how much is the same material as on AM/FM but through a digital receiver?

When you have your data, share it with other groups so you maximise the sample and then express your data in percentages and broken down by demographic groups.

AM/FM radio. The two key developments which will radically energise the digital radio industry will be the standard installation of digital radio in the car and the standard availability of digital radio through the mobile phone.

The digital radio industry is defined by multiplexes—these are bands of the broadcasting spectrum which a broadcasting institution can operate (a slice of cake is perhaps the most useful metaphor for this). The BBC dominate at present, but whichever organisation is controlling a bandwidth, the key decision that has to be made is one of quality or quantity, since the options are to broadcast more channels across the bandwidth at a lesser sound quality or fewer channels with higher quality. This is a simple matter of physics and considerably less complicated than many institutional aspects of media business!

The BBC's main rivals in the digital industry sector at present are Channel 4 and GCap (who own Digital One)—a merger of two commercial radio companies, GWR and Capital.

The advantages of digital radio to the producer and consumer are, as for all new media, obvious. More choice (but not necessarily quality) is easily enabled, as it is possible to broadcast more material at the same time through this technology. The proliferation of content allows for more diversity in programming (providing the funding source is conducive). Music radio is a very good example, as whole channels are devoted to genres and styles of music.

A DAB radio allows for a much easier listening experience because it avoids issues with better or worse reception/tuning (for example, all BBC digital radio is broadcast on the same frequency, whereas for analogue it varies for different parts of the UK). It also enables pausing of live radio (though how much this feature is actually used is something you might want to research). The on-radio screen facility allows broadcasters to transmit information through text to listeners, which may open up new opportunities for mutually beneficial promotion (for example, the name of a track and the artist appearing on the screen so the listener can purchase or download the music more easily if they don't hear the information in between songs).

Music Radio

Note: This material appears in both Chapter 2: Music and Chapter 4: Radio, highlighting its significance as an example of convergence.
The impact of the 'MP3 culture' or the 'iPod generation' on music radio is complex—they offer extraordinary challenges, making DJs and a one-dimensional play list very old fashioned—yet music radio is currently more popular than ever. The most

Radio 5 Live

BBC Radio 5 Live is very important to the BBC, as it has lost the fight for televised rights for sport over recent years, mainly to BSkyB. Radio 5 Live is the leading broadcaster of live sport on radio, with Talk Sport its main rival. It retains its market share through a number of key strategies—broadcasting simultaneously on the digital sister channel 5 Live Sports Extra allows the station to offer a similar (albeit smaller) element of choice to interactive televised sport—for example, live Test Match cricket is broadcast all day on 5 Live Sports Extra, with updates on the main channel, and when two important football matches are played at the same time this structure allows for both to be covered.

The BBC, on both TV and radio, have increasingly developed the strategy of 'spreading' material over analogue and digital services, in order to entice non digital consumers to upgrade their equipment. Combining News and Sport, 5 Live is a very interesting case study for you to develop further in relation to the audience. Starting with the BBC website and perhaps by contacting 5 Live yourself for some demographic information about who the audience is, you may like to research some answers to the following questions:

1 What strategies have 5 Live used to respond to the digital environment?
2 How much of the audience activity seems to define radio as a 'pull medium' in this case? (Also see 'The Concept Formally Known as the Audience' earlier in this section.)
3 As the BBC is a publicly funded public service broadcaster (as described earlier in this section), how does 5 Live fulfil its responsibilities to the audience?

Get together in a group of three and each student take one of the following innovations mentioned in the Radio 3.0 commentary in Case Study 3.16:

- DAB plug-ins on MP3 players (e.g. the new iPod)
- Online radio stations
- Digital radio on mobile phones.

(By the time you read this, any one of these developments may have gone mainstream, but at the time this book was written they were ideas waiting to become reality.)

Now imagine there is a space of 300 words in this book right here, for you to update the section. Each student should write 100 words on the Radio 3.0 element they have chosen. Try to adopt the same tone as the rest of this book, i.e. write for AS Media students who need to understand how these technological developments are transforming the radio industry (or not!).

Radio 3.0

Radio 3.0 is (yet another) buzz-term that describes the next generation of radio, with Radio 2.0 describing the advent of digital radio (DAB). The following commentary from James Cridland at the 2007 Radio 3.0 Conference is from BBC Radio's 'Pods and Blogs' website.

The Radio 3.0 event in London, aimed to look at where radio goes next in an increasingly competitive marketplace. Jenny Abramsky, BBC Director of Radio, opened the event revealing the launch before the end of the year of DAB plug-ins for MP3 players, a way to keep the next generation in tune with the wireless. There was a lot of talk during the day about the ongoing growth of digital radio, although Phil Riley of Chrysalis Radio was keen to point out the commercial sector is paying for digital development out of their own profits. He also likened multi platform to high stakes gambling, having to decide whether to back Sky, Freeview, mobile or online with development money. He went on to pretty much dismiss online listening, pointing out the BBC's 15 million online listening hours per month is a tiny fraction of the 1 billion listening hours per week across the whole sector. Last FM and Pandora were dismissed as 'inconsequential', along with any other online radio station. Commercial radio is alive and well according to Riley, with Galaxy in the Midlands reaching 54 per cent of the teenage population. Didn't look so healthy though an hour later, when the man in the expensive suit from Ofcom revealed that commercial radio revenues are down 4.5 per cent year on year and 40 per cent are actually losing money. He also predicted many small stations may not survive. Digital listening is now at 14 per cent but predicted to rise to 90 per cent in the next ten years. Although I did begin to think he was making stuff up to see if we were paying attention.

(*Source*: www.bbc.co.uk/blogs/podsandblogs/radio/)
(Accessed 7 September 2007)

James Cridland is Head of Future Media and Technology, Audio and Music at the BBC. Elsewhere on his blog, which can be accessed through the Pods and Blogs site, he suggests that radio is actually the most successful medium there is at evolving to survive under the threat of digital and online media forms. The examples he cites are podcasts— with the BBC in particular having made a selection of its programmes available for downloading and transferring to an MP3 player for several years already. Radio streaming is a more established trend, with listeners using their PC or laptop to access radio at work or on holiday, for example. The one aspect of the digital revolution that has not, to date, had an impact on radio is the subscription/pay per view environment, as there are no predictions yet in relation to 'pay per listen' radio or even subscription to radio channels. And a more low-tech but equally radical development has been the ease of downloading and saving audio files in comparison to taping radio, which was always much clumsier than recording from the television.

BBC 6 Music

Launched in 2002, BBC 6 Music caters for an audience wanting to listen to a range of music that is not traditionally played on its other stations—music labelled 'alternative', as well as punk, jazz, funk and hip-hop. It plays new music but also makes extensive use of the BBC's own music session archives, including the famous Peel Sessions. It can be accessed through DAB but also offers interactive features such as email, text and chat rooms that are integrated into the airtime. The idea of integrity and credibility is important for the identity of the station. Here, Ashley Layton (2007) describes the way the station combines this credibility with technological innovation, by embracing:

> . . .the next generation of radio in the digital age with online music chat rooms during live broadcasts, in-studio webcams and, of course, accessibility through radio, television and the internet. This has expanded, of course, to include podcasting, allowing an audience to listen to certain shows wherever, whenever. Before his move to sister station Radio 2, Russell Brand's 6Music podcast reached as high as second in the iTunes top 10. The audience that listens to 6Music is not concerned with the date or the genre of the music they are listening to. All they care about is that it's good music played by DJs who know their stuff. You might say that this is a niche audience: the hard core music lovers/geeks. Yet the increase in listeners would suggest this isn't the case. In the iTunes era, as the accessibility of music dramatically increases, people do slowly seem to be less interested in the charts and more concerned with hearing a variety of decent music.

(*Source*: Layton, 2007: 32–33)

tangible outcome of music radio's response to downloading has been to place more importance on the music itself and less on the presenters. This, as Miranda Sawyer (2007) points out, is an unexpected victory for the late John Peel. Some stations have dispensed with presenters entirely, while others have made the focus of conversation much more explicitly about the music and the credibility of the music played a key ingredient.

> These are strange days for radio. More and more of us are listening to it, but we're not tuning into the same station. Music radio is all over the shop. You can have non-stop oldies, never-ending alternative; you can have cheesy DJ banter, or wit and knowledge. The only problem, I find, is locating a show that does everything you want.

(Sawyer, 2007: 5)

Exam Practice Question

How has your case study institution responded to the pace of change for radio?

Production Link

The main task for radio in the Foundation Portfolio requires an understanding of local radio conventions. In order to get this right, it will be useful to employ your understanding of local radio audiences and institutional practices. In particular, will your local radio news bulletin be broadcast by a public service channel, a commercial channel or a digital channel, or via the internet (or a combination of these)? Once you have decided on this, it is sensible to carry out some research into the 'mission' and ethos of local radio providers in your area that have this profile. For example, if you decide that your news bulletin will be broadcast on the hour in the middle of a music programme catering for a wide audience in a particular region, the conventions are going to be very different to a bulletin for a regional Asian speech-based radio station. Not only the news values, but also the presentation style, the members of the public selected for the vox-pop and the tone and register of the broadcast will be specific.

Link to A2

If you progress to A2 you may study **Media in the Online Age**, **Media and Collective Identity**, **Contemporary Media Regulation** or **Global Media**. Any of these topics will allow you to develop further your understanding of contemporary radio in its institutional contexts, for example:

How is the radio industry regulated and with what effect, in comparison to previous forms of monitoring?

How does local radio support a sense of regional identity and community? How has radio responded to the global media environment and how much radio is international in its coverage and scope?

Perhaps the A2 topic that builds most clearly on the material we have covered in this section in relation to AS is **Media in the Online Age**, with regard to which you could research further Radio 3.0 and the development of web radio.

Chapter 3.5
Magazines

To succeed in this section of the Key Media Concepts exam, you need to develop a case study on a particular magazine published by an institution within the contemporary magazine industry and distributed in the UK. The focus will be on how this magazine is produced, distributed (promoted and sold in print format and online) and consumed (subscribed to, purchased or downloaded). The importance of advertising will be a major feature. This section of the book will provide an overview of contemporary magazine market, distribution and consumption in relation to UK readers and two case study starting points, one of which you may wish to pursue further for this unit.

The Big Players

There are five major publishing companies dominating the UK magazines market:

1 Emap
2 IPC Media
3 National Magazine Company
4 Conde
5 Dennis.

Publishers target a range of mainstream and niche audiences and go to great lengths to define as closely as possible the reader of each title so they can provide this information to advertisers and sell space. Advertising is by far the most lucrative element of magazine publishing, earning far more money than circulation, so this must never be forgotten when studying magazines as *products* as well as texts. For your research for this unit, it is very easy to download from any of the major publishers' websites an advertising information pack which is very useful for discovering how magazines work in the marketplace.

Case Study 3.18

Emap

Emap started out as a local newspaper company in 1947. Sixty years on, it produces over 150 consumer magazines and distributes them to a global audience. Emap Consumer Media comprises the majority of the portfolio, publishing 70 titles from *FHM* and *Heat* to *Closer*, *Empire*, *Max Power*, *Angling Times* and *Today's Golfer*. The portfolio is grouped into six sectors, as follows:

Special interest titles (Emap Active)
Bird Watching
Country Walking
Coach and Bus Week
Digital Photo
Garden Answers
Garden News
Model Rail
Practical Fishkeeping
Rail
Steam Railway
Trail
Your Horse
Natural World
Nintendo
Angling Times
Golf Weekly
Golf World
Improve your Coarse Fishing
Match
Match Angling Plus
Sea Angler
Today's Golfer
Trout and Salmon
Trout Fisherman

Automotive titles (Emap Automotive)
Car
Parker's Car Price Guide
Parker's Used and New Car Chaser
Land Rover Owner International
Max Power
Revs
Practical Classics
Classic Cars
Classic Bike
Motor Cycle News
MCN Sport
Performance Bikes
Bike
Ride
What Bike?
Automotive Management
Fleet News

Young women's titles (Emap élan)
New Woman
Top Santé
Bliss
More!

Entertainment and style titles (Emap East)
Arena
Arena Homme Plus
Pop
Empire
FHM
ZOO

Celebrity and women's weekly titles (Emap Entertainment)
Heat
Closer

Music magazines (Emap Performance)
Kerrang!
Mojo
Q
Mixmag
Sneak

It is important to recognise that editorial policy can only be fully understood in relation to institutional contexts. For example, *ZOO* is very unlike other titles in the Emap entertainment and style portfolio, but very similar to *Nuts*, which is produced by a rival publisher. So as well as delivering audiences to advertisers, publishers are also attentive to market trends and competitors' new titles.

Activity 3.11

Emap is the second most successful magazine publisher operating in the UK market. Find out who the first is, and produce a list of their portfolio like the one in the Emap case study.

The Impact of Technology

Like all media forms, web 2.0 technology has had a major impact on magazine publishing. Online magazines already exist, but as they are not as portable as hard copy magazines, media commentators predict that by 2020 only 10 per cent of magazine reading will be from hard copies on paper.

E-paper is the technology which will enable the 'e-zine', having the advantages of being small and portable, similar in aesthetics to print and fairly cheap to run from a battery. The advantages for advertisers, with the ability for ads to change, as on the internet, are obvious. A further threat to magazines, though, is the idea that 'social publishing' from peer to peer over the internet will appeal more to the public than the 'push media' of magazines produced

Case Study 3.19

Play and *PSW*

This case study on videogames magazines links to other topics and units. It is relevant for a study of the videogames industry, while the Foundation Portfolio section of this book includes guidance on producing a music magazine, with the emphasis on striking a balance between promotion and critique. The same applies for videogames magazines. For a magazine that is closely related to a commercial industry to be successful, there needs to be some 'mutual back-scratching' with the commercial players in the industry. For example, interviews or preview features might be given in exchange for free publicity (known as 'below the line' promotion). But the readership will not be attracted to a magazine that is little more than a collection of adverts, so it is essential for editors to ensure a healthy ratio of critique to promotion—this is achieved by reviews, input from readers and industry comment/monitoring.

Let's take two examples to illustrate this—the September 2007 editions of *Play* and *PSW*, both of which are exclusively targeting an audience of Playstation gamers (see Figure 36*a* & *b*).

The promotional aspects of *Play* are most notably linked to the ongoing marketing campaign for *Grand Theft Auto 4* (*GTA 4*). The magazine offers a free DVD with game trailers and screen shots, and a book—*Grand Theft Auto—the unofficial history*. In marketing terms this is a clever double strategy—the anticipation for the new game is maintained through this teaser approach and at the same time the long-running franchise context for *Grand Theft Auto* is reinforced through a celebration of the first three games in the series. While the DVD and book are produced by Imagine Publishing and not Rockstar Games, this is pure promotion.

GTA 4 also features as a below-the-line element in *PSW*, with the editor, Ian Dean, being given a 'sneak preview' playing experience. To maintain the balance between promotion and critique, there are one or two negative comments but the overall tone is very positive. A feature like this arises from what is sometimes described as a press 'junket', whereby an audience of journalists from various publications are invited to a preview or a launch.

While there is no compulsion to be positive about a new game, even the least cynical observer can identify the mutual benefits of such arrangements—the magazine sells copies on the basis of desire for the new product and the game remains in the public consciousness.

(a)

(b)

Figure 36 *Play* and *PSW*: balancing promotion and critique.

by huge corporations. As with all new forms of technology, only time will tell.

However, the magazine market remains one of the most traditional, conservative and old-fashioned media sectors, as the success of magazines with very clear gender demarcations—from *Nuts* and *Zoo* to *Glamour* and *Cosmopolitan*—seems to indicate. The male-targeted examples cited here were recently moved by supermarket chains in the UK to the top shelf, to indicate their unsuitability for children and thus their status as soft porn (rather than 'male lifestyle' as the publishers prefer).

Circulation figures in 2006 (from the Audit Bureau of Circulation) show that the magazines most adversely undermined by web 2.0 appear to be those aimed at teenagers, presumably because this is the group most likely to defect to MySpace. According to David Hepworth (2007), the changes impacting on the magazine industry are both structural and permanent. An element in the declining appeal of teen magazines is one that is less obvious at first—the recent Government legislation against junk food advertising in the wake of Jamie Oliver's media campaign for healthy eating has led to a down turn in advertising revenue for magazines aimed at teenagers: an example of one set of circumstances in the media affecting another sector entirely. On a broader scale, Hepworth argues that the demographic levelling of web 2.0 revolutionises the way advertisers think and undermines the traditional audience groupings previously used for magazine promotion.

> The economics of the magazine industry are traditionally rooted in the idea that a *Vogue* reader is worth more than a *Glamour* reader who is worth more than a *Closer* reader. The web flattens out these distinctions, which may explain why cost per thousand in that medium is so much under pressure.

(Hepworth, 2007: 33)

To fully understand Hepworth's point, we need to focus on the traditional model of advertising in magazines, which has been to group the public into the following social groupings (taken from the National Readership Survey):

A   High ranking professionals
B   Middle ranking professionals
C1   'White collar' office workers
C2   Skilled manual workers
D   Semi and unskilled manual workers
E   The unemployed or those on benefits.

Media students need to know that this is how the industry has traditionally operated, but must balance this knowledge with a more critical analysis of the implications of these categories. Some obvious issues, pointed out by Sean Offord (2007), are that disposable income is not necessarily linked to occupation. How people actually spend money is unknown and household income doesn't tell us much about teenagers for example, who do not get counted. Media profiling groups have more recently developed new ways of classifying audiences, by looking at 'consumer personality types' such as 'aspirers' or 'early adopters'. These ways of understanding audiences draw on elements of psychometric profiling. Furthermore, in the above quote, Hepworth suggests that advertising on the web cannot follow the same patterns of stratification.

Case Study 3.20

Monkey

Monkey is an online only magazine which offers a similar diet of material to *Nuts* and *Zoo*, but with the added bonus of moving image clips and sound. Given that the 'lad mag' format has a pornographic element, it is easy to see how this might appeal. This is how the magazine describes itself on its website (which *is*, of course, the magazine):

The World's first weekly digital men's magazine has arrived and it's 100% FREE forever! Yes! Give us your email address and every Wednesday you'll get a link to the latest issue of Monkey. It's honestly the best way to break the back of your week! Monkey is the first men's magazine in the world to bring you full, living, breathing, singing, dancing, stripping, and exploding video. You can watch videos and movie trailers, listen to the latest in music and share incredible stuff with your friends. To get your Monkey every week you need to sign up. Signing up is easy and free, we just need your name and email address (plus postcode if you live in the UK) and that's it. Join the Monkey party today!

(*Source*: www.monkeymag.co.uk/registration/)
(Accessed 20 September 2007)

Monkey is not the product of an alternative, independent web distributor, however. Instead it is produced by Dennis, one of the main companies and a publisher already highly prolific in the 'lad mag' sector, with such titles as *Maxim* and *Stuff*. This is an example of a big media corporation realising that the best way to compete against a perceived threat is to harness its potential for yourself, in the same way as Rupert Murdoch recently acquired MySpace and the music industry started offering legal downloads.

Discussion point

How will *Monkey* make money if it doesn't sell hard copy magazines to readers?

Production Link

The print brief for Foundation Portfolio requires the production of elements of a new music magazine. Your understanding of the magazine market from this part of your studies will be invaluable if you apply it to the following questions before you begin:

1 How will the magazine find its niche in an increasingly fragmented market?
2 Which publisher's portfolio will this magazine fit into most easily?
3 How will the audience for the magazine be sold to advertisers?

To make the most effective synoptic links between the units, you should produce an information pack for advertisers for the magazine, outlining the typical reader and her/his lifestyle.

Exam Practice Question

Describe the various strategies used by the publisher of your case study magazine to secure its survival in the current marketplace.

Link to A2

If you progress to A2 Media, you will study one or more of a range of Critical Perspectives, several of which will offer the opportunity to further develop your knowledge of the magazine market. For example, you might consider the notion that magazines develop in their readers a sense of collective identity, or consider the playful 'pick and mix' magazine audience in terms of **Post Modern Media.** Or you might look at e-zines in relation to '**We Media**' or **Media in the Online Age.**

Chapter 3.6
Videogames

To succeed in this section of the Key Media Concepts exam, you need to develop a case study on a particular game, played on one or more platforms and distributed to players in the UK, and also a case study on new game technologies (HD, Blu Ray, online gaming). The focus will be on how this game relates to:

Production: designing and constructing the game
Distribution: promoting the game and distributing it and related products to audiences via retail and online
Consumption: buying, renting, sharing, downloading.

This section of the book will provide an overview of contemporary game production, distribution and consumption in relation to UK audiences. It includes three case study starting points, one of which you may wish to pursue further for this unit.

To avoid confusion, for the AS Media specification 'videogames' is the term you will be using to describe all games played on or via games consoles, phones and computers, as well as arcade games. The terms computer games and videogames are therefore interchangeable.

As this book keeps emphasising, media industries today frequently converge and videogames are perhaps the most obvious example of this. Videogames are one of the most influential media forms, as described by Marshall (2004):

> **Via electronic games, the entertainment industry has redirected itself and moved the idea of play into the structure and meaning of other forms, from film and television to popular music and radio. This shift is very much related to incorporating the essential component of electronic games and play more widely: interactivity. The kinds of engagement embodied by electronic games have become the benchmark for popular culture.**

(Marshall, 2004: 74)

The Gaming Industry

The global videogame industry is worth £20 billion. Its own publicity frequently proclaims that it is outperforming Hollywood, but this claim is taken with a pinch of salt by industry commentators. In the UK there is a games console in over a third of homes. Increasingly, convergence is dominating the development of gaming, with consoles acting as a 'hub' for a range of other entertainment and messaging/information activities and online gaming starting to take over from the purchasing of discs, cartridges and UMDs. The 'staggered' nature of technological development in this sector is cynical and strategic. New consoles are introduced so regularly that the time for which a console is the 'best' is limited to a few months, and each major player produces portable handheld versions of their consoles to accompany the one fixed in the home. Crucially, while even Apple and Microsoft have decided to increase profits by increasing compatibility— iTunes for the PC and Windows for Mac—it is rare for a home to house both a PC and a Mac, and similarly games consoles remain mutually exclusive. As a result it is not uncommon for a family to own two or more different consoles as well as a PC with gaming capability.

In the 1980s and 1990s, arcades were normally the first place that new games could be played. This seems strange now in the context of the current 'straight to console' strategy and the proliferation of downloading and online play. But there was a time when the home was a secondary venue for gameplay.

Development

A videogame comes to be played as a result of a complex institutional set of deals. Publishers enable games to be developed by financing the work of developers. Sometimes there are separate development and publishing companies, and sometimes they are one and the same.

The games are made by developers, some of whom work directly for the big companies who own the platforms and only produce for this format; others receive partial support financially from these companies; while another group are independent developers. The latter two types of developer make multi-platform games usually. The companies who own the platforms are huge multinationals—Sony (worth approximately $70 billion), Microsoft and Nintendo—and the platforms are the various consoles, computers or other hardware devices that we play the games on.

The institutional scale of games production is described here by Newman and Oram (2006):

> **Development teams working on a single title for the current generation of videogame systems frequently consist of more than 100 people, each with very specific areas of responsibility and expertise ranging from physics engine programming (ensuring that objects in the case world move and respond 'realistically') through AI (Artificial Intelligence) programming to ensure the other characters the player meets in the game present a consistent challenge and/or appear believable, to interface design, character animation, level design, movie 'cutscene' direction and quality assurance. Importantly, the growing team sizes have necessitated more accountable management structures with each team and subteam (i.e. responsible for level design, graphics, sound, interface, etc.) having a 'lead' who reports upwards in order to coordinate development and ensure the artistic and technical vision for the game is maintained.**
>
> (Newman and Oram, 2006: 28)

Partly because most games designers are contracted to big companies (although there is an 'indie' sector, see later in this section) and partly because, like the film industry, games are increasingly being produced to successful formulae (videogames are highly generic), some games publishers might be less willing to take risks with games than at earlier points in the industry's relatively short life. When a game is so successful that it can be sustained over a number of sequels, using the same intellectual property (copyright) over and over again, this is known as a franchise. *Grand Theft Auto*, *FIFA*, *Mario* and *The Sims* are four well known examples.

Activity 3.12

This section of the book provides a range of case studies on specific games, and you may wish to take one of these as a starting point for your Key Concepts research. But in order to become expert in how a specific game has come to fruition in a range of institutional contexts, starting from scratch with another game is productive.

Because this activity concludes with you making contact with people in the games industry, it is a good idea to work in a group and to check that other groups are not contacting the same people. Better still, make sure that each group is looking at a different game, so you can come together at the end and share your findings, thus broadening everyone's knowledge of the games industry instead of duplicating the same information.

Select a game that is not covered in this section and via the internet (any games site, Amazon or Wikipedia are good places to try first), identify the following:

1 Who are the development and publishing companies (they might be the same)?
2 Who is the distribution company?
3 What is the classification given to the game?
4 What is the scope of its availability—is it multi-platform or produced exclusively for one console? Is it on general release in retail form? Is it downloadable?

Next go to a generic games site (there are a range of very comprehensive sites but Gamespot and Gamezone are two notable examples) or go to the official site of the game or the platform(s). Take a look at the marketing materials available there—trailers, gameplay sequences, interviews with developers, posters. Look at the customer reviews on the games sites and also on Amazon—these are all aspects of distribution.

Finally, work out which of the various companies involved in making this game and getting it to our attention is the smallest, and via the 'contact' section of their website, get in touch with them and ask for more information on the role they played in the process.

The increasing synergy between the gaming industry and Hollywood has further perpetuated this franchise approach, as Marshall (2004) describes here:

> *Mario* defines Nintendo games as a brand as much as *Mickey Mouse* is emblematic of Disney. Likewise, Sega's *Sonic the Hedgehog* has a value as a convertible piece of intellectual property in the same way as Warner Brothers' *Bugs Bunny*. Game manufacturers are beginning to exercise their clout across the entertainment industry. Popular music is now played in games—especially those games that are connected to a musical subcultural style. Product placement, a now routine form of promotion through film and television, is currently a successful sought-after revenue line for electronic games.

(Marshall, 2004: 66)

Electronic Arts (EA)

The American games development company EA was formed in 1982 by Trip Hawkins and is now associated with a range of very successful sports games, games with a basis in popular film and sustained franchises such as *Medal of Honor*, *The Sims* and *Command and Conquer*.

Although EA's profits have fluctuated in comparison to Rockstar Games (see the Rockstar case study later in this section), much of the company's success has been as a result of developing games for multiple platforms and the practice of designing games that are revamped annually, such as FIFA 07, FIFA 08, etc., and the same strategy for golf, ice hockey, basketball and a range of other sports games. (Such a strategy might be considered cynical perhaps, but it is certainly lucrative.)

In 2007 EA pioneered the development of some of its successful games for the Mac computer, with *Harry Potter*, *Need for Speed* and *Command and Conquer* being made available. EA has a fairly predatory track record, often acquiring smaller design companies and thus taking ownership of the intellectual property rights for the games created by the newly owned designers. For example, when EA took over Maxis, it acquired the intellectual property rights and thus the legal ability to distribute the very successful *SimCity* and *Sims* franchises. As far as convergence goes, EA were originally resistant to online gaming. They refused access to their games on the Xbox Live after failing to agree terms with Microsoft over the carving up of money acquired from online gaming. This was eventually resolved when Microsoft agreed that players would have to connect to EA's own servers to facilitate online play.

EA distribute games under a number of subsidiary labels. The EA Games label relates to all the non-sporting games, while EA Sports (with its famous 'it's in the game' tagline) distributes sports simulation titles and EA Sports Big offers extreme sports games. EA Casual Entertainment distributes games for a range of platforms, including the *Harry Potter* series. EA Mythic has seen the company diversify into Massive Multiplayer Online Role Playing Games (MMORPG) developments. This has resulted from the acquisition of Mythic Entertainment, who produced *Dark Age of Camelot*. EA Mythic's latest MMORPG is *Warhammer Online: Age of Reckoning*. EA Mobile produce games for mobile phones and iPods, the *Sims* series has its own label, Pogo.com is an online games site acquired by EA and AOL's games channel is EA branded.

To give you an idea of how complex the 'behind the scenes' practices of media institutions are, consider this description (from Wikipedia) of the development context for EA Mythic's new *Warhammer Online* game:

> *Warhammer Online* development began under the development company Climax Online. The project was officially cancelled in June 2004 when Games Workshop determined that the roll-out costs would be too expensive. However, development on the game never actually stopped as Climax Online continued the project using their own funds until the company reported in late 2004 that the *Warhammer Online* project was shut down due to difficulty in securing a publishing agreement. With the licence available again, Games Workshop was approached by EA Mythic (then known as Mythic Entertainment), who were interested in acquiring the licence and developing a new project from scratch. A long standing relationship between several Games Workshop managers and the CEO of Mythic, Mark Jacobs, ensured that a deal was quickly reached. The *Warhammer Online* licence was acquired by Mythic on May 18, 2005.

Unlike the Climax Online project, *Warhammer Online* is not a joint venture with Games Workshop. As such, it will not use rules from either Warhammer Fantasy Battles or Warhammer Fantasy Roleplay.

(*Source*: http://en.wikipedia.org/wiki/Warhammer_Online:_Age_of_Reckoning#Development_history)
(Accessed 31 August 2007)

Indie designers

Increasingly, games designers are associated with publishers or distributors rather than working freelance. This change may reduce original creativity, if it means that games are commissioned rather than being designed first and marketed second. But there is still a wide range of independent game designers who are self-financing and in total creative control. These small institutions either rely on the internet for distribution or sell their games to a larger company after production. An example of an internet-reliant company is Three Rings Design, an online game developer operating from San Francisco. Three Rings Design's most notable development is the MMORPG *Puzzle Pirates*, in which the player is represented by a pirate avatar. An example of a small scale design company selling their products on is Zootfly, operating from Slovenia, who make action adventure games for the Xbox, Xbox 360, PS3 and PC use. The most famous Zootfly products are *First Battalion, Toy Wars* and *Panzer Elite Action*.

Distributors

Distributors, as for film or any other media form, come in between production and consumption, making sure that games are promoted to an audience and sold/rented/downloaded to maximise profits. The timing of releases and 'staggered' availability are crucial aspects of 'desire creation' around new games. And just as the BBFC act as an agent in the distribution process for films (see the Film part of this section), so do they 'gatekeep' the availability of videogames. For example, *Mario Party 8* for the Wii platform (see Case Study 3.23 on page 211) has an 11 classification in the UK. This classification will exclude large sections of the existing *Mario* audience from accessing the game (assuming the law works in this case).

Technologies and 'Next Generations'

A relatively recent player in the almost forty year history of the videogame industry, Sony has come to dominate the 'console wars' since the launch of Playstation. However, Nintendo and Microsoft are a constant threat, and the range of games designed for children to be played on the DS has made Nintendo the leading light in hand-held consoles. Prior to this 'Holy Trinity', Atari and Commodore had brief periods of supremacy. It is worth noting that all three of the current major players came to design game consoles as a diversification strategy. Nintendo started life as a trading cards company; Sony was originally a producer of entertainment hardware and has more recently become involved in the distribution of music, cinema and other media forms; and Microsoft is the dominant force in home and office computing. Sony's strategy in overtaking Nintendo was developed with the launch of PS2 in 2000 and as O'Brien (2008) observes, this was achieved by effectively beating Nintendo at their own game:

> Taking an idea from what Nintendo had done with generations of its handheld Game Boy console series, the PS2 was made backwards compatible with PS1 titles, offering the potential buyer the incentive to trade up to play bigger and better games, but also offering you the facility to play your old games too (and DVDs also), thereby spreading the potential target audience for the console through the demographic brackets. It was this kind of smart thinking that enabled Sony to get to be the boss of the videogames industry.

(McDougall and O'Brien, 2008)

Microsoft entered the games industry as a reaction to the success of the other companies, and a concern that ignoring this element of computer technology would threaten the world dominance of Bill Gates' company. The Xbox console distinguished itself from the PS2 through the inclusion of internet access. While the Xbox is a success, its sales figures are way behind those of the PS2.

In 2005 Nintendo fought back with the introduction of the X360 which, due to a range of institutional problems at Sony, hit the shops a year before the PS3. Both consoles featured new elements not necessarily related to gaming—big hard drives that can be used to store still and moving images and music, Blu Ray DVD (Sony) and HD-DVD (Microsoft)—further examples of convergence for you to consider. The more recent Nintendo Wii differs from previous consoles through its kinesthetic features, with players moving through space to play some games, as opposed to sitting down with a handset. This has helped Nintendo to reach out to a new type of gamer, as they have done with their range of simulation games played by younger children on the DS, with its connectivity feature.

So far, the history of the videogame industry has been characterized by the 'console/platform wars'. But as O'Brien (2008) suggests, the future may be different, as the downloading of games onto networks that support online gaming seems to be the inevitable context for the next generation. This may mean that in a few years' time games consoles and platforms may seem as old fashioned as CDs and cathode ray televisions do today.

> As broadband connection speeds increase will we want to have to keep buying physical media which takes up storage space in homes or will we shift to online storage of games and movies and TV programmes, where we don't physically own anything, we simply rent content when we want it—a futuristic equivalent of going to a video rental store and renting a DVD and a videogame for a couple of days. Perhaps our digital TV services will become so tailored and advanced that we simply do not require the physical presence of games consoles and PCs in the home—the possibilities are limitless and it is a foolish person who tries to predict with too much certainty which way institutions and audiences will carry all of us.

(McDougall and O'Brien, 2008)

Impact of Videogames on Education and Health

A perennial challenge for the videogame industry is the negative press and occasional 'moral panic' that can surround specific games and indeed the entire world of gaming. When looking for something to blame for perceived social problems caused by

Link to A2

If you progress to A2, you may study a number of critical perspectives on the media for which the practices of the videogame industry are key examples. For instance, you might consider the *Grand Theft Auto* franchise in relation to media regulation, or look at global marketing and distribution as a feature of the games industry. You may consider the next generation of internet gaming within the area of **Media in the Online Age**, or consider the status of particular videogames as '**Post Modern Media**'.

Hannah Montana (DS)

Buena Vista Games is the interactive entertainment part of multinational conglomerate, Walt Disney Company. Disney has total assets of around $55 billion and employs roughly 40,000 people worldwide.

Buena Vista itself recently acquired the video game developer Avalanche Software, and established a new start-up development studio in Vancouver, Canada, with a number of key personnel headhunted from the Canadian sector of Electronic Arts. The *Hannah Montana* DS game (see Figure 37) is an excellent example of media convergence, and proves that it is increasingly difficult to consider the videogame, music and film industries, television and the internet as separate domains. Somewhere in the complex interplay of production, distribution and consumption they usually weave together.

Hannah Montana is a TV show produced by It's a Laugh Productions and broadcast on the Disney Channel as a spin off from *That's So Raven*. The programme is Disney's most watched series and is now broadcast in over forty countries across the world. Numerous DVDs are available, a range of merchandising and three video games, of which the DS version is the third. A journey around the internet searching for the TV show/pop star/games is a good illustration of this converged state of affairs. Starting with a Google search, we are first led to Gamespot for a 'company line' on the game:

> **Miley Stewart is living a double life as a teen pop sensation known to millions as Hannah Montana. Her best friend Lilly is the only one who knows the truth—or so she thinks. Someone is threatening to reveal Hannah's secret! Miley and Lilly investigate their school, the boardwalk, stadium and the beach to uncover clues. Help solve the mystery and keep Hannah Montana's true identity secret so the show can go on!**
>
> (Source: www.ukgamespot.com/ds/action/HannahMontana/news)
> (Accessed 31 August 2007)

We then move to Wikipedia for a description of the Hannah Montana CD:

> **Hannah Montana is the soundtrack for the Disney Channel original series of the same name, it was released on October 24, 2006 via Walt Disney Records. The first eight songs on the album are sung by the character Hannah Montana, who is played by Miley Cyrus. There are also four songs by other artists, and another track, the last on the album, that is sung by Cyrus (out of her Hannah Montana character) and her father Billy Ray Cyrus. The soundtrack was the eighth best selling album of 2006 in the USA, with nearly two million copies sold that year. An estimated 3.2 million copies were sold worldwide.**
>
> (Source: http://en.wikipedia.org/wiki/Hannah_Montana_%28album%29)
> (Accessed 31 August 2007)

Following the hyperlinks on Wikipedia, we move to the Disney Channel's website and find out more about the TV show, then end up looking at the DVDs available on Amazon. There are DVDs of the TV show, and also *Hannah Montana: the Movie*, which is a spin-off film. Amazon also offers us books, CD soundtracks from the TV show and a range of *High School Musical* products.

Every internet search for Hannah Montana products leads the browser to *High School Musical* sooner or later, due to the fact that this is another Disney Channel franchise with the same target audience. Finally we end up on YouTube watching a video for 'The Other side of Me' that has been kindly uploaded by a 13-year-old. The video (of a TV performance) includes text informing us that the Disney Channel will broadcast the show, and the Disney Channel is also credited alongside the video on the YouTube page. There are 62,700 YouTube uploads for Hannah Montana, including one that shows the cast of *High School Musical* appearing on the show.

What does this tell us about the DS game for Hannah Montana? Is this a spin-off from a TV show? Partly, but it is also intertextually related to a range of films, online media access, books and, most significantly, the music industry. As is the case also for Disney's other recent blockbuster, *High School Musical*, the audience for the media product cannot be understood in relation to one discrete media industry.

Figure 37 The Nintendo DS game for Hannah Montana cannot be analysed without bearing witness to the contemporary nature of media convergence.
(Source: © W. Disney/Everett/Rex Features)

young people, concerns about falling levels of literacy, the increase in childhood obesity and worries about young people being less socially responsible than previous generations, videogames often provide an easy scapegoat. The capitalist system makes many people more affluent but also creates desires for consumer goods that the very poor cannot access. It is possible that this alienates many young people, creating problems in our communities, with violence the manifestation of this 'tear in the social fabric'. But of course it is very hard for society to do much about this, whereas if videogames are seen as the problem, the solution (ban some of them or restrict access to them) is much simpler. This is not to say that there are no problems associated with over-exposure to violent games or that the classification of games for certain age groups is not essential. Rather, the point is that the 'effects' of games can only be really understood in a broader and more complex social context.

The videogame industry responds to these perceptions in a variety of ways. In some cases, the promoters of games have realised that concern among the parent culture and the establishment is appealing to the younger gaming generation, and have developed marketing campaigns to exploit this.

More recently, however, a range of games have been produced that develop the idea that games can be good for your health—for example, brain training games on the DS; 'edutainment' games that are of relevance to the educational curriculum; and a range of kinaesthetic games that can be used as a form of intensive exercise. Here are three examples of gaming that seem to offer a more 'healthy' experience.

1 Holyhead Secondary School in Birmingham has introduced a pilot scheme in which pupils are given PSP consoles in the classroom. This venture was designed by a Sony employee who has been recruited by Holyhead. Here is the response of the local newspaper, clearly providing very good publicity for Sony as an antidote to the usual concerns about games:

> **There won't be any shoot 'em up or football games on offer—the consoles will stay in the classroom and will be initially used to help French, History and Geography lessons.**
>
> (Tony Collins: Education Correspondent, *Birmingham Mail*, 28 March 2007)

2 A company called Immersive Education, in collaboration with the Institute of Education at the University of London have designed *Mission Maker*—software which enables children in

schools to create elements of a fantasy videogame and as a result learn how games combine narrative, character and rule systems. This software is being used by English teachers, and the children participating are involved in creativity, critical thinking, literacy skills and imagination. Quoted in a *Times Educational Supplement* article, a 14-year-old pupil here reports on the activity:

> **You have to write the game, the rules, develop the characters. You get to express how imaginative you can be. You have to use logic. You can't just do whatever you want.**
>
> (Wallace, 2006: 10)

3 In response to the idea that too much gaming can make you unhealthy, as it prevents you going outdoors and taking part in sport or exercise, a research project in Birmingham involved an experiment in a primary school where children wore heart rate monitors while playing kinaesthetic games in the lunch break. The scientific readings were then compared to the data from pupils in a PE lesson and from children playing outside during lunch:

> **In regard to heart rate monitoring, active video game play resulted in a favourable physical activity profile that is comparable or better than heart rate values recorded for regular daily physical activity or regular school lunch time physical activity. In this instance, the use of active video game play appears promising as an alternative method to enhance children's physical activity. Considering that physical activity during active game play is greater than general lunch time activity and physical activity following playground based interventions, it may be prudent for the scientific/health/educational communities to consider the potential uses of active video gaming in promoting physical activity or attracting children who are not physically active to activity in a different way.**
>
> (McDougall and Duncan, 2008: 4)

Mario Party 8

Published by Hudson Soft, a company owned by the Konami Corporation, the *Mario Party* series are exclusively made for Nintendo, and *Mario Party 8* is the first to be made for the Wii console. The Wii allows the game to be played with kinaesthetic features, such as motion control—jumping, hopping, running, rowing, punching, steering, handling a balancing pole while walking a tight rope, and using the pointer to shoot, drop and select toppings in a cake-decorating competition and select the correct answers in game show challenges.

The target audience for *Mario Party 8* is a hybrid of existing *Mario* players who have grown up with the long-running series, and owners of the Wii console, for whom this may be their first *Mario* purchase. The emphasis of the marketing campaign was very much on the social, active elements of the gaming experience.

The games industry is hugely reliant on good feedback in the form of reviews, and while videogame magazines are important, the internet is a more powerful vehicle for peer-to-peer critical comment. Here is a review of *Mario Party 8* uploaded to a games site by the brilliantly self-named 'Grim Wiiper'.

The game fits perfectly in with the Wii's image as a party-friendly console. As with all parties, the more people you get involved, the better Mario Party 8 becomes, and if you can find three friends who are willing and able to buy into the game's simplistic and charming gameplay, you're almost guaranteed to have a good time. Take a look at Nintendo's current marketing plan and you'll see that this is exactly the image they want to promote, that of the Wii as a system that people will gather around to enjoy together.

Played alone, against the computer, the game is barely worth popping out of its case. But, having even one other human opponent ups the fun exponentially—you just can't get the same satisfaction out of trash talking against a faceless computerized enemy.

There's also a definite sense of refinement to the franchise formula here, a given considering that this is the eighth instalment in the series. In case you've never played a Mario Party game before, the basics are pretty easy to grasp. In the main game mode, you and three other contestants run around a board collecting coins, competing in various mini-games and collecting Stars, which ultimately decides the game's outcome.

The biggest change from previous versions, obviously, lies in the use of the Wii Remote, and depending on the game, you'll either use it as a pointer to shoot onscreen objects, turn it sideways and use it as a simple joypad, or move it around to take advantage of the motion-sensing capabilities. The mini-games themselves are varied and have different objectives—collect the most coins, survive until the timer runs out—but it's nothing that we haven't seen before, which isn't a bad thing at all.

(*Source*: The Grim Wiiper | 05/18/2007 | 17:18:36 PM PST, posted at: http://www.gamepro.com/nintendo/wii/games/reviews/112548.shtml)
(Accessed 31 August 2007)

Rockstar Games and Grand Theft Auto 4

Rockstar Games are the producers of the hugely popular and controversial *Grand Theft Auto* (GTA) series (see Figure 2 on page 5). The company is made up of various subsidiaries located in Japan, Leeds, Lincoln, Edinburgh, San Diego, Toronto and Vancouver. The larger group is itself a subsidiary of the American company, Take Two Interactive. Although Rockstar devotes much attention to the UK market, with half of its smaller operations being based here, the commercial dividends benefit Take Two Interactive in the American economy.

The *Grand Theft Auto* franchise has been extremely lucrative for Rockstar, as have other successful and equally controversial games such as *Manhunt* and *Bully*. Altogether, over 50 million copies of the various versions (up to version 3) of GTA have been sold, and GTA3 is the biggest selling videogame of all time. The GTA series has now been established for eleven years, with the fourth version released strategically in time for Christmas 2007. This franchise is one of only a handful of game series with such longevity. As O' Brien points out (2008), there are interesting differences in the ways the games were marketed, with the first game being promoted as a car driving/racing game and GTA2 being far more explicit about the controversial crime context that led to such concern from the parent culture. For the second instalment of the series, the promotional campaign offered the gaming community the opportunity to 'carjack innocent victims, assassinate rivals, steal drug shipments' and to 'Go anywhere. Steal anything. Jack anyone.'

The remainder of this case study relates to the marketing of *Grand Theft Auto 4* in the autumn of 2007. For a more detailed account of the GTA series in relation to media concepts, debates around the effects of the games, the technological aspects of the design of the games and the way the game fits into the gaming industry, see *'Studying Videogames'* (McDougall and O'Brien, 2008).

Selling Grand Theft Auto 4

Whereas the first three GTA games were released first on the Playstation and then formatted for the Xbox and PSP, *Grand Theft Auto 4* was scheduled for release on the Playstation 3 and the Xbox 360 at the same time. O'Brien speculates on the reasons for this:

> **The simultaneous release on PS3 and X360 is a first for the series, as the titles have been PlayStation-oriented in the first instance—releases have come first for the PS consoles and then have been 'ported' or converted for other platforms such as the X-Box or PSP. This possibly indicates that Rockstar are not looking to favour either Microsoft or Sony until a winner emerges from the battle for dominance between the PS3, X360 and Nintendo's Wii, this shows how fluid and dynamic the console and videogame market is.**
>
> (McDougall and O'Brien, 2008)

Chapter 5 on magazines earlier in this section contains information about videogame magazines such as *PSW*, whose September 2007 edition carried a 'preview' feature about *GTA 4*. The report focused on four new elements of the game in particular—pedestrians will mug one another rather than just act as bystanders; a new 'physics engine' improves the movement of Niko, the new avatar hero; the game will include its own online community; and the publisher is currently auditioning gamers to be recorded for the in-game radio station. Perhaps most interestingly for your studies of *Grand Theft Auto* as a 'post modern game' there are extra-textual references, described here by Ian Dean, in a report on his preview gaming experience:

The dialogue is sharp and is filled with cultural references. This has always made GTA more than just another man-with-a-gun game. 'Guns don't kill people, videogames do' screams Goldberg, in a knowing nod to anti-game lawyer, Jack Thompson. We put a bullet in his head and watch him tumble out the window—and with it a word of warning to anyone who wants to pick a fight with Rockstar.

(Dean, 2007: 75)

However, a delay in the release of *GTA4* until 2008 was the subject of some panic in the industry, as this article (Kalning, 2007) posted on MSN describes:

'Grand Theft Auto' delay shakes industry
Both Sony and Microsoft were counting on the game to move consoles

By Kristin Kalning
Games editor
MSNBC
Updated: 8:29 p.m. ET Aug. 3, 2007

When Take-Two Interactive announced last week that it would delay 'Grand Theft Auto IV' until 2008, Wall Street punished the company's stock and sent a chill wind throughout the game industry. The much-anticipated title, along with Electronic Arts' 'Madden 08' and Bungie's 'Halo 3', was expected to account for one-third of all game sales this holiday season. And Sony and Microsoft were both counting on 'GTA IV' to help sell PlayStation 3 and Xbox 360 consoles. That was a fair bet. The gangster-adventure series, created by controversy-courting Rockstar Games, was critical to the success of the PlayStation 2.

So what does this mean for the consoles duking it out for supremacy? Or the rest of the games planned for the Christmas season? Can a delayed ship date from one game—from October to sometime in early 2008—really take the wind out of the game industry's revenue sails for 2007?

'It is a big deal from the point of view that this title was expected to be a driver of hardware—particularly PlayStation 3 hardware,' said Colin Sebastian, an analyst with Lazard Capital Markets. 'But big picture, it's more important for a title to be at a level of quality that's expected.'

In a phone conference with reporters and analysts Thursday, Take-Two declined to state the specific reason for the game's delay. Company executives from Take-Two and Rockstar would only say that the game represented a complete reinvention, and that it 'pushed the hardware to its limits.'

The 'GTA IV' delay is just the most recent bit of bad news for Take-Two, which announced in June that it would suspend distribution of its 'Manhunt 2' game after a firestorm of criticism over the title's violent content. The game received an 'Adults-Only' rating from the Entertainment Software Rating Board—the kiss of death for retail sales—and was banned in Ireland and the U.K.

Much of Take-Two's troubles, however, have come at the corporate level. In February, the company's former chairman was convicted of backdating stock options. In March, a shareholder revolt resulted in the ousting of the company's CEO and several board members. And in early April, Take-Two's CFO resigned. News of the 'GTA IV' delay—and the company's announcement that it would post a full-year loss—sent Take-Two's shares down 12.5 per cent on Thursday.

Despite the continued bad PR for the beleaguered company, industry-watchers agree that it's more important for the company, and developer Rockstar, to get this game exactly right than to hit its original ship date.

'The Rockstar guys, they're perfectionists,' said John Davison of game site 1UP.com. 'They have a very specific vision about what the game should be. And Take-Two needs "GTA" to be as perfect as it can be.'

Anyone who saw the game at E3 knows that it wasn't yet perfect. Sure, the art reached new heights of detail, but the performance was noticeably sluggish. 'Grand Theft Auto' games aren't typically characterized by their speed, but the game sites were abuzz about the reason for poor frame rates.

Analyst Michael Pachter told Web site GamesIndustry.biz that he believes Rockstar has delayed the game because it is struggling with development on the PlayStation 3.

Sony denies this charge and said that the company has a dedicated team working with Rockstar on 'GTA IV.' They say they're not that worried about the delay and would prefer that Rockstar take the time it needs to perfect the game.

'We'd love to have [it] out as soon as possible,' said Sony spokesperson Dave Karakker. 'But we've never had a single game make or break any of our platforms. That's not how we built 100 million sales of [the] PlayStation 2, and that's not how we'll build 100 million in sales of [the] PlayStation 3.'

Um, yeah. But when you think about marquee franchises on the PlayStation 2, what do you think of? 'Metal Gear,' 'Final Fantasy,' 'Gran Turismo,' and, of course, 'Grand Theft Auto'. But nearly a year into the PS3's life, not one of those critically important games has released yet for the console.

Even though the delay of 'GTA' might hit Sony hardest, Microsoft might actually be taking the news harder. Although the company's public reaction to the announcement was upbeat and included references to its other Very Important Title, 'Halo 3,'—this news is not good for Microsoft.

'Microsoft was very conscious about linking "GTA" and Xbox,' says Davison. 'With "Halo 3" coming out in September, "GTA" was like the one-two punch.' What's more, Microsoft reportedly paid $50 million for the exclusive rights to 'GTA IV' downloadable episodes—money that Take-Two has no intention of giving back, even though the title will miss the critical holiday season.

Still, most don't think the loss of 'GTA' will stall the fast-moving train that is the game industry. If anything, it provides an opening for other developers to convince retailers to give them precious shelf space.

One title that stands to gain, says Sebastian, is 'Call of Duty 4,' a shooter from Activision that might temporarily quell the 'GTA' fan's need to blow things away.

'Retailers can buy that game with a lot of certainty that they'll sell it,' he said. IGN's GamerMetrics sent out an e-mail on Friday with the list of titles it expects will be able to best capitalize on the absence of 'GTA IV.' 'Call of Duty 4' tops the list for both the PlayStation 3 and the Xbox 360—as does Ubisoft's 'Assassin's Creed,' a game that was well-received at E3 but got crowded out of the spotlight by the blockbuster sequels.

No matter what, it's unlikely that a six-month delay will do permanent damage to the 'GTA' franchise—or the game industry. It's better for everyone involved—console makers, Take-Two, Rockstar and gamers—that the title surpasses the high bar set by its predecessors. Better to wait a few months for a great title that has legs than to rush out a game that's not ready—and suffer the wrath of the fan base.

So far, gamers are taking the news in stride. Davison says that when he and his staff combed the forums, they were surprised to learn that some fans were almost relieved that their favorite game was going to be late.

'That's one less $60 game [gamers] have to buy this Christmas,' he said. 'With the titles planned for the next few months, you're going to be hard-pressed to play everything that's really good.'

© 2007 MSNBC Interactive

(*Source*: http://www.msnbc.msn.com)
(Accessed 1 September 2007)

The article above, outlining institutional reasons for, and responses to the delay in the release of *Grand Theft Auto 4*, is a rich resource for a student of the videogame industry. It shows how connected developers and platform owners are; the relationship between the publishing company and its owners at executive level (the machinations of corporate hierarchy); how crucial the timing of releases is (especially around Christmas); and the impact of the delay on retailers. Most striking is how the enormity of the gaming industry is shown by the Wall Street response to the delay of a single game.

Exam Practice Question

Describe how the videogame you have researched for your case study reaches its audience across media, platforms and markets.

Glossary

ABC
Audit Bureau of Circulation—gathers circulation figures of magazines and newspapers, primarily for advertisers but also used by students and researchers.

Aesthetic
Visual appearance, related to taste.

Ambience
Background atmosphere.

Anchorage
The 'pinning down' of the meaning of an image by text.

Audience
Collective group of people reading any media text. Digital technology has led to increasing uncertainty over how we define an audience, with general agreement that the notion of a large group of people, brought together by time, responding to a single text, is outdated and that audiences now are 'fragmented'.

Avatar
An on-screen representation of the player in a videogame.

BARB
Broadcasters' Audience Research Board—responsible for gathering TV viewing figures.

BBFC
British Board of Film Classification.

Binary
Thinking in opposites. In digital coding, binary describes the coding of digits as noughts and ones.

Blogging
Web logs, published by ordinary people. An alternative to traditional journalism.

Bollywood
Popular Indian cinema, originating in Mumbai (Bombay).

Broadband
High speed, thicker cable transmitting a powerful digital signal that can deal with complex data such as moving images, music and games.

Censorship
The practice of 'cutting' or preventing access to material.

Classification
Restricting access to material on the grounds of age.

Compression
Transferring data into less space and sending it from one place to another, through encoding data using fewer units in digital coding.

Connotations
The meanings brought to a sign or symbol by the person/people interpreting it.

Continuity
In editing, the process of disguising the construction of the scene by making it appear to 'flow' as in real life. The 180 degree rule and the eyeline match are crucial to this.

Conventions
The expected ingredients in a particular type of media text.

Convergence
Hardware and software coming together across media, and companies coming together across similar boundaries, to make the distinction between different types of media and different media industries increasingly dubious.

Copyright
The owned rights of creative or intellectual property.

Cross-cutting
Editing between two scenes that are happening at the same time—manipulating space for the audience.

DAB
Digital radio.

Data
Original information acquired in research.

Deconstruction
Investigating how texts are put together and how they can only be understood in relation to other texts.

Democracy
Society founded on equality, in which the decision-making powers are elected and are thus representative and accountable.

Demographic
Measuring people and grouping them according to characteristics such as age, gender, ethnicity, occupation, income and socio-economic status.

Diegesis
Describes what is present in the world of a text, as opposed to extra material added for the audience.

Digital
Information broken down into noughts and ones.

Discourse
A way of speaking, thinking and understanding, that becomes powerful and appears 'natural'. The ways in which we come to understand the world through ways of talking, thinking and writing that become dominant.

Download
The practice of selecting and receiving digital information from an online source on a computer, as opposed to sending it by upload.

Effects
The idea that the media have influence over people and can play a role in changing their behaviour. The suggestion that people's behaviour is influenced or altered (either directly or indirectly) as a result of exposure to media is described in terms of 'media effects'.

Ellipsis
What is left out of a narrative, but remains in the story.

Enigma
A question left unanswered to create intrigue or suspense.

Establishing shot
A shot which serves to either introduce the audience to a location and context, or remind them of it.

Ethnography
Detailed research on a particular social group.

Feminism
In a Media Studies context, the belief that we should oppose media texts that represent women as unequal to men, or as mere unthinking objects for male scrutiny.

Flow
A state of mind which happens when someone is involved in an activity that is challenging, but pleasurable and incrementally more difficult over time, with staggered rewards and feedback.

Form
The basic shape or structure of a text or product.

Gatekeeping
The role played by editors, producers, owners and regulators in opening and closing, to greater and lesser extents, the flow of media information, by selecting which information to provide and which to deny access to.

Globalisation
The shift in media distribution from local or national to international and the whole world at once. Culturally, describes the process of 'sameness' over the world, typified by the availability of McDonalds in most nations.

Hardware
The actual equipment used for media production and consumption.

HTML
Hyper Text Markup Language—a structuring language for electronic text, interfaced with links to other supplementary texts, for websites.

Hybrid
A fusion of more than one media form.

Hyperreality
A state in which images and simulations take on more reality than the state they represent, so that the distinction between reality and representation is no longer sustainable.

Icon
A sign which directly resembles what it represents.

Iconography
Familiar visual signs that establish context.

Identity
The complex way that one has a representative sense of oneself. Gauntlett's (2007) recent work on identity is the best source for a definition—'we all have a complex matrix of ideas about ourselves, who we are and what we want to be'.

Ideology
A dominant set of ideas presenting itself as common sense or truth. Power relations are reinforced through ideology.

Immersion
Used in the analysis of videogames, in two ways: perceptual (the senses are dominated by the experience of the game) and psychological (the player's imagination is drawn into the game).

Independent
A media organisation or activity that is not connected to a major company.

Interactive
Media texts which offer audiences the opportunity to choose, respond to or shape the text in some way.

Intertextual (or Intermedial)
The chain of signification, in which texts make references to one another. When one text refers to another, this is called intertextual, whereas intermedial describes a media form which relies on an understanding and experience of other media (e.g. film and music) to make meaning.

Linear
Moving in one direction in a clear and logical order.

Literacy
The ability to read and write. Media literacy extends this to include all forms of writing (for example, taking photographs) and all forms of reading (for example, listening to music), and activities which may combine them (e.g. playing a computer game).

Ludology
The study of play.

Male gaze
From Laura Mulvey (1975), an analysis of media images which suggests that the camera represents a male perspective, and as such casts men as subjects and women as objects.

Market forces
This idea likens the 'natural' flow of competition leading to consumer choice and selection, and hence the survival of the fittest, to the laws of nature.

Marxist
All theory derived from the works of Marx, founded on a belief that the ruling classes in any time and place maintain their economic and systematic power through controlling not only the means of production but also culture and ideology, including the Media.

Massive Multiplayer Online Role Play Game (MMORPG)
Online games or experiences played collectively by huge numbers of participants. Notable examples are Second Life and Club Penguin. Whether these can be analysed in the same way as offline console games is a matter of debate.

Media access
Describes the degree of ease with which citizens can be seen and/or heard in the media, respond to the media and be provided with a dialogue with institutions, and the opportunities evident for people to produce media texts themselves and for them to be distributed.

Media language
An umbrella term that describes the ways in which audiences read media texts through understanding formal and conventional structures (for example, the grammar of film editing). Media literacy describes our ability to read and write in this extended sense of language.

Media Studies 2.0
A response to web 2.0, proposed by Gauntlet (2007), in which the role of online user-generated content and sharing is seen as fundamental to how we understand media audiences.

Mise en Scène
Everything that is put into the frame (primarily the paused moving image as a still image). Includes set design, location, costume, actors and make up, non-verbal communication, colour and contrast, lighting and filter.

Mode of address
How a text, in any medium, speaks to its audience.

Moral panic
Exaggerated media response to the behaviour of a social group.

Multimedia
A text created in a variety of media.

Multimodality
A form of semiotics, using general principles that underpin all forms of communication.

NRS
National Readership Survey.

Narrative
The way information is ordered, or the story is told.

Narratology
For our purposes here, the study of videogames as stories.

News values
The idea that editors select and construct news within a framework that is influenced by political, corporate, cultural and commercial objectives.

OFCOM
Regulator of UK broadcasting and telecommunications industries.

Parody
A text which does not simply imitate the style of another (a pastiche), but instead is transformative because it either mocks or shifts in some way the original text's conventions.

PCC
Press Complaints Commission.

Peer to peer
The sharing of media material between two parties in an equal relationship.

Piracy
Distribution of media material that infringes copyright law.

Pleasure
All forms of engagement with media texts.

Plot
The parts of a narrative that we actually see or hear, as opposed to the overall story, much of which we imagine or infer.

Podcast
Uploading an MP3 file over the internet for others to access through subscription.

Point of view shot
When the camera takes the place of a character's eyes.

Polysemy
Plural meaning, as opposed to fixed, singular meaning.

Popular culture
Texts which are consumed by a wide range of people, as opposed to a smaller group that is seen as an elite; they tend to be described as 'popular' and this implies a lesser cultural status or value.

Post modern
Media that refers to itself, is transparent in its construction and blurs the boundaries between reality and representation. Describes an approach to culture which sees all texts as being intertextual and meaning as mediated, rather than representative of a state of original reality.

Post-production
The editing stage, where material is manipulated using software and transformed into a finished media product.

Pre-production
All forms of idea generation, planning and research in response to a brief.

Promotion
An aspect of distribution that creates audience interest in a media product.

Public service
Founded on principles of democracy as opposed to profit. Funded through public taxation, for example, the television licence fee.

Realism
The degree to which, and the variety of ways in which media texts represent an idea of reality.

Regulation
The monitoring and intervention in media production and consumption. Self-regulation on the part of media institutions normally precedes this.

Remix
Describes how people are able to combine and reformulate a range of information from different sources, reworking media content.

Scheduling
The strategic positioning of media texts within broadcasting time. Digital television is increasingly disrupting this approach, since viewers can choose more easily than before when to watch.

Semiotics
The science of signs and symbols, from Saussure's linguistics (1974), and Barthes' structuralism (1972). The study of the sign in terms of its connotations within cultural myth systems.

Simulation
The deliberate artificial imitation of an experience or a process with the intention of making the imitation as close as possible to the 'real thing'.

Socio-cultural
Describes considerations of how our social experiences and cultural choices combine and how meanings are constructed by audiences through experience as much as through any fixed, intended, preferred messages from producers' points of view.

Software
Programmes used on computers.

Stereotype
A blunt, overstated representation of a type of person that is usually negative.

Symbolic
When an image or sign stands for something it does not directly resemble.

Synergy
Interconnected marketing and distribution of media products across a range of platforms and sectors.

Terrestrial
Analogue broadcasts from land-based transmitters as opposed to cable or satellite digital transmissions.

Text
All media products are texts, but the term can be extended to include people, ourselves and others—anything that is made up of a range of signs that are decoded and interpreted by people.

Transgressive
A practice which transcends conventional approaches and either subverts these existing ways of working, or challenges their value.

Upload
Transferring information or material from a computer to an online network.

Verisimilitude
The logical, seemingly authentic world of a text. Not the same as 'realist', because every text has a logical, sensible world constructed through continuity, detail and recognition.

Vertical integration
When a media company profits from all aspects of production, distribution and consumption/exhibition.

Virtual
A simulation of reality or experience.

Vox-pop

'Voice of the people'—the gathering of opinion on a topic from ordinary people representing a cross-section of a community.

WAP

Wireless application protocol—the internet and email on a phone or personal device without the need for cables or wires.

Web 2.0

The second phase of the internet, where the focus shifts from people receiving information and services to people creating and sharing material.

We Media

See Gillmoor (2004). Ordinary people deciding that they want to create media, through easily accessible technologies such as blogging, digital video, podcasting and v-logging, wikis, YouTube and aspects of Second Life.

Wiki

Web-based shared authoring.

Further Study Resources for AS Media

All of the books, articles and websites mentioned in this book are listed below, together with other resources that will be of general value to the AS Media student (and one or two that teachers might make use of). You are encouraged to follow up as many of these as you can to add value to your studies.

Web Resources for Media Studies

Media UK (www.mediauk.com)
Useful for any media research related to UK institutions.

BFI Education (www.bfi.org.uk/education)
The British Film Institute's education resources are wide ranging and very useful for moving image analysis.

In the Picture (www.itpmag.demon.co.uk)
This site provides a range of very good study materials. In the Picture also run student events in the North of England.

BBC online (www.bbconline.org.uk)
Archives and daily news: an essential site for media research.

Broadcast (www.broadcast.now.com)
Website of broadcasting trade magazine.

Media Week (www.mediaweek.co.uk)
Website of trade magazine for general media.

Music Week (www.musicweek.com)
Website of music industry trade magazine.

Film Education (www.filmeducation.org.uk)
Excellent film study resources.

Internet Newspaper Directory
(www.discover.co.uk/NET/NEWS)
Global newspaper access facility.

Emap (www.emap.com)
Major magazine publisher.

British Board of Film Classification (www.bbfc.co.uk)
Regulatory body for UK film, DVD and games.

Daniel Chandler's Media and Communications site
(www.aber.ac.uk/media)
Useful academic site.

Media Zoo (www.mediazoo.co.uk)
Interesting discussions on contemporary UK media.

Theory.org (www.theory.org.uk)
David Gauntlett's excellent cultural studies and research website. Check out the Media Studies 2.0 section.

Media UK (www.mediauk.com/directory)
A gateway to websites of all the main media institutions.

English and Media Centre (www.englishandmedia.co.uk)
This organisation offers a range of high quality resources and INSET events, as well as the wonderful *Media Magazine* and the *MoreMediaMag* website, which students can subscribe to through their school or college. They also publish A level Media student work (and pay for it!).

Long Road College Media site (www.longroadmedia.com/)
Be inspired by some great Media students' production work on this site.

Community Media Association (www.commedia.org.uk)
Useful for media access research.

National Union of Journalists (www.nuj.org.uk)
Useful site for issues of journalistic practice and employment.

The Radio Site (www.i-way.co.uk/~stunova)
Links to global stations and organisations.

Media Magazine (www.mediamagazine.org.uk)
See English and Media Centre.

UK Film Council (www.ukfilmcouncil.org.uk)
Essential for statistics, as well as information on piracy.

OFCOM (www.ofcom.org.uk)
The regulatory body for broadcast media and telecommunications.

The Internet Movie Database (www.imdb.com)
Find details about any film here.

Campaign for Press and Broadcasting Freedom
(www.cpbf.org.uk)
Very useful for research on newspapers.

Gamespot (www.gamespot.com)
Offers downloads of videogame sequences and a range of other
information about videogames.

Game Culture online journal (www.game-culture.com)
Academic journal offering a range of perspectives on
videogames.

Skillset (www.skillset.org)
The National Training Organisation for broadcasting media. Useful
for employment details.

Screen International (www.screendaily.com)
Website of international trade magazine for the film industry.

UK Press Gazette (www.pressgazette.co.uk)
Website of press trade magazine.

New Media (www.newmediastudies.com)
Useful for up-to-date facts and figures, such as global internet
usage statistics.

Indymedia UK (www.indymedia.org.uk/)
Excellent for research on media access.

Media Guardian (www.media.guardian.co.uk)
Online version of the Monday supplement. Essential for
institutions and audiences.

Rajar (www.rajar.co.uk)
Radio audience research information.

Blogger.com (www.blogger.com)
You can create your own blog for free in minutes here.

Wikimedia (http://en.wikipedia.org/wiki/Wikimedia)
Great 'we media' resource.

YouTube (www.youtube.com)
Essential.

Audit Bureau of Circulation (www.abc.org.uk)
Offers updated circulation figures—essential for institutions and audiences.

National Readership Survey (www.nrs.co.uk)
Readership figures broken down demographically.

Books/Articles

Allan, S., 2000, *News Culture*, Buckingham: Open University Press.

Allen, R. and Hill, C. (eds), 2004, *The Television Studies Reader*, London: Routledge.

Barthes, R., 1972, *Mythologies*, London: Paladin.

Bignell, J., 1997: *Media Semiotics: An Introduction*. Manchester: MUP.

Bignell, J., 2004, *An Introduction to Television Studies*, London: Routledge.

Berners-Lee, T., 1999, *Weaving the Web: The Past, Present and Future of the World Wide Web*, London: Orion.

Brooker, C., 2005, *Screen Burn: Television with its Face Torn Off*, London: Guardian Books.

Bruce, C., 2002, 'Analyse This!' in *Media Magazine* 2, London: English and Media Centre.

Buckingham, D., 2003, *Media Education: Literacy, Learning and Contemporary Culture*, London: Polity.

Buckingham, D., 2007, *Beyond Technology: Children's Learning in the Age of Digital Culture*, London: Polity.

Burn, A. and Durran, J., 2007, *Media Literacy in Schools*, London: Paul Chapman Publishing.

Burn, A. and Parker, D., 2003, *Analysing Media Texts*, London: Continuum.

Carr, D., Buckingham, D., Burn, A. and Schott, G., 2006, *Computer Games: Text, Narrative and Play*, London: Polity.

Carter, M., 2005, 'Making Drama out of History' in *Broadcast*, London: emap.

Connolly, S., 2006, 'Mediaschool blog', http://mediaschool.blogspot.com (accessed 10 July 2007).

Coker, E., 2004, 'Scripting Hollyoaks' in *Media Magazine 10*, London: English and Media Centre.

Creeber, G. (ed.), 2001, *The Television Genre Book*, London: BFI.

Csigo, P., 2007, Falling apart or falling together? Audience fragmentation and audience casualization in the converging media environment. Paper presented at *Transforming Audiences* conference, University of Westminster, London.

Curran, J., 2002, *Media and Power*, London: Routledge.

Dean, I., 2007, 'To Live and Die in GTA' in *PSW* September 2007, London: Future Publishing.

Dixon, S., 2007, *Navigation and Design Issues*, Birmingham: Newman University College.

Doughty, S., 2002, 'Scarred by Soaps' in *Daily Mail*, 17 October 2002, London: Associated Newspapers Ltd.

Dovey, J. and Kennedy, H., 2006, *Game Cultures: Computer Games as New Media*, Maidenhead: Open University Press.

Dugdale, H., 2006, 'Who runs Hollywood?' in *Media Magazine* 17, London: English and Media Centre.

Edwards, C., 2001, *Radio for Media Studies*, London: Auteur.

Feldman, T., 1997, *Introduction to Digital Media*, London: Routledge.

Ferguson, M. and Golding, P. (eds), 2003, *Cultural Studies in Question*, London: Sage

Fraser, P., 'Production Work Tips' in *Media Magazine* 1, London: English and Media Centre.

Gant, C., 2007, 'Passage from India' in *Sight and Sound* 17(10), London: BFI.

Gauntlett, D., 2002, *Media, Gender and Identity—An Introduction*, London: Routledge.

Gauntlett, D., 2004, *Web Studies: Rewiring Media Studies for the Digital Age*, London: Arnold.

Gauntlett, D., 2007, *Creative Explorations*, London: Routledge.

Gauntlett, D., 2007a, *Media Studies 2.0*, www.theory.org.uk (accessed 4 September 2007).

Gee, J., 2003, *What Video Games have to Teach us about Learning and Literacy*, New York: Palgrave Macmillan.

Gibson, J., 2007, *Media Directory 2007: The Essential Handbook*, London: Guardian Books.

Gibson, J., 2007, 'Never mind the high street: Branson sells his Virgin Megastores' in *The Guardian*, 18 September 2007, London: Guardian Newspapers.

Gill, R., 2006, *Gender and the Media*, Cambridge: Polity.

Gillmor, D., 2004, *We, The Media*, California: O'Reilly.

Gonzalez, I., Martinez, R. and Fernandez, M., 2007, 'YouTube, critical mass and imagined audiences: the cultural production of contemporaries'. Paper presented at *Transforming Audiences* conference, University of Westminster, London.

Goodman, S., 2003, *Teaching Youth Media: A Critical Guide to Literacy, Video Production and Social Change*, New York: Teachers College Press.

Grahame, J., 2003, 'Just looking for Great Stories'—interview with Phil Redmond in *Media Magazine* 4, London: English and Media Centre.

Hepworth, D., 2007, 'A mighty wind of change for magazines' in Gibson (ed). *Media Directory 2007*, London: Guardian Books.

Hesmondhalgh, D., 2002, *The Cultural Industries*, London: Sage.

Holland, P., 2000, *The Television Handbook*, London: Routledge.

Horton, W., 1994, *Designing and Writing Online Documents*, New York: Wiley.

James, N., 2007, 'Greenlit unpleasant land' in *Sight and Sound*, 17:1, London: BFI.

Johnson, S., 2005, *Everything Bad is Good for You*, London: Penguin.

Kendall, A., 2008, 'Playing and resisting: re-thinking young people's reading cultures' in *Literacy* (in press).

Lacey, N., 2000, *Narrative and Genre*, London: Macmillan.

Lacey, N., 2000, *Image and Representation*, London: Macmillan.

Lacey, N., 2004, *Media Institutions and Audiences*, London: Macmillan.

Lax, S., 2004, 'The Internet and Democracy' in Gauntlett, D. and Horsley, R. (eds), *Web Studies*, 2nd edn, London: Edward Arnold.

Layton, A., 2007, 'Music that Matters: looking at 6Music' in *Media Magazine* 19, London: English and Media Centre.

Luhrs, G., 2002, 'Why Convergence Matters' in *Media Magazine* 1, London: English and Media Centre.

Luhrs, G., 2002, 'New Media Technologies: a Glossary' in *Media Magazine* 2, London: English and Media Centre.

Luhrs, G., 2005, 'The Future Will be Blogged' in *Media Magazine* 12, London: English and Media Centre.

Luhrs, G., 2007, 'Web 2.0: The Power of Collaboration' in *Media Magazine* 19, London: English and Media Centre.

McDougall, J. and Duncan, M., 2008, 'Children, Videogames and Physical Activity: An Exploratory Study', in *International Journal of Disability and Human Development* 7(1), Israel: Freund.

McDougall, J. and O'Brien, W., 2008, *Studying Videogames*, Leighton Buzzard: Auteur.

McKay J., 2000, *The Magazines Handbook*, London: Routledge.

McNair, B., 2003, *News and Journalism in the UK*, London: Routledge.

Marshall, D., 2004, *New Media Cultures*, London: Hodder Arnold.

Massey, M., 2004, 'Gripping the Light Fantastic' in *Media Magazine* 7, London: English and Media Centre.

Miller, T. (ed.), 2000, *Television Studies*, London: BFI.

Mulvey, L., 1975, 'Visual Pleasure and Narrative Cinema' in *Screen* 16(3).

Naughton, J., 'Blogging and the emerging media ecosystem', http://reutersinstitute.politics.ox.ac.uk/about/discussion/blogging.html, (accessed 2 September 2007).

Newman, J., 2004, *Videogames*, London: Routledge.

Newman, J. and Oram, B., 2006, *Teaching Videogames*, London: BFI.

O'Hear, S., 2006, 'Murdoch and MySpace' in *Media Magazine* 17, London: English and Media Centre.

Offord, S., 2007, *Introduction to Teaching about Magazines*, London: BFI conference workshop (unpublished).

Points, J., 2007, *Teaching Television Drama*, London: BFI.

Priestman, C., 2001, *Web Radio*, Oxford: Focal Press.

Randle, K. and Culkin, N., 2004, 'The digital movie revolution' in *Media Magazine* 8, London: English and Media Centre.

Ruddock, A., 2007, 'Will the Standard Survive the Freebie Onslaught?' in *Media Guardian*, 27 August 2007, London: Guardian Newspapers.

Ruddock, A., 2007, *Investigating Audiences*, London: Sage.

Sampson, A., 2004, *Who Runs this Place?*, London: John Murray.

Sawyer, M., 2007, 'Sounding Off' in *Observer Music Monthly*, September 2007, London: Guardian Newspapers.

Sohn-Rethel, M., 2003, 'Four Sets of Forces: Analysing Media Production' in *Media Magazine* 4, London; English and Media Centre.

Stafford, R., 2001, *Representation: An Introduction*, London: BFI, Keighley: itp Publications.

Stafford, R., 2003, *Audiences: An Introduction*, London: BFI, Keighley: itp Publications.

Stafford, R. and Branston, G., 2006, *The Media Student's Book*, 4th edn, London: Routledge.

Stafford, R., 2006, 'The same old song?' in *In the Picture* 55. Keighley: itp Publications.

Stewart, C., Lavelle, M. and Kowaltzke, A., 2001, *Media and Meaning: An Introduction*, London: BFI.

Strinati, D., 1995, *An Introduction to Theories of Popular Culture*, London: Routledge.

Tapscott, D., 1998, *Growing Up Digital: The Rise of the Net Generation*, New York: McGraw Hill.

Tapscott, D. and Williams, A., 2007, *Wikinomics: How Mass Collaboration Changes Everything*, USA: Atlantic Books.

Thrasher, J., 2007, *Teaching Web Design*, London: BFI conference workshop (unpublished).

Wallace, W., 2006, 'More than a Game' in *Times Educational Supplement*, 6 January 2006, London: News International.

Watson, J. and Hill, A., 2003, *Dictionary of Media and Communication Studies*, London: Arnold.

Interviews

Interviews for this book were conducted with the following producers, experts and professionals:

Huw Meredith, photographer.
Somak Raychaudry, Bollywood consultant.
Ben Andrews, music promoter.
Doug Shipton, Finders Keepers Records.
Jim Judd, Ghost Box Records.
Neil Burrows, Selectadisc, Nottingham.

Index